Great German-American Feasts

An example of *fractur,* a form of early German American folk art.

Great German-American Feasts

Nancy Gailor Cortner
with Jane Garmey

TAYLOR PUBLISHING COMPANY
Dallas, Texas

GREAT GERMAN-AMERICAN FEASTS was developed jointly by Taylor Publishing Company and Media Projects Incorporated.

Published by Taylor Publishing Company under the direction of:

Randy Marston, President
Arnie Hanson, Publisher
Robert Frese, Senior Editor
Dominique Gioia, Project Editor
Kathy Ferguson, Art Director

Produced by the Cookhouse Press of Media Projects Incorporated:

C. Carter Smith, Executive Editor
David McIntosh, Managing Editor
Ellen Coffey, Project Editor
Charlotte McGuinn Freeman, Assistant Editor
Jeff Grunewald and Dan Barba, Principal Photography
Bernard Schleifer, Designer

Library-of-Congress-Cataloging-in-Publication Data
Cortner, Nancy G.
    Great German-American feasts.

    Includes index.
    1. Cookery, German.   I. Garmy, Jane.   II. Title.
TX721.C67   1987   641.5943   87-18086
ISBN 0-87833-549-8

Printed in the United States of America

FIRST EDITION
0 1 2 3 4 5 6 7 8 9

A lavish Oktoberfest spread in Fredericksburg, Texas.

CONTENTS

INTRODUCTION

G ERMAN-AMERICAN COOKING is rich and varied—a reflection of the homes, families and traditions of German-Americans who have settled in many different parts of the country. The influence of this cuisine on American eating habits is evident in our everyday use of such words as sauerkraut, delicatessen, hamburger, frankfurter, all of which have slipped quietly into the American language.

That this influence exists is not at all surprising, for by the end of the nineteenth century, more than seven million immigrants had left the German speaking regions of Europe to come to this country. The earliest settlers came to Pennsylvania and established themselves in and around what is now Lancaster County. They soon became known to their Yankee neighbors as "Pennsylvania Dutch," mispronouncing (and then mis-spelling) the word *Deutsch*—"German."

Auccessive waves of immigrants established German-American communities in Iowa, Illinois, Indiana, Ohio, New York, Missouri, Wisconsin, and Texas. In the 1840s, largely through the intense recruitment efforts of an organization founded by members of the German nobility— who held the unlikely hope that, if populated by enough Germans, Texas could become a German settlement—thousands of immigrants sailed to Galveston and settled the towns of New Braunfels and Fredericksburg. Their descendants

German Americans in Fredericksburg, Texas, celebrate Oktoberfest.

spread across Texas, and the presence in the cuisine of basically German dishes incorporating such Tex-Mex staples as chilies, cilantro and hot peppers is testament to the melting-pot theory.

People have a way of knowing where to find good food, and twenty years ago, before there was much talk of an American cuisine and the "new" California cooking hadn't been invented yet, the cognoscenti knew that one could eat extremely well in Southeastern Pennsylvania. In fact, the word had been out for over two centuries, and the steady stream of early visitors to the inns of Lancaster County had included such notables as George Washington, Benjamin Franklin, John Hancock and Benedict Arnold.

It did not take long for the Pennsylvania Dutch—or "Sauerkraut Yankees," as they were nicknamed during the Civil War—to gain their richly deserved reputation for being good cooks and hearty eaters. The first settlers were farmers living off the land. For them frugality was a necessity. Often deprived of their favorite spices and without some of the ingredients for their best-loved dishes, they were forced to improvise, to adjust old recipes and to create new ones. The result was a rich combination of the foods of their European ancestors and those foods which they found or could grow in their new country. The emphasis on sausages and hams, the use of cabbage, dumpling and potatoes, the innumerable recipes for rich cakes and festive cookies is authentically German. The American influence is evident in the use of native grains such as buckwheat and corn, their many recipes invented to take advantage of the abundance of apples in their orchards, the frequent use of beef and veal and the interplay of sweet and salty flavors.

Today, although German-American cooking has come a long way from the Rhine Valley and the Low Countries, it is a durable hybrid that remains remarkably intact. One reason for this is that many of the first immigrants' favorite recipes were associated with festivals and feasts that they continued to observe upon arriving in this country. Families got together not just for wedding, birthdays, Christmas and Easter, but feasts such as Ascension Day, St. Martin's Day and Pentecost. And German-American communities all over the country, from Lancaster County in Pennsylvania to Fredericksburg in Texas, continue to celebrate together the traditional *Maifest* and *Oktoberfest*, times to get together to talk, to sing, and—above all—to eat. There is a wellknown Pennsylvania Dutch saying, *"die Liebe geht durch den Magen"* (love goes through the stomach). The food prepared and shared on these occasions has linked successive generations of German-Americans, preserving a common heritage, expressing a cultural identity and making a large contribution to American cuisine.

Autumn

So much of the fresh food we eat today is no longer seasonal. Stores are filled with vegetables that have been flown in from long distances, and most meats—with the exception of some game and venison—can generally be obtained all year 'round. However, people still have the urge to change their eating habits with each season, and the autumn in particular seems to be a season of transition—a time to savor the last vestiges of summer but also, as the days get shorter and the weather turns colder, a time to begin to turn again to thick soups and sauerbraten, a time when dumplings seem a necessity for many meals.

Celebrations and feasts are very much a part of the German American heritage, and wherever German Americans have settled, autumn is the time to celebrate the *Oktoberfest*. The origins of this feast go back to 1810, when Crown Prince Ludwig hosted an extravagant gala in Munich to celebrate the occasion of his wedding to a local princess. Later, the Oktoberfest evolved into a two-week-long party held in the streets of Munich to celebrate the arrival of the new beer that had been brewed the previous spring. The Munich Oktoberfest continues to be a two-week public carnival, with whole oxen roasted over open fires, intense carousing, and music and singing nonstop. In America the Oktoberfest is shorter, smaller and generally a much more private celebration, but the party is always a good one.

Early Autumn Supper

Oktoberfest Celebration

Mushroom Strudel
Lamb Paprika in Sour Cream Sauce
Spaetzle
Marinated Leek Salad
Honey Cakes

Halloween Brunch

Zesty Fruit Compote
Apple Sausage Ring
Potato Pancakes
Moravian Love Feast Buns
Black Walnut Bread

Traditional Fish Dinner

Alsatian Flounder with Cabbage
Pan-Fried Potatoes
Spinach Salad
Sour Cream Apple Pie

Hearty Sunday Supper

Dark Beer Soup
Pennsylvania Dutch Chicken Fricassee
Mustard Glazed Carrots
Potato Biscuits
Almond-Apple Crunch

Lunch for a Bunch

Vegetable Soup with Dumplings
Goulash with Sauerkraut
Buttered Egg Noodles
Green Beans and Zucchini
Plum Cake

Home Style Chicken Dinner

Leek and Potato Soup
Chicken Pot Pie
Herbed Green Beans
Buttermilk Biscuits
German Gingerbread

Early Autumn Supper

Assorted Herring Appetizers
Classic Sauerbraten
Potato Dumplings
Brussels Sprouts
Braised Red Cabbage
Frozen Raspberry Mousse

Tailgate Picnic

Hearty Tomato Soup
Grilled Marinated Chicken
Bread and Butter Pickles
Watermelon Rind Pickles
Red Potato Salad
Sour Cream Biscuits
Linzer Bars and Ginger Snaps

Winter

WINTER, with its often harsh weather, short days and dark afternoons was a time the first German-Americans put to particularly good use. It was a time for goulashes, ragouts, stews and thick, steaming soups; a time when such winter vegetables as onions, cabbages, leeks, kohlrabi and sweet potatoes all came into their own.

Winter was also the hunting season, a time to stock the larder with venison and other game. But most of all, winter was—and still is—characterized by the Christmas season. For German Americans, Christmas is not a one-day event. As it was in Germany, Christmas is a season—one that begins with the opening of the first door on the Advent calendar and does not come to an end until Twelfth Night has long passed.

The Christmas meal is traditionally a festive and elaborate family affair. Usually a goose will be served, but a roast of venison, pheasant or turkey is also acceptable. (In Texas, many German-Americans feast on wild turkey—a dish that would never have been eaten in Germany.) There are a vast array of accompanying dishes—relishes, puddings, vegetables, some more traditional than others. There are no rigid rules, but the likelihood is that on every Christmas table there will be at least one recipe from the Old Country that has been handed down from generation to generation—whether it be the stuffing, the Christmas stollen or a brew of spiced cider.

Rolf's Yuletide Goose

Festive Yuletide Dinner

Crabmeat and Anchovy Canapes
Rolf's Yuletide Goose
Gingered Carrots
Potato Dumplings
Apple Sauerkraut Salad
Assorted Christmas Cookies and
  Christmas Stollen

Twelfth Night Dinner

Biersuppe
Pork Loin with Juniper Berries
Stuffed Onions
Scalloped Potatoes
Apple Strudel

Game Dinner Supreme

German Potato Soup
Saddle of Venison
Allerlei
Plum Dumplings
Amish Creamy Raisin Pie

Traditional Midwinter Fare

Potato and Watercress Soup
Swabian Pork Chops
German Potato Salad
Sweet Potato Rolls
Green Tomato Mincemeat
Dill Pickles
Pecan Maple Pie

Friday Fish Dinner

*Marinated Mushrooms and
    Artichoke Hearts*

Grilled Salmon with Dill

Hashed Brown Potatoes

Wilted Lettuce Salad

Apples Baked in Apricot Sauce

Elegant New Year's Dinner

New Potatoes with Caviar

Pheasant in Green Peppercorn Sauce

Wild Rice Pilaf with Almonds

Herbed Green Beans

Watercress and Endive Salad

Taimi's Dobosch Torte

Winter Solstice Celebration

Crocked Beer Cheese

Winter Chicken and Potato Casserole

Braised Red Cabbage

Braised Brussels Sprouts with Bacon

Herb Bread

Bundt Kuchen

Sunday Ski Brunch

Westphalian Ham Bread

Sausage Links in Cornmeal Pudding

Sauteed Apple Slices

*Pennsylvania Dutch-Style Sauteed
    Peaches*

Philadelphia Sticky Buns

Spring

SPRING is the season for change; a time to break out of winter habits and experiment with new recipes and new food combinations. The urge for new vegetables and crisp salads comes from our deep past. The first appearance of green leaves, both cultivated and wild, heralds the arrival of spring and the promise of fresh foods after the dwindling preserves of a long hard winter. Here again we run counter to the stereotype of German American cooking as heavy and hearty.

A nineteenth century German-American family relished the first cauldron of light Spring Beet Borscht that arrived on their table. True, they would probably have followed it with meat and potatoes, but today it can be the main course of a light and very German vegetarian lunch or dinner. Accompany it with Sour Cream Onion Biscuits; follow it with a Caledonian Salad—that luscious combination of raw cabbage, mushrooms, raisins and pineapple bits—and celebrate the new arrival of spring.

Easter Sunday Dinner

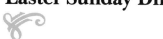

German Wine Soup
Country Roast Leg of Lamb
New Peas with Scallions
Potato Kugel
Vanilla Bavarian Cream with
    Raspberry Sauce

Pot Luck Supper

Choucroute Garni
Herb Bread
Wilted Lettuce Salad
German Chocolate Cake

A Meatless Meal

Spring Beet Borscht
Sour Cream Biscuits
Caledonian Salad
Gooey Shoofly Pie

Mother's Day Dinner

Smoked Salmon Rolls with
    Horseradish Cream
Roast Pheasant with Purple Plum Sauce
Glazed Baby Carrots
Cabbage in White Wine
Bitter Chocolate Torte

The Sweet & Sour Influence

Roast Pork Stuffed with
*   Apricots and Raisins*
Cranberry Orange Chutney
Green Tomato Relish
Zucchini Nut Cake

Lenten Fish Dinner

Fresh Mushroom Soup
Baked Mackeral with Mustard Sauce
Asparagus with Dill
Sour Cream Apple Tart

Light Buffet Lunch

Kirschsuppe (Cold Cherry Soup)
Chicken with Grapes
String Beans Vinaigrette
Fresh Apricot Ice Cream

Contemporary Dining Al Fresco

Roast Duck with Melon
Potato Pancakes
Shredded Carrots
Lemon Meringue Torte

Summer

MANY of the eighteenth and early nineteenth century German-American immigrants were farmers who lived off the land. They knew how to appreciate summer's bounty—that glorious profusion of fruit and vegetables—and how to preserve it for the winter months when the harvests were long past; summer was a season not only of picking and cooking, but of "putting away." In a society where frugality was considered not only a virtue but a creative art, nothing was wasted. Recipes were devised to make use of the rinds of the watermelon, the tomato that somehow stayed green, the less than perfect apple. Summer was the season to prepare the larder for the winter and to fill it with jams, preserves, relishes and dressings.

Today we think of summer as a time to enjoy the simple pleasures of eating outdoors—summer picnics and informal barbecues. German-American cuisine, with its extensive variety of salads and breads—to say nothing of *wursts* and hamburgers—has contributed much to this tradition.

Fourth of July Backyard Cookout

Grilled Brats in Beer
Grilled Beer Burgers
Cole Slaw
Picnic Potato Salad
Sliced Watermelon
German Chocolate Pound Cake

Summerfest Spread

Best Ever Terrine
Grilled Chicken and Shrimp
Grilled Baby Vegetables
Parker House Rolls
Red Fruit Fruit Pudding

Brunch on the Porch

Pecan Griddle Cakes
Midwest Scrapple
Fresh Melon Slices
Moravian Sugar Coffee Bread

Cocktails Alfresco

Steak with Beer Dip
Veal Terrine
Walnut Liver Pâté
Sweet Pickles
Crudité Patchwork Salad

Sunday Seafood Supper

*Salmon Fingers with Pine Nuts
and Basil Sauce*

Baked Stuffed Bass

Asparagus with Dill Sauce

Watercress and Hearts of Palm Salad

German Apple Pancake

German Country Lunch

*Pan-Fried Weisswurst with
Dusseldorf Mustard*

Boiled New Potatoes

Marinated Celeriac Salad

*Mixed Vegetables in
Tarragon Mustard Vinaigrette*

Rhubarb Custard Pie

Cool Dinner for Company

Watercress Soup

Baked Martini Chicken

Rotkrautsalat

New Potato and Red Bean Salad

Peach Cobbler

Memorial Day Dinner

Spring Beet Borscht

Hofbrau Steak

Potato and Apple Pancakes

Mixed Green Salad

*Apricot Ice Cream and
German Ginger Bars*

Stuffed Edam Cheese

Sausage Soup

Root Soup

Celery Soup

Sauerkraut Soup

Leek and Potato Soup

Kirschsuppe

Summer Salad

Root Vegetable Salad

Cucumber Salad

Fish and Caviar Mousse

Bacon Salad

Roast Pheasants with Purple Plum Sauce

Traditional Roast Duck

Brussels Sprouts, Red Cabbage with Apples

Green Cabbage in Wine, Mustard Glazed Carrots

Sauerbraten and Potato Balls

Rolf's Veal Shank Dinner

Roast Pork with Dill

Saffron Breads

Graham Crescents

Poppy Seed Cake

Assorted Breads

Mocha Cake

Bitter Chocolate Torte

Frozen Raspberry Mold

APPETIZERS

*I*N Germany it is the tradition to begin the main meal of the day with *vorspeisen*, or appetizers. The custom is to serve one rather than several, carefully garnished and well presented. In this country, too, *vorspeisen* are the pride of the German American cook; herring appetizers, steak tartare, smoked sausages and mushroom delicacies are all extremely popular. And here, where the trend for a while has been toward lighter meals, these delicious dishes are often served as main courses for luncheon or supper.

Apple Sausage Ring

1½   *cups saltine cracker crumbs*
½   *cup milk*
2   *eggs, lightly beaten*
2   *pounds bulk pork sausage*
⅓   *cup minced onion*
2   *tablespoons brown sugar*
1   *teaspoon grated lemon rind*
1¾   *cups peeled and chopped tart apples*
   parsley sprigs
   toasted rounds of white and rye bread

In a small bowl soak the cracker crumbs in the milk for 5 minutes. Add the eggs, sausage, onion, brown sugar, lemon rind, and apples. Butter a 10-cup ring mold and press the sausage mixture into it. Refrigerate the mold for 8 hours or overnight.

Preheat the oven to 350° F.

Set the mold in a pan of hot water for a few seconds, rap it sharply against the counter to loosen the contents, and unmold the apple-sausage ring onto a jelly-roll pan. Bake the ring for 1 to 1¼ hours, or until it is browned and cooked through. If the sausage becomes too brown, cover the ring with foil during the last 30 minutes of cooking time.

Transfer the apple-sausage ring to paper towels to drain. Set it on a serving plate, garnish it with parsley sprigs, and arrange the toast rounds around it. Makes 20 appetizer servings.

Rollmops

2 tablespoons Dijon mustard
8 fillets Matjes herring
1 large half-sour dill pickle, julienned
1 large Bermuda onion, sliced thin and
     separated into rings
32 capers
2 cups white wine
1 cup white vinegar
1½ tablespoons pickling spices

Spread a thin layer of mustard over each herring fillet. Arrange 2 strips of pickle, 3 onion rings, and 4 capers on each fillet. Roll the fillets jelly-roll fashion and secure them with toothpicks.

In a shallow dish combine the white wine, vinegar, pickling spices, and the remaining onion rings. Place the rollmops in the marinade and refrigerate them, covered, for 3 to 4 days. Makes 8 rollmops.

Salmon Rolls with Horseradish Cream

1 cup cream cheese
1 cup sour cream
1 cup horseradish
½ teaspoon salt
1 teaspoon lemon juice
12 slices smoked salmon
6 slices rye bread
   butter
   parsley sprigs
   lemon slices
   capers

In a mixing bowl combine the cream cheese and sour cream. Add the horseradish, salt, and lemon juice. Spread the salmon slices with the horseradish cream and roll them up loosely. Remove the crusts from the bread slices, cut each slice into two triangles, and butter the triangles. Arrange the salmon rolls and rye bread triangles on a platter and garnish the platter with parsley, lemon slices, and capers. Makes 12 appetizers.

Miniature Sausage Cakes

1 cup crushed saltine cracker crumbs
¾ cup milk
1 pound bulk pork sausage
1 beaten egg
1–2 tablespoons horseradish
1 tablespoon mustard seed
   toast rounds
   parsley sprigs

Preheat the oven to 350° F.

In a bowl, soak the cracker crumbs in the milk for 5 minutes. Add the sausage, egg, horseradish, and mustard seed and combine the mixture well. Pack the mixture into miniature muffin tins and bake the appetizers for 12 to 15 minutes, or until they are well browned. Carefully remove the sausage cakes from the muffin tins, drain them on paper towels, and arrange them on a platter. Surround them with toast rounds and garnish the platter with parsley sprigs. Makes 24 appetizers.

Salmon Fingers with Pine Nuts and Basil Sauce

1   *pound salmon fillets, cut about ½ inch thick*
    salt and white pepper
¼   *cup pine nuts*
3   *tablespoons butter*
3   *ounces white vermouth*
1½ *cups heavy cream*
12 *fresh basil leaves*

Preheat the oven to 350° F.

Cut the salmon into 3½- x 1½-inch strips, season the strips with salt and white pepper to taste, and set them aside.

Spread the pine nuts in a baking pan and toast them in the oven, shaking the pan once or twice, for 10 to 12 minutes, or until they are browned.

Melt the butter in a heavy skillet, add the salmon strips, and sauté them over medium heat for 5 minutes, turning once. Transfer them to a heated platter and keep them warm. Pour the vermouth into the skillet and stir to scrape up any brown bits from the pan. Add the cream and cook the sauce over moderate heat, stirring often, until it is thick and heated through, but be careful not to let it boil. Chop 4 of the basil leaves and stir them into the sauce. Adjust the seasoning, adding salt and pepper if necessary, and heat the sauce for another 2 to 3 minutes.

Spoon an equal amount of sauce onto each of 4 plates and arrange 3 or 4 salmon fingers on the sauce on each plate. Sprinkle the appetizers with the toasted pine nuts and garnish them with the remaining basil leaves. Makes 4 appetizers.

Crabmeat and Anchovy Canapés

4   *tablespoons (½ stick) butter*
½   *pound crabmeat*
2   *teaspoons chopped shallots*
2   *tablespoons flour*
1   *cup milk, heated*
1   *egg yolk*
½   *cup grated Parmesan cheese*
½   *cup bread crumbs*
    cayenne
6   *slices homemade-style white bread*
12 *anchovy fillets, halved*
    chopped parsley
    lemon wedges

Melt 2 tablespoons of the butter in a heavy skillet, add the crabmeat and shallots, and sauté the mixture for 5 minutes. Set the skillet aside.

In a saucepan over medium heat melt the remaining 2 tablespoons butter. Add the flour and cook the roux, stirring constantly, for 2 or 3 minutes, being careful not to let it brown. Add the hot milk in a stream, whisking until the mixture is smooth and thickened; turn off the heat under the white sauce.

Put the egg yolk in a bowl and beat it lightly. Slowly add 3 tablespoons of the white sauce to the egg yolk, whisking constantly. Pour the egg yolk mixture into the white sauce, stirring to blend. With a slotted spoon transfer the crabmeat and shallots to the saucepan and simmer the mixture, stirring, for 3 minutes, or until it is heated through. Stir in half of the grated cheese and half of the bread crumbs. Season the sauce with cayenne to taste and keep it warm.

Preheat the broiler.

Toast the bread, remove the crusts, and cut the slices into quarters. Spread 1 tablespoon of the crabmeat mixture on each toast square. Place the squares on a cookie sheet, sprinkle them with the remaining Parmesan cheese and bread crumbs, and top them with anchovies and chopped parsley. Broil the canapés for 3 to 5 minutes, until they are nicely browned. Arrange them on a serving platter and garnish them with lemon wedges. Makes 24 canapés.

Caviar Sour Cream Pie

1	*medium-size sweet onion, grated*
5	*hard-cooked eggs*
4	*tablespoons mayonnaise*
	salt and pepper
1¼	*cup sour cream*
2	*ounces red caviar*
2	*ounces black caviar*
½	*cup minced scallions, greens included*
	toast points or pumpernickel triangles

Butter the bottom and sides of a 9-inch springform pan or a shallow glass serving dish or pie pan.

Spoon the onion onto paper towels to drain.

Peel four of the hard-cooked eggs and grate them into a mixing bowl. Peel one of the remaining eggs, set the yolk aside for use in the topping, and grate the white into the bowl. Stir the mayonnaise into the eggs and season the mixture with salt and pepper to taste. Spread the egg mixture over the bottom of the pie pan or serving dish. Scatter the grated onion over the egg mixture. Drop the sour cream on top of the onion by the tablespoonful and spread the cream out evenly. Refrigerate the pie for 2 hours.

Pile the red and the black caviar in separate mounds on paper towels to drain; divide each mound into four roughly equal parts. Grate the reserved egg yolk and set it aside. With a knife score the top of the pie into 8 wedges. Scatter one of the portions of black caviar over one of the wedges and a portion of red caviar over the adjacent wedge; repeat the procedure until all of the wedges are garnished. Fill the scored gashes between the wedges with minced scallion. Scatter a thin border of grated egg yolk around the outside of the pie; sprinkle any remaining egg yolk in the center of the pie.

If using a springform pan, unmold the caviar pie and set it on a serving dish, or set the glass pie pan or serving dish on a larger plate, and arrange the toast points or pumpernickel triangles around the appetizer. Makes 8 appetizer servings.

Sausage-Stuffed Mushrooms with Garlic-Tomato Sauce

18   large, well-shaped mushrooms
½   pound bulk sausage
1   cup tomato sauce
1   cup dry white wine
½   clove garlic, minced
½   teaspoon oregano
3   cups watercress

Preheat the oven to 350° F.

Remove and finely chop the mushroom stems; trim the top of each cap, if necessary, so that the stuffed mushrooms will not tip over. In a heavy skillet over medium-high heat, brown the sausage. Add the chopped mushroom stems and cook the mixture until the mushrooms are soft and slightly browned. Drain the fat from the skillet. Fill the mushroom caps with the sausage mixture, packing each cap quite full. Arrange the stuffed mushrooms on a greased cookie sheet so that they do not touch one another and bake them for 30 minutes, or until they are bubbly and lightly browned.

In a saucepan combine the tomato sauce, wine, garlic, and oregano. Heat the mixture through and cook it at just below the simmering point for 10 minutes to blend the flavors.

Arrange 3 stuffed mushrooms on a bed of watercress on each of 6 appetizer plates. Spoon about 4 teaspoons of the garlic-tomato sauce over each serving. Makes 18 stuffed mushrooms.

Stuffed Mushrooms with Cheese

1   pound medium-size, well-shaped mushrooms
½   pound bulk pork sausage
1   small onion, minced
2   cloves garlic, minced
½   cup bread crumbs
⅔   cup grated Parmesan cheese parsley sprigs

Remove the mushroom stems and mince half of them, reserving the rest for another use; trim the top of each cap, if necessary, so that the stuffed mushrooms will not tip over.

In a heavy skillet lightly brown the sausage over medium-high heat. Reduce the heat to medium, add the onion, mushroom stems and garlic, and cook the mixture for another 10 to 12 minutes, until the vegetables are soft.

Preheat the broiler.

Drain the fat from the skillet and stir in the bread crumbs and ⅓ cup of the cheese; cook the stuffing over medium heat until it is hot. Pack the mushroom caps quite full of the sausage mixture and sprinkle about 1 teaspoon of the remaining cheese on top of each one. Place the appetizers on a cookie sheet so that they do not touch one another and broil them for 3 to 5 minutes, until they are bubbly and lightly browned. Arrange the mushrooms on a serving platter, spear each one with a large canapé pick, and garnish the platter with parsley. Makes 16–20 stuffed mushrooms.

Sausage Biscuits

1 **pound bulk pork sausage**
1¼ **cups sharp Cheddar cheese**
3 **cups biscuit mix**
butter (optional)

Preheat the oven to 375° F.

In a large mixing bowl thoroughly combine the sausage, cheese, and biscuit mix. Shape the dough into 1-inch balls and place them on a cookie sheet. Bake the biscuits for 12 minutes. Serve the sausage biscuits piping hot, with butter, if desired. Makes about 40 appetizers.

Kielbasa Vinaigrette

1 **large kielbasa**
1 **cup dry red wine**
1 **cup water**
1 **medium onion, thinly sliced**
1 **teaspoon Dijon mustard**
⅓ **cup red wine vinegar**
½ **teaspoon salt**
⅛ **teaspoon black pepper**
¼ **cup snipped fresh dill**
1 **clove garlic, minced**
⅔ **cup olive oil**
6 **scallions, green parts included, thinly sliced**
¼ **cup finely chopped parsley**
1 **large tomato, peeled, seeded, and cut into large chunks**
8 **large, well-shaped lettuce leaves**

Place the kielbasa in an enameled or stainless steel skillet and add the wine, water, and onion slices. Bring the liquid to a boil, lower the heat, and simmer the sausage, covered, for 30 minutes. Let it cool in the poaching liquid.

Put the mustard, vinegar, salt, pepper, dill, and garlic in a blender or a food processor, turn on the motor, and let it run for a few seconds, just until the ingredients are combined. Pour in the olive oil, a little at a time, blending until all of the oil is incorporated and the vinaigrette is thick.

When the kielbasa is cool enough to handle, carefully remove the skin and cut the sausage into thin slices. Place it in a large mixing bowl and add the scallions, parsley, and tomato. Add the vinaigrette, toss the mixture thoroughly, and refrigerate for at least 1 hour.

Place a lettuce leaf on each of 8 appetizer plates and spoon some kielbasa vinaigrette onto each leaf. Makes 8 appetizer servings.

New Potatoes with Caviar

12 **very small new potatoes**
¾ **cup sour cream**
4 **tablespoons red caviar**
4 **tablespoons finely snipped chives**

Preheat the oven to 350° F.

Prick the skins of the potatoes and bake them for 25 minutes, or until they are soft.

Cut the potatoes in half and trim the ends, if necessary, so that the halves will not tip over. Place 1 tablespoon sour cream on the cut side of each potato. Top the sour cream with ½ teaspoon red caviar and ½ teaspoon snipped chives. Makes 24 appetizers.

Veal Terrine

2 *pounds ground veal*
2 *teaspoons salt*
¼ *cup chopped chives*
2 *eggs*
1 *cup heavy cream*
1 *tablespoon chopped fresh thyme, or ¼*
    teaspoon dried thyme
1 *tablespoon chopped fresh rosemary, or ⅛*
    teaspoon dried rosemary
1 *tablespoon chopped fresh sage, or ¼*
    teaspoon dried sage
½ *cup chopped pistachios*
10 *strips bacon*
    thyme, rosemary, and sage sprigs
    bread rounds

Preheat the oven to 350° F.

Put the veal, salt, and chives in a large bowl. In a small bowl beat the eggs lightly with a fork; stir in the cream, and pour the mixture into the large bowl. Add the thyme, rosemary, sage, and pistachios. Combine the ingredients well.

Lay 8 of the bacon strips across the bottom and sides of a 1½-quart loaf pan or terrine, letting the ends of the strips hang over the edges of the pan. Pack the veal mixture into the pan and fold the loose bacon ends over the top. Halve the 2 remaining bacon strips and lay them on top of the loaf. Pour about 1 inch of hot water into a shallow baking pan and set the loaf pan in the water. Cover the loaf pan with foil, pressing to seal it well. Place the pans in the oven and bake the terrine for 1 hour, adding water to the shallow baking pan if necessary. The meat is cooked when the juices run clear.

Remove the terrine from the oven and place a weight on top of the foil; leave it in place for about 5 minutes to press out some of the fat and eliminate air pockets. Remove the weight and the foil, carefully pour off the fat, and refrigerate the terrine overnight or for at least 8 hours.

Turn the chilled terrine out onto a serving plate, slice it, and garnish it with herb sprigs. Arrange bread rounds around the veal. Makes 16 appetizer servings.

Walnut Liver Pâté

2 *ounces shelled walnuts*
½ *cup cream cheese, softened*
¼ *pound liverwurst*
2 *tablespoons cognac*
½ *teaspoon tarragon*
    Finely chopped parsley
    Toast points or crackers

Preheat the oven to 350° F.

Half fill a small saucepan with water. Bring the water to a boil and add the walnuts. Let the water come to a second boil, lower the heat, and simmer the walnuts, uncovered, for 3 minutes. Drain the nuts on paper towels, spread them on a cookie sheet, and toast them in the oven for 8 to 10 minutes, shaking the pan often. Let the walnuts cool and chop them coarsely.

In a large bowl thoroughly combine the

cream cheese, liverwurst, cognac, tarragon, and walnuts. Mound the pâté on a serving plate, cover it loosely with plastic wrap, and refrigerate it for at least 3 hours. Garnish the pâté with chopped parsley and arrange toast points or crackers around it. Makes 4–6 appetizer servings.

Swabian Pork Liver Pâté

2	*tablespoons butter*
2	*tablespoons flour*
2	*cups milk*
1/4	*teaspoon salt*
1/8	*teaspoon pepper*
1/2	*teaspoon allspice*
1/4	*teaspoon ground cloves*
1	*pound pork liver, cut into chunks*
3/4	*pound salt pork, cut into chunks*
4	*anchovy fillets*
1	*large onion, quartered*
2	*large eggs, lightly beaten*
	bread rounds or crackers

In a saucepan melt the butter over medium heat, stir in the flour, and cook the roux, whisking constantly, for 3 minutes. Add the milk and cook the mixture, whisking rapidly, until the white sauce is smooth and thickened. Stir in the salt, pepper, allspice, and cloves. Set the sauce aside and let it cool for about 10 minutes.

Preheat the oven to 350° F.

In a large mixing bowl combine the liver, salt pork, anchovies, and onion and put the mixture through the coarse blade of a meat grinder three times. Add the white sauce to the liver mixture and combine the ingredients well. Add the eggs, a little at a time, and mix them into the pâté thoroughly. Transfer the mixture to a 2½-quart loaf pan. Set the loaf pan in a shallow pan filled with hot water to a depth of 1 inch, and bring the water to a boil on top of the stove. Place the pans in the oven and bake the pâté for 1¼ hours, or until the juices run clear.

Refrigerate the pâté for 8 hours or overnight and serve it with bread rounds or crackers. Makes 6–8 appetizer servings.

Tongue with Eggs and Celery

1	*beef tongue, cooked, trimmed, and cut into chunks*
2	*large celery stalks, thickly sliced*
6	*hard-cooked eggs, peeled and thickly sliced*
6	*gherkins, thickly sliced*
1/2	*cup mayonnaise*
6	*sprigs watercress*
	carrot, green pepper, and celery sticks
	scallions
	rye and pumpernickel rounds

In a large mixing bowl loosely combine the tongue, celery, eggs, and pickle. Run the mixture through the coarse blade of a meat grinder. Stir in the mayonnaise and mound the spread on a serving plate. Garnish the mound with watercress and arrange the vegetables and bread around it. Makes 16–20 appetizer servings.

Best Ever Terrine

¾   pound ground veal
½   pound ground pork
½   pound ground beef
½   pound calves' brains
¼   pound chicken livers
4   eggs
¼   cup water
½   teaspoon savory
½   teaspoon marjoram
½   teaspoon coriander
½   teaspoon salt
¼   teaspoon pepper
⅓   cup pistachios
½   pound salt pork in one piece
white and rye bread triangles

Put the veal, pork, and beef in a large mixing bowl. Carefully trim the brains and chicken livers, put them through the coarse blade of a meat grinder twice, and add them to the bowl. In a smaller bowl beat the eggs with the water and add them to the meats along with the savory, marjoram, coriander, salt, pepper, and pistachios. Combine the ingredients thoroughly and refrigerate the mixture for 8 hours or overnight to combine the flavors.

Preheat the oven to 450° F.

Trim the skin from the salt pork, slice it very thin, and cut it into long strips about 1½ inches wide. Line a 2½-quart loaf pan or terrine with the salt pork strips. Pack the meat mixture into the loaf pan and fold any loose ends of salt pork over the top of the loaf. Cover the pan with foil and place it in a shallow baking pan filled to a depth of 1 inch with hot water. Place the pans in the oven and bake the terrine for 1½ hours, adding water to the shallow pan if necessary. The meat is cooked when the juices run clear.

Remove the terrine from the oven and place a weight on top of the foil; press down gently and leave it in place for about 5 minutes to press out some of the fat and eliminate air pockets. Remove the weight and the foil, carefully pour off the fat, and refrigerate the terrine overnight or for at least 8 hours. Slice the loaf and serve it from the terrine, or turn it out onto a serving plate and cut it into slices. Arrange triangles of white and rye bread around the terrine. Makes 14–16 appetizer servings.

Steak with Beer Dip

1   cup beer
¼   cup olive oil
1   clove garlic, minced
2   pounds sirloin steak, 2 inches thick
½   cup butter
1   teaspoon Worcestershire sauce
½   teaspoon dry mustard
2   tablespoons dry red wine
salt and pepper

In a small mixing bowl combine the beer, olive oil, and garlic. Put the steak in a shallow baking dish, pour the beer mixture over it, and refrigerate the steak in the marinade for 8 hours or overnight.

Preheat broiler or prepare a charcoal grill.

Remove the steak from the baking dish, reserving the marinade. Broil or grill the steak to the desired degree of doneness and cut it into bite-size pieces. Transfer the meat to a chafing dish and keep it warm.

In a saucepan combine the butter, Worcestershire sauce, dry mustard, wine, and the remaining marinade. Cook the mixture over medium heat until the butter is melted and the sauce is heated through. Adjust the seasonings, adding salt and pepper to taste. Pour the sauce into a bowl and serve it with the steak. Makes 8–10 appetizer servings.

Steak Tartare Salzburg

1   *2-ounce tin flat anchovy fillets*
2   *pounds lean ground beef, ground twice*
2   *tablespoons Worcestershire sauce*
1   *tablespoon Dusseldorf or Dijon mustard*
3   *tablespoons capers*
1   *small onion, minced*
2   *tablespoons chopped parsley*
2   *egg yolks*
    salt
    cayenne
    parsley sprigs
    rye, white, and pumpernickel bread, sliced thin

Transfer the anchovy fillets to paper towels to drain; measure out and reserve 1 tablespoon of the oil. Place the ground beef, anchovies, anchovy oil, Worcestershire sauce, and mustard in a large bowl. If the capers are large, mince

them; add them to the beef mixture along with the onion, parsley, and egg yolks. Mix the ingredients lightly. Season the beef mixture with salt and cayenne to taste.

Mound the steak tartare in the center of a serving plate and garnish it with parsley. Remove the crusts from the bread slices and cut each slice into rounds or triangles; arrange the bread around the steak tartar. Makes 16 appetizer servings.

Fried Potato Skins

6   *medium-size Idaho potatoes*
    vegetable oil for deep frying
    salt and pepper
1½ *cups grated Cheddar cheese*

Preheat the oven to 350° F.

Prick the potato skins with a fork, wrap the potatoes in foil, and bake them for 50 minutes, or until they are tender. Remove the foil from the potatoes, halve them lengthwise, and scoop out centers, leaving a lining about ¼ inch thick.

Pour about 3 inches of oil into a large saucepan and heat it to 385° F. Fry the potato skins, one or two at a time, until they are crisp and golden brown. Drain them on paper towels and season them with salt and pepper to taste.

Preheat the broiler.

Sprinkle about 2 tablespoons grated cheese into each potato skin, arrange the skins on a broiler pan so that they do not touch one another, and broil them until the cheese becomes runny. Makes 12 appetizer servings.

Mushroom Strudel

3/4 cup (1½ sticks) butter
½   cup chopped onion
1   pound mushrooms, chopped
3/4 cup sour cream
1   teaspoon snipped fresh dill
½   teaspoon salt
1/8 teaspoon pepper
¼   teaspoon nutmeg
6   strudel or phyllo leaves at room
     temperature

In a large skillet over medium heat melt ¼ cup (½ stick) of the butter. Add the onion and sauté it for 8 to 10 minutes until it is soft but not brown. Stir in the mushrooms and cook them, tossing often, until all the liquid has evaporated. Remove the skillet from the heat and stir in the sour cream, dill, salt, pepper, and nutmeg. Set the mixture aside.

In a small saucepan melt the remaining ½ cup (1 stick) butter. Unfold the strudel leaves; carefully lift off one leaf and place it on a cloth towel. Brush it lightly with melted butter and place a second leaf directly on top of it. Brush the second leaf with butter. Repeat the procedure with the third leaf, and cover the remaining leaves with a damp towel to prevent them from drying out. Spread half of the mushroom mixture along one end of the stack of buttered strudel leaves, leaving ½-inch margins. Fold over the sides of the dough and roll the strudel up jelly-roll fashion, lifting the dough with the towel to prevent the dough from splitting.

Preheat the oven to 375° F.

Lightly grease a jelly-roll pan or a shallow baking pan. Place the strudel in the pan seam side down and brush it with melted butter. Make a second strudel and put it in the jelly-roll pan. Bake the appetizers for 30 minutes, or until they are golden. Cut each strudel in thirds and serve each portion on a small appetizer plate. Makes 6 appetizer servings.

Dilled Vegetables

1   teaspoons salt
1½ cups cauliflower florets
1½ cups whole green beans
3   teaspoons snipped fresh dill
4   strips bacon
6   tablespoons olive or peanut oil
2   tablespoons red wine vinegar
½   teaspoon minced garlic
¼   teaspoon pepper

Fill two large saucepans with water, bring the water to a boil, and add ½ teaspoon salt to each pan. Plunge the cauliflower into one saucepan and the beans into the other. Cook the cauliflower for 8 minutes, or until it is tender but still crisp; drain it well, sprinkle it with 1 teaspoon of the snipped dill, and refrigerate it, covered, for at least 2 hours. Cook the green beans for 5 minutes, or until they are tender but still crisp; drain them well, sprinkle them with 1 teaspoon of the dill, and refrigerate them, covered, for at least 2 hours.

Cook the bacon until it is crisp; drain it on paper towels.

In a small jar with a tight lid combine the oil,

vinegar, garlic, pepper, and the remaining 1 teaspoon dill; shake well. Pour half of the dressing over the cauliflower; toss well. Pour the rest of the dressing over the beans and toss well. Mound the beans and cauliflower in twin serving dishes and crumble the bacon over them. Makes 6 appetizer servings.

Onion Herb Kuchen

     1   *cup flour*
    ³⁄₄   *teaspoon salt*
    ¹⁄₈   *teaspoon sugar*
    ¹⁄₄   *pound (1 stick) butter at room*
          temperature
     2   *tablespoons milk*
     6   *strips bacon*
     3   *cups chopped onion*
     3   *eggs*
    ³⁄₄   *cup light cream*
     1   *teaspoon chopped chives*
    ¹⁄₈   *teaspoon pepper*
    ¹⁄₂   *teaspoon caraway seeds*

Sift the flour, ¼ teaspoon of the salt, and the sugar into a large mixing bowl. Cut in the butter until the mixture is mealy. Add milk, a little at a time, until the dough becomes manageable. Mix the dough well and shape it into a ball. Wrap it in plastic and chill it for at least 1 hour.

Preheat the oven to 350° F.

Roll out the pastry between two sheets of wax paper. Fit it into a 9-inch pie plate and prick the crust with a fork. Bake the pie shell for 10 minutes, or until it is lightly browned.

In a heavy skillet cook the bacon until it is crisp; drain it on paper towels. Add the onion to the skillet and sauté it for 8 to 10 minutes, until it is soft and just beginning to brown. With a slotted spoon transfer the onion to paper towels to drain.

In a large mixing bowl combine the eggs, cream, and chives; stir in the remaining ½ teaspoon salt and the pepper. Add the sautéed onions and beat the mixture briefly until it is smooth. Crumble the bacon over the bottom of the pie shell. Pour the egg mixture over the bacon, and sprinkle the caraway seeds over the top. Bake the quiche for 30 to 35 minutes, until it is set. Makes 8 servings.

Artichoke Hearts with Blue Cheese Fondue

     2   *14-ounce cans artichoke hearts*
    ¹⁄₂   *cup (1 stick) butter*
    ¹⁄₂   *cup blue cheese*
    1¹⁄₂   *tablespoons lemon juice*

Put the artichokes and their liquid in a saucepan and heat them thoroughly over medium heat.

In a heavy saucepan melt the butter over medium heat. Add the cheese and lemon juice and heat mixture, stirring, until cheese is melted.

Pour the cheese mixture into a fondue pot and keep it warm over the flame. Drain the artichokes well and arrange them around the fondue. Provide fondue forks for dipping. Makes 4–6 appetizer servings.

Roquefort Mousse

½ pound Roquefort cheese
4 ounces cream cheese
4 tablespoons (½ stick) butter
¼ cup water
1 tablespoon unflavored gelatin
½ cup heavy cream
1 egg
½ teaspoon Dijon mustard
   crackers

Unwrap the cheeses and the butter, cut them into small pieces, and let them come to room temperature.

Pour the water into a small dish, sprinkle the gelatin over the water, and let it soften for 10 to 15 minutes.

Whip the cream until it is stiff and set aside.

Separate the egg. In a small bowl beat the egg white until it holds stiff peaks; set it aside. In a large bowl beat the egg yolk until it is smooth; add the Roquefort to the egg yolk, a few pieces at a time, and beat the mixture until it is smooth. Add the cream cheese and butter all at once and beat the mixture until it is smooth.

Butter a gelatin mold.

Fill a small skillet with water to a depth of ½ inch and bring the water almost to a boil. Turn off the heat, place the dish of softened gelatin in the hot water, and stir until the gelatin is dissolved. Stir the gelatin mixture and the mustard into the cheese mixture. Fold in the beaten egg white and then the whipped cream. Pour the mixture into the gelatin mold and chill it for 6 hours or overnight.

Dip the bottom of the gelatin mold in a pan of warm water for a few seconds, rap the mold sharply on the work surface, and unmold the mousse onto a serving plate. Serve the mousse with the crackers. Makes 10–12 appetizer servings.

Crocked Beer Cheese

1   12-ounce bottle beer
1½   pounds Cheddar cheese
2   tablespoons Worcestershire sauce
2   cloves garlic, minced
3–4 drops hot pepper sauce
     salt and pepper (optional)
     crackers or pumpernickel

Pour the beer into a blender or food processor and let it stand for 20 minutes, or until it is flat. Unwrap the cheese, cut it into small pieces, and let it come to room temperature.

Put the cheese in the blender with the beer. Add the Worcestershire sauce, garlic, and hot pepper sauce. Turn on the motor and blend the ingredients to a coarse purée. Season the mixture with salt and pepper to taste, if desired. Pack the beer-Cheddar in a crock and refrigerate it for at least 8 hours to blend the flavors.

Let the beer-Cheddar come to room temperature and serve it with crackers or pumpernickel. Makes 12–16 servings.

Note: This cheese will keep for several weeks in the refrigerator, and this method can be used for other cheeses or for a combination of leftover cheeses.

Westphalian Asparagus Quiche

1   pound asparagus
8   tablespoons (1 stick) butter
4   tablespoons minced onion
1½ cups saltine cracker crumbs
½   pound Westphalian ham,
        thinly sliced
3   eggs
½   cup milk
⅓   cup Gruyère cheese
¼   teaspoon nutmeg
¼   teaspoon salt
⅛   teaspoon pepper
        grated Parmesan cheese

Cook the asparagus in lightly salted water to cover for 10 minutes, or until it is just tender; drain it well.

In a small skillet melt 2 tablespoons (¼ stick) of the butter over medium heat. Add the onion and sauté it for 8 minutes, or until it is soft and just beginning to brown. Transfer the onion to paper towels to drain.

Wipe out the skillet and it in melt the remaining 6 tablespoons (¾ stick) butter. Pour the melted butter into a large mixing bowl, add the cracker crumbs, and stir to combine thoroughly. Press the mixture into a 9-inch pie plate. Line the pie shell with ham slices, trimming the edges to fit, if necessary. Arrange the asparagus spears, tips outward like spokes in a wheel, on top of the ham.

Preheat the oven to 350° F.

In a large bowl beat the eggs lightly; add the milk and beat the mixture until it is smooth.

Pour the mixture into a saucepan and heat it through over medium heat, stirring often. Add the cheese and stir constantly until it is melted. Add the onion, nutmeg, salt, and pepper and stir until the mixture is hot, but do not let it boil. Let the mixture cool for 5 minutes and carefully pour it over the asparagus spears. Sprinkle the tart with the grated cheese and bake it for 25 to 30 minutes, or until it is set. Makes 8 servings.

Liptauer Cheese

8   ounces butter, softened
16 ounces cream cheese,
        softened
1   tablespoon grated onion
2   teaspoons chopped capers
1½ teaspoons Dijon mustard
1½ teaspoons caraway seeds
2   teaspoons chopped parsley
2   teaspoons chopped chives
        crackers

Combine the butter and cream cheese. Add the onion, capers, mustard, and caraway seed and mix the ingredients well. Pack the Liptauer into a crock or shape it into a mound and sprinkle it with parsley and chives, or mold the cheese mixture into a ball and roll it in the parsley and chives. Serve the cheese with crackers. Makes 8–10 appetizer servings.

Variation: Add 2 or 3 minced anchovy fillets to the Liptauer cheese.

Marinated Mushrooms and Artichoke Hearts

2   *9-ounce packages frozen*
    artichoke hearts
2   *pounds small whole mushrooms*
1½ *cups water*
1   *cup vinegar*
½   *cup olive oil*
½   *teaspoon salt*
¼   *teaspoon pepper*
½   *teaspoon thyme*
½   *teaspoon oregano*
½   *teaspoon chervil*
1   *bay leaf*
2   *tablespoons chopped parsley*

Cook the artichoke hearts according to the package directions. Drain them thoroughly and let them cool for 15 minutes.

In a large bowl combine the mushrooms, water, vinegar, and artichoke hearts. Sprinkle the oil, salt and pepper, thyme, oregano, and chervil over the mixture. Add the bay leaf, stir to combine the ingredients, and refrigerate the mixture, covered, for at least 24 hours, stirring occasionally.

Pour off the marinade; arrange the artichoke hearts and mushrooms on a serving platter and sprinkle them with the chopped parsley. Makes 6–8 appetizer servings.

Filled Edam Cheese

1   *Edam cheese*
½   *pound bacon, cooked and crumbled*
4   *scallions, minced*
3   *ounces cream cheese, softened*
    Worcestershire sauce to taste

Scoop out the cheese and grate it by hand or in a food processor. Combine it with all the other ingredients and fill the shell of the Edam with the mixture.

Serve the cheese with crackers.

Note: Any leftovers can be spread on crackers and baked until bubbly for delicious hot hors d'oeuvres.

Stuffed Gouda Cheese

1   *small Gouda cheese*
3   *tablespoons sherry*
1   *teaspoon caraway seed*
    crackers

With a sharp knife, cut a ¼-inch slice off the top of the cheese. Scoop out the inside of the cheese, leaving a ½-inch shell, and put the scooped-out cheese in a blender or food processor. Add the sherry and caraway seeds and blend the mixture until it is light and fluffy. Pile the cheese mixture back into the shell and serve the stuffed gouda with crackers. Makes 4 appetizer servings.

SOUPS

SOUPS—superb budget stretchers that magically transform whatever ingredients are at hand—have always been an important part of any ethnic cuisine, particularly that of an immigrant group striving to make ends meet. The stockpot was the most often used kitchen utensil in the kitchens of eighteenth and nineteenth century German American immigrants. Therein simmered those hearty meat soups remembered from the Old Country, so thick they were probably served in dinner plates rather than soup bowls. The stockpot was also used for making delicate consommés, soups flavored with beer, and rich-tasting soups of fruit. Whether as a meal in itself, or the starter course of a truly hearty dinner, soup is a genuine staple of German American cooking.

Veal Stock
(White Stock)

2½   *pounds meaty veal bones, cut in several*
        pieces
3   *quarts water*
1   *large onion, peeled*
1   *large carrot*
2   *celery stalks, leaves intact*
1   *parsnip*
1   *tablespoon beef bouillon granules*
4   *peppercorns*

Preheat the oven to 450° F.

Put the veal bones in a roasting pan and brown them in the oven, uncovered, for 30 minutes. Remove the pan from the oven, add ½ cup of the water, and with a wooden spoon loosen the crusty bits from the bottom of the pan. With a slotted spoon transfer the bones to a kettle. Pour the pan liquid and the browned bits over the bones and add the remaining water. Bring the stock to a boil and add the onion, carrot, celery, parsnip, bouillon, and peppercorns. Reduce the heat and simmer the stock for 5 hours, uncovered.

Strain the stock through a sieve lined with two layers of cheesecloth and refrigerate it overnight. Lift off the fat from the top of the stock.

Use the veal stock in cream soups in place of about half of the milk. Makes 1½ pints.

Fish Stock (Court Bouillon)

2 pounds white-fleshed fish bones and
    heads, thoroughly rinsed
1½ quarts water
1 small onion, peeled
1 stalk celery, leaves intact
2 parsley sprigs
1 small bay leaf
½ cup white wine vinegar
6 peppercorns
½ teaspoon salt

Put all of the ingredients in a large saucepan
and bring the water to a boil. Lower the heat
and simmer the stock, uncovered, for 20
minutes. Strain the court bouillon through 2
layers of cheesecloth. Use the fish stock in fish
soups and sauces and as a poaching liquid for
fish. Makes 8 cups.

Beef Stock

6 pounds meaty beef bones
2½ quarts water
2 large onions, peeled
2 large celery stalks, leaves intact
1 large carrot
1 turnip
1 parsnip
3 parsley sprigs
6 peppercorns
1 bay leaf
    salt (optional)

Put the bones in a large kettle and cover them
with the water. Bring it quickly to a simmer

and skim off any foam from the top. Simmer
the bones, uncovered, for 3 hours. Add the
onions, celery, carrot, turnip, parsnip, parsley,
peppercorns, and bay leaf and simmer the
stock for 2 more hours. Season the stock with
salt, if desired.

    Strain the broth, pressing hard on the solids
to extract all the liquid. Refrigerate the stock
for 1 hour and lift off the fat. Use the stock as
a base for gravies and for soups that call for
beef broth or stock. Makes 2–2½ pints.

Chicken Stock

3 pounds chicken wings,
    necks, and backs
2 quarts water
1 large onion, peeled
1 large carrot
1½ large celery stalks,
    leaves intact
1 small turnip
3 parsley sprigs
    salt and pepper

Put the chicken in a large kettle and cover it
with the water. Add the onion, carrot, celery,
turnip, and parsley and bring the water to a
boil. Skim off any foam, reduce the heat, and
simmer the chicken, covered, for 2 hours.
Season the stock with salt and pepper to taste.
Strain the broth and reserve the chicken meat
for another use. Refrigerate the stock for 1
hour and skim off the fat. Use the broth as a
base for gravies and for soups that call for
chicken stock or broth. Makes 6 cups.

Beef Consommé

6   cups beef stock
1   egg white, lightly beaten
1   crushed eggshell
¼   cup water
     salt and pepper
2   tablespoons chopped chives

In a large saucepan bring the beef stock to a simmer. In a small bowl stir together the egg white, the crushed eggshell, and the water. Add the mixture to the hot stock and simmer the stock without stirring for 10 minutes. Push the foam aside with a wooden spoon and strain the consommé into a clean saucepan through a sieve lined with two layers of cheesecloth. Heat the consommé almost to a boil, add salt and pepper to taste, and sprinkle the consommé with the chives. Makes 6 servings.

Chicken Consommé

6   cups chicken stock
2   egg whites, lightly beaten
2   eggshells, crushed
     salt and pepper
2   tablespoons minced fresh parsley

In a large saucepan bring the chicken stock to a simmer. In a bowl stir together the egg whites and the crushed eggshells. Add the mixture to the hot stock and simmer the stock without stirring for about 15 minutes. Do not skim off the thick, crusty foam that appears on top of the broth. Remove the saucepan from the heat and let it cool for 1 hour. Line a large fine-mesh strainer with a double thickness of cheesecloth. Push the foam aside with a wooden spoon and ladle the stock through the strainer into a clean saucepan. Reheat the consommé, add salt and pepper to taste, and sprinkle the consommé with the parsley. Makes 6 servings.

Fresh Mushroom Soup

4   tablespoons butter
½   cup minced onion
½   pound mushrooms, sliced
2   tablespoons flour
6   cups chicken stock
1   egg yolk
1   cup sour cream

In a large kettle melt the butter over medium heat. Add the onion and sauté it for 5 minutes, until it is soft. Add the mushrooms and cook them, tossing often, for 10 minutes, or until they are golden brown. Push the mushrooms and onions aside and stir the flour into the butter. Cook the roux, stirring constantly, for 3 or 4 minutes. Gradually add the chicken stock and simmer the mixture, stirring constantly, until it is smooth and bubbly. Cook the soup slowly for 30 minutes, stirring often.

In a small bowl beat the egg yolk lightly; blend in the sour cream and pour the mixture into a soup tureen. Carefully pour the hot soup into the tureen. With a wooden spoon swirl the sour cream mixture into the soup. Makes 6 servings.

German Wine Soup

6   tablespoons butter
1   large onion, peeled and separated into
      rings
2½ tablespoons flour
6   cups beef stock
4   slices day-old white bread
½   cup white wine
2   egg yolks
      salt and pepper
½   cup sour cream
1½ teaspoons chopped chives
1½ teaspoons chopped dill

Melt 3 tablespoons of the butter in a large heavy kettle over medium heat. Add the onion rings and sauté them for 8 minutes, or until they are soft but not browned. Push the onions aside, sprinkle the flour into the kettle, and cook the roux, stirring constantly, for 3 minutes. Add about ½ cup of the stock and cook the sauce, stirring, until it is smooth and bubbly. Add the rest of the stock and cook the soup, stirring constantly, until it is smooth and somewhat thickened. Simmer the soup for 20 minutes more, stirring often.

Remove the crusts from the bread and cut the slices into crouton-size cubes. In a small skillet over medium-high heat, melt the remaining 3 tablespoons butter, add the bread cubes, and brown them, tossing often. With a slotted spoon transfer the croutons to paper towels to drain and keep them warm. Add the wine to the skillet and cook it, stirring, for 3 minutes, scraping up the brown bits from the pan. Add the wine to the soup. In a small bowl,

beat the egg yolks lightly and beat in one cup warm soup. Slowly whisk the yolk mixture into the kettle and stir the soup until it is smooth and hot but not boiling. Taste the soup and add salt and pepper to taste.

Pour the soup into a tureen and serve it with the sour cream, chives, dill, and croutons. Makes 6 servings.

Root Soup

1   large carrot
3   large fresh beets
1   large parsnip
1   large knob celeriac
2   medium potatoes
1   small onion, chopped
2   tablespoons butter
2   tablespoons all-purpose flour
2   cups strong beef broth
2   cups water
      pepper
      sour cream to garnish

Peel all the vegetables except the onion and grate them coarsely by hand or in a food processor. Set them aside.

In a large heavy saucepan melt the butter and sauté the onion until it is translucent. Add the flour and stir the roux until it is a pale golden color. In another saucepan bring the broth and water to a boil. Add the boiling stock all at once to the roux, stirring. Add vegetables and pepper to taste. Bring soup to a simmer and cook until vegetables are just tender.

Serve the soup garnished with sour cream. Makes 4 servings.

Dark Beer Soup

½ loaf dry pumpernickel, diced
4½ cups strong dark beer
½ cup maple syrup
½ teaspoon powdered ginger
    salt and pepper

In a food processor or blender combine the pumpernickel cubes and 1½ cups of the beer. Run the motor just until the mixture is coarsely puréed.

In a saucepan heat the remaining 3 cups beer. Stir in the maple syrup and the ginger and bring the soup almost to a boil. Add the puréed bread and beer and cook the soup for 10 minutes more, stirring often. Season the soup with salt and pepper to taste. Makes 4 servings.

Biersuppe

1 cup milk
1 stick cinnamon
1 tablespoon sugar
2 teaspoons cornstarch
1 egg yolk
1½ cups dark beer

Put the milk in a saucepan with the cinnamon stick and bring the milk almost to a boil. In a small bowl combine the sugar and cornstarch. Add the egg yolk and beat the mixture with a whisk until it is smooth. Add about ¼ cup of the hot milk and stir to incorporate it. Pour the egg yolk mixture into the saucepan and cook the soup, stirring constantly, until it is smooth and thickened. Add the dark beer and reheat the soup, but do not let it boil. Makes 2 servings.

Creamed Asparagus Soup

1 pound fresh asparagus, washed, trimmed, and chopped
3 cups chicken broth
2 cups water
3 tablespoons butter
3 tablespoons flour
⅓ cup dry white wine
    juice of ½ lemon
1 cup half-and-half
    salt and pepper

In a saucepan combine the asparagus, the broth, and the water. Bring the mixture to a boil, reduce the heat, and cook the asparagus for 5 minutes. With a slotted spoon transfer the asparagus to a food processor fitted with the steel blade, or to a blender, reserving the stock. Purée the asparagus, return it to the stock, and keep the soup warm over low heat.

In a small skillet melt the butter over medium heat. Stir in the flour and cook the roux for 5 minutes, stirring constantly. Pour the wine into the skillet and stir the sauce until it is smooth and bubbly. Add the lemon juice and about ¼ cup of the hot stock and stir the sauce until it is well combined and heated through. Gradually add the sauce to the soup, stirring constantly, and simmer the soup for 15 minutes. Add the half-and-half, reheat the soup, and season it with salt and pepper to taste. Makes 4 servings.

Watercress Soup

3   bunches watercress
3   tablespoons butter
¼   cup minced onion
1   cup water
6   cups chicken broth

Rinse the watercress, drain it well, and remove any tough stems. In a large heavy saucepan over medium heat, melt the butter. Add the onion and cook it for 10 minutes, or until it is golden. Stir in the watercress and cook the mixture over low heat for 5 minutes more. Add the water and broth and cook the soup over medium heat for 10 minutes; let it cool for 10 minutes. Pour the soup, in batches if necessary, into a food processor fitted with the steel blade, or into a blender, and purée it. Return the soup to the kettle and heat it through. Makes 6 servings.

German Potato Soup

6   large potatoes, peeled and quartered
2   medium-size onions, peeled and coarsely chopped
½   cup chopped celery
6   cups chicken stock
4   cups water
1   cup light cream
¼   cup chopped parsley
¼   teaspoon minced dill

In a large saucepan combine the potatoes, onions, and celery. Add the chicken stock and water and bring the mixture to a boil. Lower the heat and simmer the stock for 20 to 25 minutes, or until the potatoes are tender.

Strain the soup through a coarse sieve into a soup kettle and keep the stock warm over low heat. Put the vegetables in a food processor fitted with the steel blade, or in a blender. Add 2 cups of the stock and purée the mixture. Slowly add the purée to the kettle, beating with a wire whisk until the soup is smooth and well blended. Stir in the cream and reheat the soup, taking care not to let it boil.

Serve the soup, hot or chilled, garnished with the parsley and dill. Makes 8–10 servings.

Potato and Watercress Soup

2   tablespoons butter
2   leeks, white parts only, sliced thin
3   medium-size potatoes, cooked, peeled, and diced
1   bunch fresh watercress, chopped
6   cups chicken broth
1   cup heavy cream
    salt and pepper
12–16   whole watercress leaves

Melt the butter in a large saucepan over medium heat. Add the leeks and sauté them for 10 minutes, or until they are soft but not brown. Add the potatoes, the watercress, and the chicken broth. Bring the soup to a boil, lower the heat, and simmer it for 5 minutes. Let the soup cool for 10 minutes. Pour it, in batches if necessary, into a food processor fitted with the steel blade or into a blender, and purée it. Return the purée to the saucepan, add the cream, and heat the soup through, stirring constantly, without letting it boil. Season the soup with salt and pepper to taste.

Garnish the soup with the whole watercress leaves and serve it hot, or refrigerate it for 4 hours and serve it cold. Makes 6–8 servings.

Vegetable Soup with Dumplings

2 *quarts beef stock*
2 *medium-size potatoes, peeled and diced*
4 *carrots, sliced*
2 *large celery stalks, chopped*
1 *large onion, sliced and separated into*
    rings
1/4 *cup cooked lima beans*
1/4 *cup cooked whole-kernel corn, drained*
1 *cup cooked peas*
2 *cups tomato juice*
    salt and pepper
1 *cup sifted flour*
2 *teaspoons baking powder*
1/2 *teaspoon salt*
3/4 *cup milk*
2 *tablespoons vegetable oil*

In a large kettle bring the stock to a boil and add the potatoes, carrots, celery, and onion. Return the stock to a boil, reduce the heat to low, and simmer the vegetables for 15 minutes. Stir in the lima beans, corn, peas, and tomato juice and cook the soup for another 10 minutes. Add salt and pepper to taste.

Into a large bowl sift together the flour, baking powder, and ½ teaspoon salt. In a measuring cup mix the milk and the oil. Pour the mixture into the dry ingredients, stirring just until the flour is thoroughly moistened.

Increase the heat under the soup to medium and drop the dumpling batter by the tablespoonful into the bubbling soup. Cover the kettle and cook the dumplings for 10 minutes. Makes 8–10 servings.

Leek and Potato Soup

3 *tablespoons butter*
1 *large onion, diced*
4 *leeks, white parts only, sliced*
2 *large potatoes, peeled and diced*
2 *carrots, sliced*
8 *cups chicken stock*
1/2 *cup heavy cream*
    salt and pepper
1½ *cups croutons*

In a soup kettle melt the butter over medium heat. Add the onion and leeks and sauté them for 10 minutes, or until they are golden. Add the potatoes and carrots and stir to coat them with butter. Pour the chicken stock into the kettle and simmer the soup, partly covered, for 25 minutes, or until the vegetables are tender. Pour the soup in batches into a blender or a food processor fitted with the steel blade and purée it. Return the soup to the kettle, stir in the cream, and heat it through. Season the soup with salt and pepper to taste and serve it with the croutons. Makes 6 servings.

Bavarian Lentil Soup

1   pound lentils, washed
3   quarts water
1   meaty ham bone
2   whole onions
3   celery stalks, leaves intact
1   bay leaf
½   teaspoon thyme
1   large potato
3   large carrots, sliced
6   strips bacon
1   cup coarsely chopped onion
1   cup sliced celery
    salt and pepper

Soak the lentils overnight in water to cover. Drain them well and put them in a large kettle with the 3 quarts water. Add the ham bone, the whole onions, the celery stalks, and the bay leaf and thyme. Peel the potato, grate it, and stir it into the lentil mixture. Bring the mixture to a boil, reduce the heat, and simmer the soup for 4 hours, stirring often.

In a small saucepan cook the carrots in water to cover for 15 minutes, or until they are very tender. Drain them well.

In a heavy skillet cook the bacon thoroughly; transfer it to paper towels to drain. Stir the chopped onion and sliced celery into the bacon drippings and sauté them over medium heat for 15 minutes, or until they are very tender, but take care not to let them brown. With a slotted spoon transfer the vegetables to paper towels and drain them well.

Remove the ham bone, the whole onions, the celery stalks, and the bay leaf from the kettle and keep the soup warm over very low heat. Discard the bay leaf, onions and celery stalks. Cut all of the meat from the ham bone, break it into manageable pieces, and return it to the kettle. Stir the carrots and the sautéed onion and celery into the kettle. Season the soup with salt and pepper to taste.

Pour the soup into a tureen and crumble the bacon over the top. Makes 8–10 servings.

Lentil Beer Soup

2   cups dried lentils
4   cups beer
4   cups water
4   cups chicken broth
1   meaty ham bone
2   tablespoons butter
2   medium onions, minced
2   stalks celery, very thinly sliced
3   medium carrots, very thinly sliced
    salt and pepper

Soak the lentils overnight in water to cover. Drain them well and pour them into a large kettle. Stir the beer, water, and broth into the kettle, add the ham bone, and bring the mixture to a boil. Reduce the heat and simmer the lentils, covered, for 3 hours, stirring occasionally. Remove ham bone, strip off meat, break into small pieces, and return to the kettle.

In a small skillet melt the butter over medium heat. Add the onions, celery, and carrots and sauté them for 10 minutes, or until they are soft but not browned. With a slotted spoon transfer the vegetables to the soup kettle and cook the soup for 30 minutes more. Season the lentil beer soup with salt and pepper to taste. Makes 8–10 servings.

Hearty Tomato Soup

4 tablespoons (½ stick) butter
2 medium-size onions, chopped
1 clove garlic, minced
2 celery stalks, chopped
2 carrots, sliced
4 tablespoons flour
4 cups veal stock
4 cups chicken broth
4 large tomatoes, peeled, seeded, and chopped
2 cups tomato purée
1 tablespoon sugar
5 peppercorns
   salt

Melt the butter in a large kettle. Stir in the onions, garlic, celery, and carrots and sauté the vegetables for 10 minutes, or until they are soft. Push the vegetables to one side of the kettle, stir in the flour, and cook the roux, stirring constantly, for 5 minutes, or until it is golden. Gradually add 1 cup of the veal stock and cook the mixture, stirring in some of the vegetables, until it is smooth and slightly thickened. Add the rest of the veal stock and all of the chicken broth and return the soup to a simmer. Stir in the tomatoes, the tomato purée, the sugar, and the peppercorns. Simmer the soup for 25 minutes and season it with salt to taste. Makes 8–10 servings.

Spring Beet Borscht

8 small beets, washed, trimmed, and julienned
1 medium-size onion, minced
1 carrot, julienned
6 cups beef broth
½ cup tomato juice
1 cup water
2 stalks celery, tops included, chopped
1 small tomato, peeled, seeded, and minced
½ cup chopped green beans
2 cups shredded cabbage
1 tablespoon fresh lemon juice
1 tablespoon flour
1 cup sour cream
   salt and pepper
1 tablespoon chopped dill

Put the beets, onion, and carrot in a large kettle. Add the beef broth, tomato juice, and water. Bring the mixture to a boil, lower the heat, and simmer the vegetables, covered, for 15 minutes. Stir in the celery, tomato, green beans, and cabbage and simmer the soup for another 10 minutes. Add the lemon juice. In a measuring cup stir together the flour and ½ cup of the sour cream. Add about ¼ cup of the soup and stir the mixture well. Gradually spoon the mixture into the hot soup, stirring constantly, until the soup is smooth, and taking care not to let it boil. Season the soup with salt and pepper to taste and garnish it with the remaining ½ cup sour cream and the dill. Makes 6 servings.

Sauerkraut Soup

1   *16-ounce can sauerkraut*
¼   *pound salt pork*
1   *tablespoon butter*
1   *medium yellow onion, chopped*
4   *cups strong chicken broth*
2   *cups water*
½   *teaspoon marjoram*
½   *teaspoon thyme*
2   *carrots*
4   *potatoes*

Pour the sauerkraut into a sieve and rinse it well. Set it in the sink to drain. Cut the salt pork into cubes. In a heavy saucepan brown the salt pork. Drain off the fat and in the same saucepan melt the butter. Add the onion and sauté until translucent. Add the chicken broth, water, and herbs and bring the broth to a boil.

Peel the carrots and potatoes, cut them into chunks, and add them to the soup. Add the rinsed sauerkraut to the soup and simmer until the vegetables are tender. Serve immediately. Makes 4 servings.

Celery Soup

3   *cups strong chicken broth*
3   *cups water*
1   *medium onion, minced*
2   *cups chopped celery*
1   *tablespoon butter*
2   *tablespoons all-purpose flour*
1   *egg yolk*

1   *cup heavy cream*
    watercress to garnish

In a saucepan boil the chicken broth and the water. In another large heavy saucepan melt the butter and sauté the onion and celery until the onion is translucent. Stir in the flour and cook the roux until it turns a pale golden color. Add the boiling stock all at once and stir to combine. Simmer the soup for 10 minutes and remove it from the heat.

In a small bowl mix the egg yolk and cream. Whisk in ½ cup of the hot soup and add the egg mixture, stirring well to combine. Serve the soup garnished with watercress. Makes 4 servings.

Oven Fish Chowder

2   *pounds haddock fillets cut into serving-size pieces*
4   *cups fish stock*
½   *cup dry white wine*
3   *medium-size onions, chopped*
4   *medium-size potatoes, peeled and diced*
1   *bay leaf*
½   *teaspoon salt*
¼   *teaspoon pepper*
2   *cups light cream*
4   *tablespoons chopped parsley*

Preheat the oven to 375° F.

Put the haddock in a large ovenproof casserole and pour the fish stock and wine over it. Add the onions, potatoes, bay leaf, salt, and pepper and bake the chowder for 45 minutes, or until the fish flakes easily. Remove the bay leaf, stir in the cream, and return the casserole to the oven for 5 minutes. Garnish the chowder with the chopped parsley and serve it with garlic bread and a green salad. Makes 4 servings.

Creamy Spinach Soup

2   tablespoons butter
1/2 cup chopped scallions, green part
    included
2   pounds cooked spinach, well drained
6   cups chicken broth
    dash nutmeg
1   cup light cream
    salt and pepper
1   hard-cooked egg, grated

In a large saucepan melt the butter over medium heat. Add the scallions and sauté them for about 2 minutes, or until they are soft. Add the spinach, and cook it, tightly covered, for 5 minutes, or until it is heated through. Stir in the broth and nutmeg, and bring the soup to a simmer. Cook the soup 5 minutes more, or until the spinach is soft. In a food processor or blender, puree the soup until it is smooth and green. Return the soup to the saucepan, add cream, and reheat the soup but do not let it boil.

Sprinkle the hard-cooked egg over the soup just before serving. Makes 6 servings.

Dilled Fish Soup

3   tablespoons butter
1   onion, chopped
2   celery stalks, diced
1 1/2 cups water
4   medium-size potatoes, diced
2   cups fresh peas
2   teaspoons dill
4 1/2 cups fish stock
1   pound cod or whitefish fillets, cut into
    2-inch pieces
    salt and pepper
2   tablespoons chopped parsley
2   strips bacon, cooked and crumbled

In a large heavy saucepan melt the butter over medium heat. Add the onion and sauté it for 5 minutes. Stir in the celery and cook the vegetables for 10 minutes more, taking care not to let them brown. Add the water, the potatoes, the peas, and the dill. Heat the water almost to a boil, reduce the heat, and simmer the vegetables, covered, for 20 minutes.

While the vegetables are cooking, pour the fish stock into a heavy skillet, add the fish and the salt and pepper to taste, and bring the stock to a boil. Lower the heat and poach the fish for 5 to 8 minutes, until it flakes easily.

With a slotted spoon carefully transfer the fish to a soup tureen. Pour the fish stock into the saucepan and stir it into the vegetable liquid. Slowly pour the soup and vegetables into the tureen and garnish the soup with the parsley and crumbled bacon. Makes 4 servings.

Sausage Soup

½   *medium cabbage, shredded*
4   *medium carrots, peeled and sliced*
3   *medium potatoes, peeled and cubed*
3   *celery stalks with leaves, chopped*
1   *turnip, cubed (optional)*
1   *large onion, peeled and thinly sliced*
2   *quarts beef stock*
4   *tablespoons tomato paste*
2   *tablespoons vinegar*
1   *teaspoon salt*
½   *teaspoon dried thyme, crushed*
¼   *teaspoon black pepper*
1   *pound kielbasa, cut in ¼-inch slices*

In a large kettle or Dutch oven combine the cabbage, carrots, potatoes, celery, turnip and onion. Add the stock, tomato paste, vinegar and seasonings. Bring to a boil. Reduce the heat and stir in the sausage. Simmer, covered, for 35 to 45 minutes, or until vegetables are tender. Makes 12 servings.

Kirschsuppe

4   *cups fresh pitted cherries, puréed in food*
    processor or blender
⅓   *cup sugar*
1   *lemon, halved lengthwise and sliced thin*
2   *cups water*
1   *cinnamon stick*
1   *cup dry red wine*
1   *cup heavy cream, whipped*

In a saucepan gently simmer the cherry purée, sugar, lemon slices, water, and cinnamon for 25 minutes, stirring frequently. Remove from the heat. Cool. Remove the cinnamon stick. Stir in the wine and chill at least 4 hours. Stir well. Serve topped with whipped cream. Makes 6 servings.

SALADS AND SALAD DRESSINGS

What American doesn't think of Cole Slaw or Potato Salad when planning picnic fare? But look into the history of such American staples and you will find German origins. German and German American cooking are noted for marvelous salads served with hot dressings, unusual winter salads of shredded kohlrabi or red beets, and other salads for all seasons featuring a variety of ingredients such as marinated leeks and other piquant vegetables and combinations.

Cabbage Slaw with Cooked Dressing

2   cups sugar
1½   cups vinegar
½   cup water
1   tablespoon Dijon mustard
½   tablespoon celery seeds
1   medium-size cabbage
1   tablespoon salt
1   small sweet red pepper, chopped
1   small green pepper, chopped
2   carrots, grated
1   onion, chopped
1   cup diced celery
    pepper

In a saucepan combine the sugar, vinegar, and water; remove the pan from heat and stir in the mustard and celery seeds. Set the dressing aside at room temperature for 2 hours.

Grate the cabbage into a large bowl and toss it with the salt; set the mixture aside at room temperature for 2 hours.

Add the red pepper, green pepper, carrots, onion, and celery to the cabbage. Pour the dressing over the salad and toss the mixture very well. Season the salad with pepper to taste and refrigerate it for at least 1 hour. Makes 8–10 servings.

Coleslaw

4 cups grated cabbage
1 cup grated carrots
½ cup chopped green pepper
¼ cup chopped scallion
⅔ cup mayonnaise
¼ teaspoon salt
⅛ teaspoon pepper
½ teaspoon sugar
1 tablespoon vinegar
1 tablespoon lemon juice
1 tablespoon milk
2 drops hot pepper sauce

In a large bowl toss together the cabbage, carrots, pepper, and scallion. In a bowl combine all of the remaining ingredients and stir the dressing well. Spoon the dressing over the vegetables, toss the salad again, and refrigerate it for at least 1 hour. Makes 4–6 servings.

Kohlsalat

3 cups grated cabbage
4 cups boiling water
3 tablespoons vegetable oil
¼ cup vinegar
¼ cup water
½ teaspoon salt
1 teaspoon sugar
2 tablespoons caraway seeds

Put the cabbage into a large bowl, pour the boiling water over it, and let it stand for 3 minutes. Drain the cabbage in a colander, return it to the bowl, and set it aside at room temperature to cool.

In a small saucepan combine the oil, vinegar, water, salt, and sugar. Bring the dressing to a boil, stirring to dissolve the sugar. Set the pan aside and let the dressing cool to room temperature.

Pour the cooled dressing over the cabbage, sprinkle the caraway seeds over the top, and toss the slaw thoroughly. Makes 4–6 servings.

Rotkrautsalat

4 cups grated red cabbage
½ teaspoon salt
¼ teaspoon pepper
4 strips bacon
1 teaspoon sugar
2 tablespoons vinegar
¼ cup white wine (optional)
2 tablespoons olive oil

Put the red cabbage in a large bowl, add the salt and pepper, and toss the salad well.

In a large skillet cook the bacon until it is crisp and transfer it to paper towels to drain, reserving 3 tablespoons of the drippings. Wipe out the skillet and return the reserved drippings to the pan. Add the sugar, vinegar, wine if desired, and oil and heat the dressing to a boil, stirring constantly. Pour the hot dressing over the red cabbage, toss the salad well, and serve it immediately. Makes 4–6 servings.

Pennsylvania Dutch Red Cabbage Salad

3   cups coarsely grated red cabbage
⅔   cup grated carrot
½   cup thinly sliced celery
1   cup minced green pepper
⅓   cup water
¼   cup vinegar
2½ tablespoons sugar
1   teaspoon salt

In a large bowl combine the cabbage, carrot, celery, and green pepper. Put the water, vinegar, sugar, and salt in a jar with a tight lid and shake the dressing well. Pour the dressing over the vegetables, toss the salad well, and chill it for at least 1 hour. Makes 6–8 servings.

Caledonian Salad

1   16-ounce jar herring in wine sauce
1   large sweet onion, sliced
1   can seedless white grapes
1   3-ounce package blanched almonds
1   tablespoon sugar
2   medium apples, sliced
2   tablespoons fresh lemon juice
1   pint sour cream, whipped to soft peaks

Wash herring well in cold water, squeeze, and pat dry. Cut each herring in half. Mix the herring halves with the onion, grapes, almonds, sugar, apples, and lemon juice, fold in sour cream. Refrigerate one hour or until chilled.

Serve the salad on lettuce leaves with rye rounds for luncheon. Makes 4 servings.

Apple Sauerkraut Salad

2   cups sauerkraut, well rinsed and drained
1   large unpeeled apple, cored and chopped
1   large onion, chopped
1   green pepper, chopped
1   cup chopped celery
¼   cup chopped pimientos
¼   cup vegetable oil
½   cup vinegar
1   cup sugar

In a large bowl toss together the sauerkraut, apple, onion, pepper, celery, and pimientos. In a jar with a tight lid combine the oil, vinegar, and sugar. Pour the dressing over the vegetables, toss the salad well, and refrigerate it, covered, for 24 hours. Makes 8–10 servings.

Bacon Salad

2   pounds bacon, sliced thick
1½ pounds Cheddar cheese
1   pound green grapes
2   cups sliced celery
¼   cup chopped parsley
    Bavarian Cucumber Dressing
1   head Boston lettuce

Cut the bacon strips in four pieces and fry them until crisp. Drain the bacon on paper towels. Cut the cheese into small cubes. Wash the grapes and remove them from the stems. In a large bowl combine the bacon, cheese, grapes, celery, and parsley and toss them with dressing. Line salad bowl with lettuce and fill with bacon-cheese mixture. Makes 12 servings.

Sauerkraut Salad

1½   cups sugar
¾   cup vinegar
2   cups chopped celery
1   cup chopped onion
2   large carrots, coarsely grated
1   green pepper, minced
3   cups sauerkraut, well rinsed and drained

In a saucepan combine the sugar and vinegar and bring the dressing to a boil. Lower the heat and simmer the mixture, stirring, until the sugar is melted. Set the dressing aside and let it cool to room temperature.

In a large bowl combine the celery, onion, carrots, pepper, and sauerkraut. Pour the cooled dressing over the vegetables and toss the salad well. Refrigerate the salad, covered, for 8 hours or overnight. Makes 4 servings.

German Potato Salad

6   medium-size potatoes
1   medium-size onion, diced
½   teaspoon salt
¼   teaspoon pepper
1   teaspoon celery seed
3   tablespoons white vinegar
6   strips bacon
2   teaspoons sugar

Cook the potatoes in water to cover for 30 to 40 minutes, or until they are tender. Drain them and submerge them in cold water until they are cool enough to handle. Peel and cube them, put them in a large bowl, and add the onion. Sprinkle the potatoes and onion with the salt, pepper, celery seed, and vinegar and toss the mixture two or three times.

In a skillet cook the bacon until it is crisp. Transfer it to paper towels to drain, reserving ¼ cup of the drippings. Sprinkle the sugar over the reserved drippings and cook the mixture, stirring, until the sugar is dissolved. Pour the hot drippings over the salad and toss it well. Crumble the bacon over the salad and serve it immediately. Makes 6–8 servings.

Kartoffelsalat

8   large potatoes, cubed
8   strips bacon
½   cup minced onion
½   cup chopped celery
¼   cup minced dill pickles
⅓   cup water
¾   cup vinegar
2   teaspoons sugar
¼   teaspoon salt
½   teaspoon paprika
½   teaspoon dry mustard
1   tablespoon chopped parsley
1   tablespoon chopped chives

In a saucepan cook the potatoes in water to cover for 10 to 15 minutes, or until they are tender. Drain them and let them cool for 10 minutes.

In a skillet cook the bacon until it is crisp. Transfer it to paper towels to drain, reserving 3 tablespoons of the drippings. To the drippings add the onion and celery and sauté them over medium heat for 5 minutes, or until they are translucent. Add the pickles and heat them through. Turn off the heat and let the mixture cool for 5 minutes.

In a small saucepan combine the water and vinegar; bring the mixture to a boil and reduce the heat. Stir in the sugar and salt and simmer the dressing, stirring, until the sugar is dissolved. Remove the saucepan from the heat and let it cool for 5 minutes.

Transfer the potatoes to a large serving bowl, pour the onion and celery over them. Add the vinegar mixture, the paprika, and the mustard and toss the salad well. Sprinkle the parsley and chives over the salad and serve it at once. Makes 8–10 servings.

Austrian Salad

2   large Idaho potatoes
1   tablespoon vegetable oil
3   cups escarole, torn into bite-size
      pieces
4   strips bacon
3   tablespoons white vinegar
     salt and pepper

Preheat the oven to 350° F. Prick the potatoes with a fork, oil the skins, and bake them for 1 hour, or until they are tender. Set them aside until they are cool enough to handle.

Drop the escarole into a large bowl of ice water and let it soak for 20 minutes. Drain it well, pat it dry, and put it in a large salad bowl.

In a skillet cook the bacon until it is crisp. Transfer it to paper towels to drain. Pour the drippings into a measuring cup, let the solids settle to the bottom, and reserve 4 tablespoons of the clearer drippings.

Peel the potatoes and cut them into ½-inch cubes. Add the potato cubes to the salad bowl. Crumble the bacon over the escarole and potatoes. Sprinkle the salad with the vinegar and the reserved bacon drippings and season it with salt and pepper to taste. Toss the salad well and serve it immediately. Makes 4 servings.

Red Potato Salad

16–24   small russet potatoes
1¼   cups olive oil
⅓   cup tarragon vinegar
1   tablespoon Dijon mustard
1   tablespoon snipped dill
½   teaspoon salt
¼   teaspoon pepper

Peel a strip around the center of each potato and cook the potatoes in water to cover for 20 to 25 minutes, or until they are tender.

Put the oil, vinegar, mustard, dill, salt, and pepper into a blender or a food processor fitted with the steel blade. Run the motor just long enough to blend the dressing well.

Drain the potatoes, halve or quarter them, and put them in a large bowl. Pour the dressing over the warm potatoes and refrigerate the salad for 1 hour. Makes 4–6 servings.

Potato and Smoked Herring Salad

½ *pound smoked herring, boned and diced*
6 *new potatoes, cooked, peeled, and diced*
1 *small onion, chopped*
1 *tablespoon lemon juice*
1 *cup mayonnaise*
   salt and pepper
6 *cup-shaped lettuce leaves*

In a large bowl combine the herring, potatoes, and onion. Sprinkle the salad with the lemon juice. Spoon the mayonnaise into the bowl and toss the salad well. Season the mixture with salt and pepper to taste, mound the salad in the lettuce leaves, and serve it immediately. Makes 6 servings.

New Potato and Bean Salad

10   *unpeeled new potatoes*
1½ *cups cooked navy beans, rinsed and drained*
¾   *cup sliced scallions, green parts included*
¾   *cup olive oil*
¼   *cup vinegar*
3   *tablespoons Dijon mustard*
½   *teaspoon salt*
¼   *teaspoon pepper*
1   *tablespoon fresh thyme, or ¼ teaspoon dried thyme*
1   *teaspoon fresh chervil, or ⅛ teaspoon dried chervil*
½   *teaspoon fresh marjoram, or ⅛ teaspoon dried marjoram*

In a large saucepan cook the new potatoes in water to cover for 20 minutes, or until they are tender. Cool them in cold water, drain them well, and pat them dry. Halve them, leaving the skins intact, and put them in a large salad bowl. Add the navy beans and the scallions.

In a small jar with a tight lid combine the oil, vinegar, mustard, salt, pepper, and herbs. Shake the dressing well, pour it over the vegetables, and toss the salad well. Makes 4–6 servings.

Picnic Potato Salad

6   *medium-size potatoes*
    salt and pepper
½ *cup sliced scallion, white parts only*
¼ *cup chopped green pepper*
¼ *cup chopped dill pickle*
1   *cup mayonnaise*
1   *teaspoon strong mustard*
2   *tablespoons vinegar*
2   *teaspoons paprika*

In a large saucepan cook the potatoes in water to cover for 30 to 40 minutes, or until they are tender. Cool the potatoes in cold water, peel them, and cut them into ½-inch cubes. Put the cubed potatoes into a large bowl, season them with salt and pepper to taste, and add the scallion, green pepper, and pickle.

In a small bowl combine the mayonnaise, mustard, and vinegar. Spoon the dressing over the vegetables and toss the salad until it is well combined. Sprinkle the paprika over the salad and serve it immediately or refrigerate it, covered, for 8 hours or overnight. Makes 6–8 servings.

Cucumbers in Cream

3 *large cucumbers, peeled and sliced*
3 *tablespoons minced onion*
½ *teaspoon sugar*
½ *teaspoon salt*
¼ *teaspoon pepper*
2 *tablespoons lemon juice*
1 *cup sour cream*
1 *teaspoon snipped dill*

In a large bowl combine the cucumber, onion, sugar, salt, and pepper. Cover the bowl with a plate and set it aside for 20 minutes.

Pour about half of the liquid off the cucumber mixture. Stir in the lemon juice and sour cream and chill the salad for 30 minutes. Sprinkle the salad with dill just before serving. Makes 6 servings.

Jerusalem Artichoke Salad

½ *pound Jerusalem artichokes, peeled and sliced thin*
   bibb or Boston lettuce leaves
⅓ *cup olive oil*
2 *tablespoons tarragon vinegar*
1 *teaspoon Dijon mustard*
¼ *teaspoon salt*
1–2 *drops hot pepper sauce*

Plunge the artichoke slices into a large saucepan of boiling water, lower the heat and simmer them for 8 to 10 minutes, or until they are just tender. Plunge them in cold water to refresh them, drain them on paper towels, and arrange the artichoke slices on the lettuce leaves.

In a jar with a tight lid, combine the oil, vinegar, mustard, salt, and hot pepper sauce. Shake the dressing well and drizzle it over the artichokes. Let the salad marinate in the refrigerator for 3 hours. Makes 2 servings.

Marinated Leek Salad

6 *leeks, white parts only*
¾ *teaspoon salt*
½ *cup sour cream*
1 *teaspoon Dusseldorf Mustard*
2 *tablespoons lemon juice*
½ *teaspoon horseradish*
⅛ *teaspoon pepper*

Wash the leeks thoroughly, slitting them open and removing all of the grit. Bring a saucepan of water to a boil, add the leeks and ½ teaspoon of the salt. Lower the heat and simmer the leeks for 15 to 20 minutes, or until they are tender. Drain them on paper towels, reserving ¼ cup of the cooking liquid, and refrigerate them for at least 1 hour.

In a small bowl stir together the sour cream and the reserved cooking liquid. Add the mustard, lemon juice, and horseradish, and season the dressing with the remaining ¼ teaspoon salt and the pepper.

Arrange the leeks on a serving plate and spoon the dressing over them. Makes 2 servings.

Root Vegetable Salad

1   head Boston lettuce
1   cup finely shredded white cabbage
1   cup finely shredded red cabbage
1   medium carrot, grated
1   medium knob celeriac, cooked and
    julienned
3   medium beets, peeled and grated
1   small white turnip, peeled and grated

On a large platter make a bed of lettuce. Arrange the vegetables decoratively on the lettuce, chill for 1 hour, and serve with Dill Vinaigrette. Makes 4–6 servings.

Cucumber Salad

¾   cup sour cream
1   tablespoon vinegar
1   tablespoon lemon juice
1   tablespoon minced fresh dill
1   teaspoon tarragon
2   medium-sized cucumbers

Blend all ingredients except cucumbers in a bowl. Peel the cucumbers and slice them ¼ inch thick. Toss the cucumbers with the dressing. Cover and chill the salad for 2 hours. Toss again and serve the salad on a bed of lettuce. Makes 4 servings.

Marinated Celeriac Salad

3   knobs celeriac (celery root)
¾   teaspoon salt
½   cup vegetable oil
2   tablespoons vinegar
2   tablespoons lemon juice
1   teaspoon sugar
½   teaspoon dry mustard
    dash cayenne
6–8   cup-shaped lettuce leaves
½   teaspoon paprika

Trim the root fibers and stems from the celeriac. Scrub the knobs, peel, and cut them into jullienne strips. Pour about 3 inches of water into a large saucepan; add ½ teaspoon of the salt and the celeriac. Bring the water to a boil, lower the heat, and simmer the celeriac for 15 minutes, or until it is tender. Drain the celeriac knobs and cool them in cold water.

In a jar with a tight lid, combine the oil, vinegar, lemon juice, sugar, and dry mustard. Add the remaining ¼ teaspoon salt and the cayenne and shake the dressing vigorously. Pour it over the celeriac, toss the salad well, and let it marinate in the refrigerator, covered, for at least 3 hours.

Place a lettuce leaf on each of 6 or 8 individual salad plates. Spoon some of the salad into each leaf cup and sprinkle it with the paprika. Makes 6–8 servings.

Wilted Lettuce Salad

6   strips bacon
¼   cup vinegar
1½   tablespoons sugar
½   teaspoon salt
¼   teaspoon pepper
1   head leafy lettuce torn into bite-size
    pieces
4   hard-cooked eggs, sliced

In a skillet cook the bacon until it is crisp. Transfer it to paper towels to drain. To the skillet add the vinegar, sugar, salt, and pepper. Cook the dressing, stirring constantly, until the sugar is dissolved and the mixture is hot.

Put the lettuce in a large salad bowl and crumble the bacon over it. Pour the hot dressing over the salad, add the sliced eggs, and toss the mixture well. Makes 6 servings.

Winter Vegetable Salad

1   *pound green beans, trimmed*
2   *large celery stalks, sliced*
3/4 *pound mushrooms, thinly sliced*
2   *tablespoons chopped scallions, white*
        parts only
2   *tablespoons capers*
1/3 *cup vegetable oil*
1/3 *cup olive oil*
1/4 *cup red wine vinegar*
1   *tablespoon Dijon mustard*
2   *tablespoons minced parsley*
        salt and pepper
6   *cup-shaped lettuce leaves*
1   *8-ounce can beets, drained and cut into*
        julienne strips

Plunge the green beans into a large saucepan of boiling water, lower the heat, and simmer the beans for 5 to 7 minutes, or until they are just tender. Drain the beans, plunge them into cold water, and drain them on paper towels. In a large bowl combine the beans with the celery, mushrooms, scallions, and capers.

In a small bowl whisk together the oils, vinegar, mustard, parsley, and salt and pepper to taste. Pour the dressing over the vegetables, toss the salad gently, and refrigerate it for 1 hour.

Just before serving, place a lettuce leaf on each of 6 salad plates and divide the salad among the leaves. Garnish each serving with some of the julienned beets. Makes 6 servings.

Crudité Patchwork Salad

2   *cups bean sprouts*
1   *large cooked beet*
1   *daikon radish*
2   *sweet red peppers*
2   *yellow peppers*
2   *carrots*
1   *medium-size zucchini*
1/2 *pound cooked green beans*
1   *cup olive oil*
4   *tablespoons lemon juice*
2   *tablespoons lime juice*
2   *tablespoons Dijon mustard*
1   *teaspoon sugar*
4   *basil leaves, shredded (optional)*
1/4 *teaspoon salt*
1/8 *teaspoon pepper*

Spread the bean sprouts on a platter. Cut the beet, radish, peppers, carrots, and zucchini into julienne strips, keeping the vegetables separate, and arrange them and the green beans on the bean sprouts in a patchwork pattern. In a jar with a tight lid, combine all of the remaining ingredients and drizzle the dressing over the vegetables. Makes 4–6 servings.

Summer Salad

½ head iceberg lettuce
¾ pound fresh spinach
1 bunch scallions, chopped,
    including tops
1 10½-ounce package frozen peas, thawed
2 teaspoons sugar
    salt and pepper
1 cup grated Swiss cheese
1½ cups sour cream
1½ cups mayonnaise

Wash, drain and tear lettuce into pieces. Wash the spinach well, remove the stems, pat dry and tear into pieces.

To make the dressing, in a small bowl, combine the sour cream and mayonnaise.

In the bottom of a large glass salad bowl or souffle dish, layer half of each of the ingredients in the following order: lettuce, spinach, scallions, and peas. Sprinkle with 1 teaspoon of the sugar, and salt and pepper to taste. Cover with half of the dressing mixture. Repeat the layers, using the remaining ingredients, and top with the remaining sugar and dressing. Sprinkle the grated cheese on top. Cover and refrigerate overnight. Makes 8–10 servings.

Mixed Green Salad

2 cups olive oil
1 cup red wine vinegar
2 tablespoons minced onion
2 teaspoons chopped pimiento

6 ripe olives, chopped
6 green olives, chopped
½ cup chopped green pepper
1 teaspoon capers
½ teaspoon salt
¼ teaspoon pepper
1 small head romaine, torn into bite-size
    pieces
1 bunch spinach, washed, stemmed, and
    patted dry
1 bunch escarole, torn into bite-size pieces
2 bunches watercress, tough stems removed

In a jar with a tight lid combine the oil, vinegar, onion, pimiento, olives, green pepper, capers, salt, and pepper. Shake the dressing very well and refrigerate it for at least 24 hours.

In a large bowl combine the romaine, spinach, escarole, and watercress. Pour the dressing over the greens and toss the salad well. Makes 6 servings.

Green Salad with Beer Dressing

3 carrots, cut into 1-inch pieces
1 cup cauliflower florets
1 cup broccoli florets
½ cup thinly sliced fresh mushrooms
1 cup firmly packed spinach leaves,
    washed, stemmed, and patted dry
1 cup firmly packed romaine, torn into
    bite-size pieces
½ cup mayonnaise
¼ cup Dijon mustard
¼ cup beer
1 tablespoon horseradish
2 drops hot pepper sauce (optional)
2 tablespoons catsup (optional)

Plunge the carrots into a large saucepan of boiling water. Lower the heat and simmer the carrots for 5 minutes. With a slotted spoon transfer them to paper towels to drain. Bring the water to a boil, add the cauliflower, and cook it for 5 minutes. Transfer it to paper towels to drain. Repeat the process with the broccoli.

In a large bowl combine the carrots, cauliflower, broccoli, mushrooms, spinach, and romaine.

In a 2-cup measure combine the mayonnaise, mustard, beer, and horseradish. Stir in the hot pepper sauce and the catsup, if desired. Spoon the dressing over the vegetables and toss the salad well. Makes 6–8 servings.

Belgian Endive Salad with Mustard Dressing

2   *Belgian endives, trimmed and separated into sheaves*
10 *pimiento strips*
½   *teaspoon salt*
½   *teaspoon pepper*
½   *teaspoon sugar*
½   *teaspoon dry mustard*
1   *teaspoon Dijon mustard*
½   *teaspoon lemon juice*
2   *tablespoons tarragon vinegar*
2   *tablespoons olive oil*
½   *cup vegetable oil*
3   *egg yolks*
½   *teaspoon minced garlic*
2   *drops hot pepper sauce*
¼   *teaspoon celery salt*

Arrange the endive sheaves decoratively on 2 salad plates and garnish them with the pimiento strips. In a 1-pint jar with a tight lid combine all of the remaining ingredients and shake the jar to combine the dressing. Drizzle the dressing over the endive leaves and pimiento strips. Makes 2 servings.

Watercress and Endive Salad

2   *bunches watercress*
3   *Belgian endives*
1   *bunch radishes*
1   *cup olive oil*
¼   *cup red wine vinegar*
¼   *cup white wine*
4   *tablespoons Dijon mustard*
½   *teaspoon chopped fresh tarragon (or ⅛ teaspoon dried tarragon)*
1   *teaspoon chopped fresh parsley*

Wash the watercress, pat it dry, and remove the tough stems. Wash the endives, pat them dry, trim off the bottoms, and separate them into sheaves. Trim the radishes, wash and dry them, and cut them into thick slices.

In a large bowl whisk together the oil, vinegar, wine, mustard, and herbs. Toss the endive sheaves in the dressing and arrange them on 6 small salad plates in a star pattern, with the root ends in the center. Toss the watercress in the dressing and arrange clusters of it in the center of each plate. Toss the radish slices in the remaining dressing and arrange them around the watercress clusters. Makes 6 servings.

Watercress and Hearts of Palm Salad

2 *bunches watercress*
6 *stalks hearts of palm, well drained and cut into pieces*
¾ *cup salad oil*
2 *tablespoons vinegar*
½ *teaspoon dry mustard*
  salt and white pepper

Trim the tough stems from the watercress and put it in a salad bowl with the hearts of palm.

In a measuring cup stir together the oil, vinegar, mustard, and salt and white pepper to taste. Pour the dressing over the vegetables and toss the salad well. Makes 4 servings.

Spinach Salad

1¼ *cups water*
¼ *cup plus 2 tablespoons vinegar*
¾ *cup sugar*
1 *chicken bouillon cube*
6 *strips bacon*
¼ *cup flour*
¾ *pound spinach, washed, stemmed, and patted dry*
¼ *cup chopped red onion*
¼ *pound mushrooms, sliced*
1 *hard-cooked egg, sliced*

In a saucepan combine the water, vinegar, sugar, and bouillon cube. Bring the water to a boil, lower the heat, and simmer the mixture, stirring, until the sugar and the bouillon cube are dissolved. Keep the vinegar mixture hot over very low heat.

In a skillet cook the bacon until it is crisp. Transfer it to paper towels to drain. Stir in the flour and cook the mixture for 2 or 3 minutes, stirring constantly. Pour the vinegar mixture into the saucepan a little at a time and cook the dressing over medium heat, stirring constantly, for 5 minutes, or until it is smooth.

Put the spinach in a serving bowl with the onion, mushrooms, and hard-cooked egg and crumble the bacon over it. Pour the hot dressing over the salad and serve it at once. Makes 6 servings.

Dressings for Green Salads

Bavarian Cucumber Dressing

1 *tablespoon red wine vinegar*
½ *cup olive oil*
3 *tablespoons grated onion*
1 *small cucumber, peeled, seeded, and grated*
1 *teaspoon chopped parsley*
1 *clove garlic, minced*
1 *teaspoon sugar*
1½ *teaspoons salt*
½ *teaspoon pepper*

In a blender or a food processor fitted with the steel blade, combine all of the ingredients and process until smooth. Set the dressing aside and let the flavors ripen at room temperature for at least 6 hours. Makes 1 cup salad dressing.

Tarragon Mustard Vinaigrette

1½ cups olive oil
¼ cup tarragon vinegar
1 tablespoon Dijon mustard
½ teaspoon minced fresh tarragon (or ⅛
    teaspoon dried tarragon)
½ teaspoon salt
⅛ teaspoon pepper

Combine all of the ingredients in a jar with a
tight lid. Shake dressing well and refrigerate it,
covered, for up to 24 hours. Makes 1¾ cups.

Scallion Vinaigrette

1 cup olive oil
¼ cup lemon juice
1 tablespoon Dijon mustard
½ cup minced green onion

Combine all of the ingredients in a jar with a
tight lid and shake the dressing vigorously.
Sprinkle over salad immediately or refrigerate,
covered, for up to 3 hours. Makes 1¾ cups.

Raspberry Vinaigrette

¼ cup olive oil
¼ cup vegetable oil
2 tablespoons vinegar
1 teaspoon raspberry vinegar
    Salt and pepper

In a jar with a tight lid combine the oils and
vinegars. Shake the dressing very well, season it
with salt and pepper to taste, and shake it
again. Makes 1 cup salad dressing.

Mayonnaise

¼ teaspoon salt
½ teaspoon dry mustard
    dash cayenne
2 egg yolks
1 tablespoon vinegar
1 cup olive oil
1 tablespoon lemon juice

In a blender or a food processor fitted with the
steel blade combine the salt, dry mustard, and
cayenne. Add the egg yolks and run the motor
until the mixture is smooth. Pour in the
vinegar and blend the mixture until the
ingredients are combined. With the motor
running, add ¼ cup of the oil in a thin stream.
Turn off the motor, scrape down the sides of
the container with a rubber spatula, and add
the rest of the oil in a stream with the motor
running until the mayonnaise is thick and
creamy. Pour in the lemon juice and blend the
dressing just until it is incorporated. Makes 1
cup salad dressing.

Tomato Mayonnaise

1 cup mayonnaise
3 tablespoons tomato paste
¼ cup plus 1 tablespoon peeled, seeded,
    and chopped tomato
1 tablespoon chopped parsley

In a small bowl thoroughly combine the
mayonnaise and tomato paste. Fold in the
chopped tomatoes and the parsley. Makes 1½
cups salad dressing.

FISH AND SEAFOOD

Most of the early German American settlements were not in parts of the country close to the sea. But this is a nation of lakes and rivers, and there is fish in abundance even far away from the coast of either ocean or the Gulf of Mexico. Canals, railroads, local markets and fish peddlers who drove their wagons door to door made it possible for fish and seafood to appear on the tables of newly arrived Americans in even the most rural of communities. The cooking of fish tends to be simple now as it was in the days of the pioneers; slightly piquant sauces created with mustard and capers are often used to enhance the subtle flavors of fish and seafood dishes.

Grilled Salmon with Dill

4   salmon steaks, cut 1 inch thick
    salt and pepper
3   tablespoons lemon juice
3   teaspoons vegetable oil
4   small sprigs fresh dill
1   lemon, cut into wedges
2   sticks (1 cup) butter, softened
2   tablespoons chopped fresh dill
1/4   teaspoon Worcestershire sauce
1/2   teaspoon mustard

Oil a charcoal grill or a broiler pan and set it on a working surface. Prepare a charcoal fire and let it reach the glowing-coal stage, or preheat the broiler.

Season the salmon steaks with salt and pepper to taste and sprinkle them with 2 tablespoons of the lemon juice and the vegetable oil. Place them on the cold grill, set the grill over the hot coals, and grill the steaks for 5 minutes on each side, or broil them for 5 minutes on each side, or until they flake easily when tested with a fork. Transfer the salmon steaks to a heated platter, garnish them with dill sprigs and lemon wedges, and keep warm.

In a mixing bowl combine the butter, chopped dill, Worcestershire sauce, mustard, and the remaining tablespoon of lemon juice. Spoon the dill butter into a small serving bowl, and serve it with the salmon steaks. Makes 4 servings.

Salmon Steaks with Caper Sauce

 2   *tablespoons butter*
 ¾   *cup finely sliced carrots*
 ½   *cup finely sliced celery*
 ½   *cup finely sliced shallots*
 2   *tablespoons chopped fresh parsley*
 ¾   *teaspoon fennel seed*
 ¼   *teaspoon thyme*
 6   *salmon steaks, cut 1 inch thick*
      salt and pepper
 ¼   *cup dry white wine*
 ¼   *cup chicken broth*
 3   *egg yolks, lightly beaten*
 2   *tablespoons capers*
 6   *sprigs parsley*

In a large skillet melt the butter over medium heat. Add the carrots, celery, and shallots and sauté the vegetables for 2 to 3 minutes, stirring constantly. Stir in the chopped parsley, fennel seed, and thyme. Cover the skillet and cook the vegetable mixture for 10 more minutes. Spread the vegetables in the bottom of a large greased flameproof baking dish.

Preheat the oven to 450° F.

Arrange the salmon steaks on top of the vegetables and season them with salt and pepper to taste. Pour in the wine and broth and bring the liquid to a simmer over low heat. Cover the baking dish tightly with foil and bake the salmon for 10 minutes, or until it flakes easily when tested with a fork. Transfer the salmon steaks to a heated platter and keep them warm.

Strain the cooking liquid into a saucepan, pressing down on the vegetables to extract all of the court bouillon. Place the saucepan over low heat, slowly add the egg yolks, whisking constantly, and cook until the sauce is smooth and thickened, being careful not to let the sauce come to a boil. Season the sauce with salt and pepper to taste, fold in the capers, and spoon the sauce over the salmon steaks. Garnish the platter with the parsley sprigs. Makes 6 servings.

Halibut and Potatoes au Gratin

 2   *pounds halibut steak*
 1   *quart cooked potatoes, diced*
 6   *tablespoons butter*
 6   *tablespoons flour*
 3   *cups milk, heated*
      salt and pepper
 ½   *cup grated sharp Cheddar cheese*
 4   *slices bacon, cooked and crumbled*

Preheat the oven to 325° F.

Put the halibut steak in the center of a shallow greased baking dish and arrange the potatoes around it. In a heavy saucepan, melt the butter. Stir in the flour and cook it over medium-low heat for 3 to 5 minutes, but do not let it brown. Turn the heat up to medium and gradually add the hot milk, stirring constantly until the sauce thickens and comes to a boil. Season the sauce with salt and pepper to taste and pour it over and around the fish. Sprinkle the cheese and bacon over the fish and potatoes and bake the dish for 45 minutes. Makes 6 servings.

Halibut Ring with Dill Sauce

1½ *pounds fresh halibut*
3 *cups water*
2 *sprigs parsley*
4 *celery tops*
1 *small onion, sliced*
1 *slice lemon*
1 *bay leaf*
½ *teaspoon salt*
¼ *teaspoon pepper*
5 *tablespoons butter*
5 *tablespoons flour*
2¼ *cups milk, heated*
6 *dashes hot pepper sauce*
3 *eggs*
4 *teaspoons chopped fresh dill*
1 *teaspoon lemon juice*
3–4 *cups cooked peas, chopped broccoli, or*
   sliced green beans

Place the halibut in a large saucepan and cover it with the water. Add the parsley, celery tops, onion, lemon slice, bay leaf, salt, and pepper. Bring the water to a boil; lower the heat and poach the fish just below the boiling point for 12 to 15 minutes, until the fish is opaque. Let the fish cool for 10 to 15 minutes in the cooking liquid or court bouillon. Carefully transfer the halibut to a cutting board, reserving the court bouillon. Remove the skin and bone from the halibut, flake the fish with a fork, and set it aside. Reduce the court bouillon over high heat to about one-third of its volume; strain it and set it aside.

Preheat the oven to 325° F.

In a skillet over medium heat cook 3 tablespoons of the butter until it bubbles. Add 3 tablespoons of the flour and cook the roux, stirring constantly, for 3 to 4 minutes without letting it brown. Add 1½ cups of the hot milk and cook the sauce, whisking constantly, until it is thick and bubbly. Season with hot pepper sauce, add more salt and pepper if necessary, and cook the sauce for 1 to 2 minutes longer.

In a large bowl beat the eggs well. Stir the sauce and flaked fish into the eggs and mix the ingredients well. Pour the mixture into a greased 5-cup ring mold. Set the mold in a pan of hot water and bake it for 45 minutes, or until it has set.

In a large saucepan melt the remaining butter. Add the remaining flour and cook the roux, stirring, until it bubbles, but do not let it brown. Add the reduced court bouillon and the remaining ¾ cup hot milk, and cook the sauce over medium heat, stirring constantly, until it is thickened and bubbly. Stir in the dill and lemon juice and cook the sauce for another 1 to 2 minutes.

Unmold the halibut ring onto a heated platter and fill the center with cooked peas, broccoli, or green beans. Pour some of the sauce over the fish and vegetables and serve the rest in a gravy boat. Makes 6 servings.

Grilled Herring with Bacon

vegetable oil
¼ *cup white wine vinegar*
4 *serving-size fresh herring*
8 *strips bacon*

Oil a charcoal grill or a broiler pan and set it on a working surface. Prepare a charcoal fire and let it reach the hot-coal stage, or preheat the broiler.

Place the herring in a shallow dish and pour the vinegar over them. Cover the dish and let the herring marinate in the refrigerator for 10 minutes. Pat the fish dry and wrap a strip of bacon in a spiral around each one, securing it with toothpicks. Place the bacon-wrapped herring on the cold grill or broiler pan and grill or broil them for about 10 minutes per inch of thickness, turning at least twice. Makes 4 servings.

Alsatian Flounder with Cabbage

½	cup water
1	tablespoon lemon juice
1	clove garlic, pressed
1¼	teaspoons salt
1½	pounds fresh or frozen flounder fillets
1	onion, sliced
5	tablespoons butter
8	cups shredded cabbage
¼	cup dry white wine
¼	teaspoon pepper
3	tablespoons flour
⅛	teaspoon nutmeg
⅛	teaspoon white pepper
1½	cups milk, heated
⅔	cup shredded Swiss cheese

Preheat the oven to 350° F.

In a shallow baking dish combine the water, lemon juice, garlic, and half of the salt. Add the fish fillets and the onion slices. Cover the dish with foil and poach the fish in the oven for 15 to 20 minutes, until it is opaque and flakes easily.

In a large skillet melt 2 tablespoons of the butter. Add the cabbage and cook it over medium heat, stirring occasionally, until it is tender but not soft. Add the wine, ½ teaspoon of the remaining salt, and the pepper. Cover the skillet and simmer the mixture for 10 minutes. Transfer the cabbage and its liquid to a shallow baking pan. Gently remove the fish from the baking dish, place it on top of the cabbage, and keep the casserole warm. Strain the court bouillon and reserve ¼ cup.

Preheat the broiler.

In a small saucepan, melt the remaining 3 tablespoons butter and stir in the flour, nutmeg, white pepper, and the remaining ¼ teaspoon salt. Cook the roux for 2 to 3 minutes, stirring constantly, but do not let it brown. Add the hot milk and the poaching liquid and cook the sauce over medium heat, stirring briskly with a wire whisk, until it is smooth and bubbly; continue cooking for another 2 minutes. Stir in half of the cheese, remove the saucepan from the heat and continue to stir until the cheese has melted and the sauce is smooth. Spoon the sauce over the fish and cabbage. Sprinkle the remaining cheese on top and broil the casserole for 2 to 3 minutes, or until all of the cheese is melted and the top is very lightly browned. Makes 6–8 servings.

Carp in Aspic

3 cups water
2 large carrots, julienned
2 leeks, white parts only, julienned
3 scallions, both the green and the white
    parts, julienned
1 bay leaf
2 tablespoons chopped fresh dill
4 peppercorns
    juice of ½ lemon
1 2-pound whole carp
    salt and pepper
2 cups chicken broth
1 tablespoon unflavored gelatin
3 sprigs fresh dill
1 hard-cooked egg, peeled and thinly sliced
2 gherkins, thickly sliced

Pour the water into a fish poacher or a kettle. Add the carrots, leeks, and scallions and bring the water to a boil. Turn down the heat and simmer the vegetables for 8 to 10 minutes, or until the carrots are just tender. With a slotted spoon transfer the vegetables to a platter, cover them with plastic wrap, and refrigerate them. Add the bay leaf, chopped dill, peppercorns, and lemon juice to the liquid in the fish poacher. Place the carp on a rack over the water and steam the fish for 15 to 20 minutes, until it flakes easily when tested with a fork. Carefully transfer the fish to the platter, season it and the vegetables with salt and pepper to taste, and return the platter to the refrigerator.

Strain the fish stock into a heavy saucepan and reduce it over high heat to 1 cup. Add the chicken broth and reduce the combined liquids

to 2 cups. In a measuring cup soften the gelatin in 2 or 3 tablespoons of the hot broth and add the gelatin mixture to the saucepan, stirring until the gelatin is dissolved. Refrigerate the mixture for several hours, until it sets.

Place the steamed carp on a chilled platter, arrange the julienned vegetables around it, and garnish the fish with dill sprigs, sliced egg, and sliced gherkins. Spoon a thin layer of aspic over the fish and vegetables and refrigerate the fish and the aspic until the coating has set. Repeat the procedure until the fish and vegetables are uniformly coated with aspic. Makes 4 servings.

Baked Stuffed Bass

2 strips bacon
2 tablespoons melted butter
1 cup dry bread crumbs
1 hard-cooked egg, chopped
1 large onion, chopped
1 teaspoon chopped parsley
½ teaspoon thyme
1 teaspoon Worcestershire sauce
3 tablespoons chicken broth
    salt and pepper
1 1½–2 pound whole bass
2–3 tablespoons salad oil
½ cup flour
1 tablespoon butter, cut into small pieces

In a heavy skillet cook the bacon until it is crisp and drain it on paper towels. Crumble it into a mixing bowl and stir in the melted butter, bread crumbs, egg, onion, parsley, and thyme.

Add the Worcestershire sauce and chicken broth, season the mixture with salt and pepper to taste, and set it aside.

Preheat the oven to 450° F.

Brush the bass inside and out with salad oil, sprinkle it with salt and pepper, and dredge it in the flour. Stuff the fish with the bacon mixture and skewer the edges together securely. Place the fish on a well-buttered baking pan, dot it with butter, and bake it for 15 to 20 minutes, or until fish flakes easily when tested with a fork. Makes 4 servings.

Shrimp Fromage

2   pounds small shrimp
    pepper
1   tablespoon minced fresh dill
1¼   cups heavy cream
1   package gelatin
2   tablespoons sherry
    black lumpfish roe to garnish

Shell, devein, and wash the shrimp. In a large bowl combine the shrimp, pepper, dill, and cream. Cover the mixture with plastic wrap and let it marinate in the refrigerator for 10 to 12 hours.

Dissolve the gelatin in the sherry. Strain the cream from the shrimp mixture and combine it with the gelatin-sherry mixture. Whip the cream-sherry mixture until it is stiff and fold in the shrimp. Pour the mixture into a ring mold. Refrigerate the mold 3 hours, or until it is set.

Rap the mold on a hard surface, run it under warm water, and unmold it onto a serving platter. Garnish with lumpfish roe. Makes 4 appetizer or light luncheon servings.

Trout with Almonds and Lemon Sauce

3   large trout fillets (lake, steelhead, or salmon trout)
½   cup flour
    salt and white pepper
2–3   eggs, lightly beaten
½   cup sliced almonds
¾   cup (1½ sticks) butter
1   tablespoon fresh lemon juice
¼   teaspoon Worcestershire sauce
1   lemon cut into wedges
    parsley sprigs

Cut each trout fillet into four pieces. Dip the pieces in flour seasoned with salt and pepper to taste, then in the beaten eggs, then in the sliced almonds; set the trout aside on a sheet of wax paper.

In a large heavy skillet heat ¼ cup (½ stick) of the butter. Add the trout to the skillet, a few pieces at a time, and sauté it for 2 to 3 minutes, until golden. Turn and sauté for 2 minutes more. Arrange the fish on a heated platter and keep it warm.

In a saucepan melt the remaining ½ cup (1 stick) butter over medium heat. Add the lemon juice and Worcestershire sauce and whisk until blended and heated through. Season the sauce with salt and white pepper to taste and pour it over the fish. Garnish the platter with lemon wedges and parsley sprigs. Makes 6 servings.

Shad and Roe with Lemon-Caper Sauce

1	pair shad roe
1¼	teaspoons salt
3	tablespoons lemon juice
1	shad fillet
	pepper
½	cup milk
¼	cup flour
½	cup peanut or corn oil
1	lemon, thickly sliced
3	tablespoons butter
3	tablespoons capers
	chopped parsley

Rinse the roe well and place it in a saucepan; cover it with boiling water, 1 teaspoon of the salt, and 1 tablespoon of the lemon juice. Bring the water to a boil, lower the heat, and simmer the roe for 5 to 8 minutes, until it is opaque. Drain the roe, plunge it into cold water for about 30 seconds, and drain it on paper towels. Carefully separate the two halves of the roe, taking care not to cut the membrane, and prick the membrane in several places with the tip of a fine pin to prevent the eggs from exploding when they are sautéed.

Cut the fillet in half, season it and the roe with the remaining salt, and sprinkle them with pepper to taste. Dip the shad and roe in the milk and dredge them in the flour. Heat the oil in a large skillet over medium-low heat. Turn the heat to low and sauté the roe very gently for about 6 minutes on each side, or until it is browned and crisp; transfer the roe to a heated platter. Increase the heat to medium, adding more oil if necessary, and sauté the shad for 6 minutes on each side, or until it is crisp and golden brown. Arrange the fish beside the roe and keep the platter warm.

Cut the rind from the lemon slices and remove the seeds; with a small sharp knife, cut between the membranes to separate the lemon sections. In a saucepan, melt the butter and add the capers, the lemon sections, and the remaining 2 tablespoons lemon juice. Cook the sauce until it is smooth and bubbly. Pour the lemon-caper sauce over the shad and roe and garnish the platter with parsley. Makes 2 servings.

Baked Mackerel with Mustard Sauce

6	mackerel fillets (½ pound)
¼	cup melted butter
3	tablespoons plus 1 teaspoon lemon juice
	salt and pepper
2	tablespoons butter
1	tablespoon flour
1	tablespoon dry mustard
1	cup milk, heated
2	teaspoons Dijon mustard
¼	cup heavy cream

Preheat the oven to 400° F.

Arrange the mackerel fillets skin side down in a buttered baking dish. Brush them with about half of the melted butter, sprinkle them with about 1½ tablespoons of the lemon juice,

and season them with salt and pepper to taste.
Cover the baking dish with a well-buttered
sheet of wax paper and bake the mackerel for
15 minutes.

In a heavy saucepan melt the 2 tablespoons
butter over medium heat and stir in the flour
and dry mustard. Cook the roux, stirring
constantly, for 2 to 3 minutes until it just begins
to brown. Pour in the hot milk and cook the
sauce, stirring constantly, until it is smooth and
bubbly. While continuing to stir the sauce, add
the mustard, the cream, and 1 teaspoon of the
remaining lemon juice; cook the sauce,
stirring, for another 2 to 3 minutes over low
heat. Season the sauce with salt and pepper to
taste.

Transfer the fish to a heated serving dish,
pour the remaining melted butter and lemon
juice over it, and serve the mackerel with the
mustard sauce. Makes 2 servings.

Baked Fish Mousse

3	pounds flounder, cod, or haddock fillets
2	onions, peeled and halved
3	parsley sprigs
1	bay leaf
1/2	teaspoon salt
4–5	peppercorns
3	lemons
1	cup cream or milk
1 1/4	cups fine cracker crumbs
1/3	cup melted butter
6	eggs, separated

Place the fillets in a large saucepan and cover
them with water. Add the onions, parsley
sprigs, bay leaf, salt, and peppercorns. Halve
one of the lemons; squeeze one of the halves
and add the juice to the saucepan; slice the
other half and add the slices to the saucepan.
Bring the court bouillon to a boil, immediately
lower the heat, and cook the fish just below the
boiling point for 12 to 15 minutes, until it is
opaque. Let the fillets cool in the court bouillon
for 10 to 15 minutes.

Transfer the fish to a large mixing bowl and
flake it with a fork. Add the cream, cracker
crumbs, and melted butter. Halve the
remaining 2 lemons, squeeze them, and add
the juice to the fish mixture. Stir the mixture
with a fork until the ingredients are finely
mashed and well blended. Beat the egg yolks
until they are smooth and creamy and stir
them into the fish mixture. In a separate bowl,
with clean beaters, beat the egg whites until
they are stiff; gently fold them into the fish
mixture.

Preheat oven to 350° F.

Grease a 9- x 5- x 2¾-inch loaf pan, fill it with
the mixture, and smooth it out. Cover the loaf
pan with aluminium foil and set it in a pan of
hot water. Bake the mousse for 1 hour until it
is firm to the touch. Loosen the edges with a
spatula and turn the mousse out onto a heated
platter. Makes 6–8 servings.

VEGETABLES

*T*o the German cook, a vegetable is never simply an accompaniment to an entree. Vegetable dishes are often complex creations intended to stand on their own as separate courses. While German Americans are not infrequently stereotyped as being of the "meat and two veg" school, they nevertheless rarely forget the Old Country's abundance of vegetable presentations. Recipes range from the ubiquitous sauerkraut to fresh vegetables simply cooked, elaborate casseroles, soufflés and stuffed vegetables accompanied by special sauces.

Cheese-Asparagus Custard

1	*pound asparagus, cut into 1-inch pieces*
2	*tablespoons butter*
½	*cup sliced mushrooms*
4	*eggs*
1	*cup shredded Gruyère cheese*
1	*cup mayonnaise*
1	*cup heavy cream*
½	*teaspoon salt*
¼	*teaspoon pepper*

Steam the asparagus over boiling water for 15 minutes, or until it is tender but still bright green.

In a small skillet melt the butter over medium heat. Add the mushrooms and sauté them for 10 minutes, tossing often, or until they are soft and golden.

Preheat the oven to 350° F.

Turn the asparagus and the mushrooms into a blender or a food processor and purée them until they are smooth. Drop in the eggs and run the motor until the mixture is blended. Add the cheese, mayonnaise, cream, salt, and pepper and blend the mixture until it is smooth. Pour the mixture into a lightly buttered 1½-quart soufflé dish or casserole. Set the baking dish in a larger pan and pour 2 inches of hot water into the pan. Bake for 55 to 60 minutes, until the custard is firm on top. Makes 6 servings.

Asparagus with Dill

28 asparagus spears, trimmed
    Salt and pepper
1   tablespoon butter
1   tablespoon snipped dill

Steam the asparagus over boiling water for 10 to 15 minutes, until it is just tender. Transfer the asparagus to a heated serving dish, season it with salt and pepper to taste, and top it with the butter and the snipped dill. Makes 4 servings.

Stangenspargel (Asparagus Spears)

3   cups water
½   teaspoon salt
2   pounds asparagus, trimmed
4   tablespoons butter
½   cup bread crumbs
    grated rind of ½ lemon

In a skillet bring the water to a boil and add the salt. Plunge the asparagus into the boiling water and cook it, partly covered, for 6 to 8 minutes, or until it is tender but still bright green. Drain the asparagus, transfer it to a heated platter, and keep it warm.

In the same skillet melt the butter over medium heat. Add the bread crumbs and sauté them, stirring occasionally, until they are lightly browned. Spoon the toasted crumbs over the asparagus and sprinkle the grated lemon rind over the crumbs. Makes 6–8 servings.

Beets and Red Cabbage

3   medium-size beets
½   teaspoon salt
4   cups coarsely grated red cabbage
1   small onion, sliced
⅓   cup water
¼   cup vinegar
4   teaspoons cornstarch
¼   teaspoon cinnamon
⅛   teaspoon ground cloves
½   cup sour cream (optional)

Trim the beets, leaving 1 inch of the greens intact; scrub them well but do not peel them. Put the beets in a saucepan, cover them with water, and add ¼ teaspoon of the salt. Cook the beets, covered, for 25 to 30 minutes, or until they are almost tender.

Preheat the oven to 325° F.

Drain the beets and submerge them in cold water until they are cool enough to handle. Cut off the greens, peel the beets, and cut them into julienne strips.

In a 4-quart casserole combine the beets, cabbage, and onion. Bake the mixture for 20 minutes, stirring once. In a measuring cup combine the water, vinegar, cornstarch, cinnamon, cloves, and the remaining ¼ teaspoon salt. Stir the mixture into the casserole and bake the beets and cabbage for 20 minutes more, or until the cabbage is tender. Serve the beets and red cabbage with the sour cream. Makes 6 servings.

Green Beans and Zucchini

4 slices bacon
1 onion, diced
1 pound fresh green beans, cut into 1-inch pieces
½ teaspoon salt
¼ teaspoon pepper
1 cup water
½ pound zucchini, sliced

In a deep heavy skillet or kettle sauté the bacon until it is crisp. Transfer it to paper towels to drain. Add the onion to the bacon drippings and sauté it for 8 minutes, or until it is translucent. Add the beans, salt, pepper, and water. Bring the water to a boil, reduce the heat, and simmer the green beans for 15 minutes. Stir in the zucchini and simmer the mixture, covered, for 10 minutes more. Drain vegetables, turn them into a serving bowl, and crumble bacon over them. Makes 4–6 servings.

Beets with Apples

16 ounces canned diced beets, drained
2 cups diced tart apples
⅓ cup thinly sliced onion
2 teaspoons brown sugar
2 tablespoons butter, cut into small pieces

Preheat the oven to 325° F.
Combine the beets, apples, and onion in a baking dish. Sprinkle the brown sugar over them and scatter the butter over the sugar. Cover and bake for 45 minutes, or until the apples are tender. Makes 4 servings.

String Beans Vinaigrette

1 teaspoon salt
2 pounds fresh string beans
1 cup olive oil
¼ cup lemon juice
1 tablespoon Dijon mustard
½ cup sliced scallions, white part only

Half fill a large saucepan with water, add the salt, and bring the water to a boil. Plunge the string beans into the boiling water, reduce the heat, and simmer the beans for 20 minutes, or until they are tender but still bright green. Drain them, transfer them to a heated serving bowl, and keep them warm. In a jar with a tight lid combine the oil, lemon juice, and mustard. Pour the vinaigrette over the beans and toss them to coat them well. Scatter the scallions over the beans and serve them at once. Makes 8 servings.

Swiss-Style Green Beans

2 pounds green beans, trimmed
6 strips bacon
2 medium onions, sliced
2 tablespoons butter
2 tablespoons flour
1 cup chicken broth
2 tablespoons vinegar
Salt and pepper

Steam the green beans over boiling water for 15 to 20 minutes, until they are tender.

Transfer them to a heated serving dish and keep them warm.

In a skillet cook the bacon until it is crisp. Transfer it to paper towels to drain. Stir the onions into the bacon drippings and cook them over medium heat, stirring, for 8 to 10 minutes, until they are translucent. Drain off the bacon drippings, add the butter to the onions, and melt it over medium-low heat. Stir in the flour and cook the roux for 5 minutes. Gradually add the chicken broth and simmer the sauce, stirring constantly, until it is thickened and bubbly. Stir in the vinegar, simmer the sauce for 5 minutes more, and season it with salt and pepper to taste.

Pour the sauce over the green beans and crumble the bacon over the sauce. Makes 6–8 servings.

Herbed Green Beans

½	teaspoon salt
1	pound green beans, cut diagonally into 2-inch pieces
4	tablespoons butter
½	cup chopped onion
½	teaspoon minced garlic
¼	cup chopped celery
½	cup chopped parsley
1	teaspoon fresh rosemary, or ¼ teaspoon dried
1	teaspoon fresh basil, or ¼ teaspoon dried

Half fill a large saucepan with water, add the salt, and bring the water to a boil. Plunge the green beans into the boiling water, reduce the heat, and simmer the beans for 15 to 20 minutes, until they are tender but still bright green.

In a large skillet melt the butter over medium heat. Stir in the onion, garlic, and celery and sauté the vegetables, stirring often, for 8 to 10 minutes, until they are translucent. Add the parsley, rosemary, and basil and combine the mixture well.

Drain the green beans and turn them into the skillet. Toss them with the vegetables and herbs and heat them through. Serve the herbed green beans immediately. Makes 4 servings.

Braised Brussels Sprouts with Bacon

4	cups Brussels sprouts, trimmed
¾	cup chicken broth
1	small clove garlic, minced
4	strips bacon

In a saucepan combine the Brussels sprouts, chicken broth, and garlic. Bring the broth to a boil, reduce the heat, and simmer the sprouts for 10 to 15 minutes, or until they are tender but still bright green.

In a skillet cook the bacon until it is crisp. Transfer it to paper towels to drain.

Drain the sprouts well, turn them into a heated serving bowl, and crumble the bacon over them. Makes 4–6 servings.

Brussels Sprouts

2   1-pint containers, Brussels sprouts
1½ cups boiling water
    salt and pepper
2   tablespoons butter

Trim stems, remove withered leaves, and cut an x in the base of each sprout to ensure even cooking. Place sprouts in a saucepan with the boiling water and salt to taste. Boil gently for 10 to 15 minutes or until the sprouts are crisp-tender and bright green. Drain the sprouts, season them with pepper and butter, and serve immediately. Makes 4–6 servings.

Braised Red Cabbage

1   small red cabbage, shredded medium fine
½ large Spanish onion, peeled and sliced thin
4   tart cooking apples, peeled, cored, and sliced thin
¼ cup firmly packed dark brown sugar
1-2 teaspoons salt
½ cup dry red wine or red wine vinegar
2   tablespoons butter or margarine pepper

In a large heavy kettle combine cabbage, onion, apples, sugar, 1 teaspoon salt, and wine. Cover and boil slowly, stirring once or twice, for 20 to 25 minutes, or until the cabbage is just tender. Mix in the butter, pepper and remaining salt, if desired. Makes 4–6 servings.

Viennese-Style Cabbage

1   medium-size head cabbage, cored and cut into thin wedges
1   cup water
½ teaspoon salt
2   tablespoons butter, cut into small pieces and softened
⅛ teaspoon white pepper
1   cup sour cream
2   teaspoons poppy seeds

Put the cabbage in a heavy kettle, pour the water over it, add the salt, and bring the water to a boil. Reduce the heat and simmer the cabbage for 20 to 25 minutes, adding more water if necessary, until it is tender but not limp. Drain the cabbage well and transfer it to a heated platter. Scatter the butter over the cabbage, sprinkle with the white pepper, and keep warm.

Spoon the sour cream into the kettle and heat it through, but take care not to let it boil. Ladle the hot cream over the cabbage and sprinkle the cream with the poppy seeds. Makes 4–6 servings.

White Cabbage in Sour Cream

4   cups coarsely shredded white cabbage
1   medium-size onion, thinly sliced and separated into rings
1   cup beef stock or broth
1   tablespoon cornstarch or arrowroot
1   tablespoon butter
½ cup sour cream

In a large saucepan combine the cabbage, onion rings, and beef stock. Bring the mixture to a boil, reduce the heat, and simmer the vegetables for 15 minutes. With a slotted spoon transfer the cabbage and onions to a heated serving platter, reserving the cooking liquid, and keep them warm.

In a measuring cup mix the cornstarch or arrowroot with about ¼ cup of the cooking liquid. Stir the paste into the remaining broth and cook the sauce over medium heat, stirring constantly, until it is hot and thickened. Add the butter and cook the mixture until it is melted. Turn off the heat, spoon the sour cream into the sauce, and beat the mixture with a whisk until it is smooth. Pour the sauce over the cabbage and onions. Makes 4–6 servings.

Country-Style Sauerkraut

4 *tablespoons lard, butter, or bacon*
   drippings
1 *large onion, chopped*
2 *apples, cored, peeled, and chopped*
8 *cups sauerkraut, well rinsed and*
   drained
4 *cups beef stock*
6 *juniper berries or 1 tablespoon*
   caraway seeds
1 *large raw potato*
¾ *cup dry white wine or cider*

In an enameled Dutch oven or casserole melt the fat over medium heat. Add the onion and

sauté it for 5 minutes, or until it is just soft. Stir in the apples and cook them, stirring occasionally, for 10 minutes. Add the sauerkraut, toss it with the onion and apple, and cook the mixture, covered, over low heat for 10 minutes. Pour in enough of the stock to half-cover the sauerkraut and add the juniper berries or caraway seeds. Cover the pot and simmer the sauerkraut for 1 hour and 15 minutes, adding more broth if necessary.

Peel the potato and grate it into a 2-cup measure. Stir the potato and its juice into the sauerkraut and cook the mixture over medium heat until it is slightly thickened. Stir in ½ cup of the wine or cider and cook the sauerkraut for 20 minutes more, adding the remaining ¼ cup wine if more liquid is needed. Makes 10 servings.

Glazed Baby Carrots

1 *pound baby carrots*
1½ *cups boiling water*
   salt to taste
2 *tablespoons butter*
¼ *cup light brown sugar*
   freshly ground black pepper

Boil carrots, covered, for 8 to 10 minutes. In a heavy skillet melt the butter and mix in the brown sugar and pepper to taste. Cook over low heat until the sugar dissolves. Drain the carrots and add them to the skillet. Cook the mixture 5 minutes, turning the carrots to coat them with the glaze. Makes 3–4 servings.

Carrot Soufflé

½ teaspoon plus a pinch of salt
5 medium-size carrots, cut into 1½-inch
   pieces
4 tablespoons butter
2 tablespoons minced onion
3 tablespoons flour
1 cup milk
3 egg yolks
¼ teaspoon nutmeg
   pinch cayenne
3 egg whites

Half fill a saucepan with water, add the ½ teaspoon salt, and bring the water to a boil. Plunge the carrots into the boiling water, reduce the heat, and cook the carrots for 25 minutes, or until they are tender. Drain the carrots, turn them into a blender or a food processor fitted with the steel blade, and purée them until they are smooth.

In a small skillet melt the butter over medium heat, add the onion, and sauté it for 8 minutes, or until it is golden but not browned. Stir in the flour and cook the roux for 3 or 4 minutes, taking care not to let it brown. Slowly add the milk and stir the sauce until it is smooth and thickened. Fold in the carrots, turn off the heat, and let the mixture cool to lukewarm.

Preheat the oven to 350° F.

In a bowl beat the egg yolks until they are smooth. Beat in the nutmeg and the cayenne. In another bowl with an electric mixer beat the egg whites until they are foamy. Add the remaining pinch of salt and continue to beat the whites until they hold stiff peaks.

Stir the beaten yolks into the skillet, combining the two mixtures very well. Fold in the beaten egg whites and turn the soufflé into a buttered casserole or a soufflé dish. Bake the soufflé for 35 to 40 minutes, until it is puffy and the top is firm. Makes 2 servings.

Carrot-Potato Purée

4 tablespoons butter
½ cup chopped onion
4 large Idaho potatoes, peeled, cut into
   ½-inch slices
8 carrots, cut into 1-inch pieces
1 cup chicken broth
   salt and pepper
¼ teaspoon nutmeg

In a large heavy skillet melt 2 tablespoons of the butter over medium heat. Add the onion and sauté it for 8 minutes, stirring often, until it is translucent. Add the potatoes, carrots, and broth and simmer the mixture for 25 to 30 minutes, until the carrots and potatoes are tender. Let the vegetables cool for 10 minutes.

Turn the vegetables and the cooking liquid into a blender or a food processor fitted with the steel blade and purée the mixture until it is smooth. Season the purée with salt and pepper to taste and add the remaining 2 tablespoons butter. Return the purée to the skillet and cook it over low heat until it is very hot. Transfer the purée to a serving dish and garnish it with the nutmeg. Makes 8 servings.

Gingered Carrots

1/4   cup (1/2 stick) butter
2   tablespoons lemon juice
2   tablespoons water
20   medium-size carrots, scraped and halved
      lengthwise
1   tablespoon sugar
1   tablespoon ground ginger
      salt and pepper
2   teaspoons snipped dill

In a large skillet melt the butter over low heat. Add the lemon juice, water, and carrots. Cover the skillet and cook the carrots, stirring often, for 15 to 20 minutes, or until they are tender. Sprinkle the sugar and ginger over the carrots, season them with salt and pepper to taste, and cook them for 5 minutes more, turning them often, until they are glazed and tender. Turn the carrots into a heated serving dish and sprinkle them with the dill. Makes 4 servings.

Mustard-Glazed Carrots

1/2   teaspoon salt
2   pounds carrots
3   tablespoons butter
3   tablespoons Dijon mustard
1/4   cup brown sugar
2   tablespoons chopped parsley

Half fill a saucepan with water, add the salt, and bring the water to a boil.

Trim the carrots, scrape them well, halve them lengthwise, and cut the halves into 2-inch pieces. Drop them in the boiling water, reduce the heat, and simmer the carrots, covered, for 15 to 20 minutes, or until they are tender. Drain them well.

In a skillet melt the butter. Stir in the mustard and brown sugar and cook the glaze over low heat until it is syrupy. Add the carrots, toss them with the glaze, and heat them through. Transfer the carrots to a serving dish and sprinkle them with the parsley. Makes 6 servings.

Corn Casserole

6   ears fresh corn or 2 cans whole-kernel
      corn
2   cups milk
3   eggs
1   cup cracker crumbs
1/2   cup chopped onion
1/4   cup chopped pimiento
1/2   teaspoon salt
1   large green pepper cut into rings

Preheat the oven to 350° F.

Using a sharp knife scrape the corn from the cob, or thoroughly drain the canned corn. In a large saucepan combine the corn and the milk and bring the mixture to a simmer over medium heat.

In a large bowl lightly beat the eggs. Stir in the cracker crumbs, onion, pimiento, and salt. Stir the egg mixture into the corn and milk, pour the combination into a buttered 2-quart casserole, and top it with the green pepper rings. Bake the corn casserole for 50 to 60 minutes. Makes 6 servings.

New Peas with Scallions

2½   cups shelled peas
6   scallions, white part only, cut into 1-inch
      pieces
½   teaspoon salt
⅛   teaspoon pepper
1   teaspoon sugar
¾   cup boiling water
1   tablespoon chopped parsley
2   teaspoons chopped chives
⅛   teaspoon dried or 1 teaspoon fresh
      tarragon
⅛   teaspoon dried or ½ teaspoon fresh
      chervil
2   tablespoons butter, cut into small pieces

In a saucepan combine the peas, scallions, salt,
pepper, and sugar. Pour the boiling water over
the peas and scallions and simmer them,
covered, over low heat for 5 minutes. Stir in
the parsley, chives, tarragon, and chervil and
cook the mixture, uncovered, for 10 minutes
more, stirring occasionally. Drain the peas, toss
them with the butter, and serve them
immediately. Makes 4–6 servings.

Country Baked Beans

4   cups navy beans
10   cups water
1   large onion, peeled and chopped
½   cup molasses
½   cup (1 stick) butter
1   teaspoon salt
2   teaspoons dry mustard
1   cup catsup

Put the beans in a large enameled kettle, pour
the water over them, and let them soak
overnight. Drain the beans, cover them with
fresh water, and bring the water to a boil.
Reduce the heat and simmer the beans,
uncovered, for 2 hours, or until they are
tender.

Preheat the oven to 300° F.

Spread the onion over the bottom of a well-
buttered bean pot. Drain the beans and reserve
the cooking liquid, adding water if necessary to
make 1¾ cups. Turn the beans into the bean
pot and add the molasses, butter, salt, dry
mustard, and catsup. Stir in the reserved
cooking liquid and bake the beans, covered, for
3 hours, adding more water if necessary.
Uncover the beans and cook them for 30
minutes more. Makes 10–12 servings.

Sweet-and-Sour Onions

1   cup water
¼   cup white wine vinegar
3   tablespoons olive oil
¼   cup sugar
3   tablespoons tomato paste
20   very small onions, peeled
6   parsley sprigs
1   teaspoon fresh thyme, or ¼ teaspoon
      dried
1   small bay leaf
      salt and pepper
¼   cup Madeira

In a large saucepan combine the water,
vinegar, oil, sugar, and tomato paste. Bring the

mixture to a boil, reduce the heat, and simmer the liquid, stirring, until the sugar is dissolved and the ingredients are well combined. Add the onions and return the liquid to a simmer.

Tie the parsley, thyme, and bay leaf inside a square of cheesecloth and drop the bouquet garni into the cooking liquid. Simmer the onions, uncovered, for 20 minutes, or until they are tender. Pour the Madeira over the onions, heat it almost to a simmer, and cook the onions for 5 minutes more. Remove the bouquet garni and transfer the onions and Madeira to a serving bowl. Serve the onions hot or let them cool to room temperature. Makes 4 servings.

Stuffed Onions

6   medium-size onions, trimmed
      and peeled
1/2 cup water
1   cup fresh bread crumbs
1/2 cup chopped parsley
1   cup chopped spinach, cooked and
      drained
1   clove garlic, minced
1/4 teaspoon salt

Preheat the oven to 375° F.

Put the onions in an 8-inch round glass or enameled baking dish. Pour 1/4 cup of the water around them, bake them for 25 minutes, and set them aside at room temperature until they are cool enough to handle. With a small metal spoon or a melon ball cutter carefully scoop out the center of each onion, leaving a shell 1/4 inch thick.

In a bowl combine the bread crumbs, parsley, spinach, garlic, and salt. Spoon the stuffing into the onion shells and return the shells to the baking dish. Pour the remaining 1/4 cup water around them and bake them for 20 minutes, or until the filling is slightly browned and the onions are tender. Makes 6 servings.

Leek Tart

4   eggs
1 1/2 cups half-and-half
1 1/2 cups grated Gruyère or Swiss cheese
1/4 cup (1/2 stick) butter
2   cups coarsely chopped leeks, including 1/2
      inch of the green parts
      salt and pepper
1   baked 9-inch pie shell
      nutmeg

In a large bowl beat together the eggs and half-and-half. Stir in the cheese and set the mixture aside.

Preheat the oven to 375° F.

In a heavy skillet melt the butter over medium heat. Add the leeks and sauté them for 10 minutes, or until they are soft but not quite translucent. Season the leek mixture with salt and pepper to taste and turn it into the pie shell. Pour the cheese sauce over the leek mixture and smooth it with a spatula. Sprinkle the tart with nutmeg and bake it for 30 minutes. Makes 6–8 servings.

Turnips with Caraway Seeds

5   *medium-size turnips, scraped and cut*
into 1-inch cubes
1   *teaspoon salt*
3   *tablespoons sugar*
1/4 *teaspoon white pepper*
3   *teaspoons caraway seeds*
6¼ *cups water*
2   *cups white wine vinegar*
1   *tablespoon cornstarch*
1   *tablespoon butter*
1/4 *sweet red pepper, minced*

In a large saucepan combine the turnips, salt, sugar, white pepper, and 2 teaspoons of the caraway seeds. Add 6 cups of the water and bring it to a boil. Reduce the heat and simmer the turnips for 20 minutes, or until the cooking liquid is reduced by about half. Stir in the vinegar and cook the turnips for 15 minutes more, or until they are tender.

In a measuring cup combine the cornstarch with the remaining ¼ cup water and stir the paste into the turnips. Cook the mixture, stirring, for 8 to 10 minutes, until the sauce is thickened and glossy. Spoon the turnips and sauce into a heated serving bowl and keep them warm.

In a small skillet melt the butter over medium heat. Add the red pepper and sauté it for 5 minutes, or until it is soft. Pour the red pepper and butter over the turnips and sprinkle them with the remaining 1 teaspoon caraway seeds. Makes 4 servings.

Teltower Rübchen (Glazed Turnips)

2   *pounds turnips*
5   *tablespoons butter, softened*
1   *tablespoon sugar*
1   *cup beef broth*
3/4 *cup flour*

Trim and scrape the turnips and halve them lengthwise and crosswise if they are large. In a heavy skillet melt 2 tablespoons of the butter over medium heat. Add the turnips and sauté them for 5 minutes, turning them occasionally. Sprinkle the sugar over the turnips and toss them lightly to coat them well. Reduce the heat to low and cook the turnips, covered, for 5 more minutes. Add the broth to the skillet, bring it to a simmer, and cook the turnips for about 20 minutes, or until they are tender.

In a bowl combine the flour with the remaining 3 tablespoons softened butter. Shape the mixture into marble-size balls and drop the balls into the cooking liquid. Cook the turnips, stirring, for 5 more minutes. Makes 6 servings.

Turnip Pudding

8   *medium-size turnips, scraped and cut*
into 1-inch cubes
2   *medium onions, quartered*
salt and pepper
1/2 *cup heavy cream*
2   *tablespoons butter*
2   *egg whites*

Steam the turnips and onions over boiling water for 30 to 35 minutes, or until they are tender. Drain the vegetables well and purée them in a blender or a food processor fitted with the steel blade. Transfer the turnip-onion purée to a heavy saucepan, season it with salt and pepper to taste, and stir in the cream and the butter. Cook the mixture over low heat until it is smooth and bubbly. Set the mixture aside to cool.

Preheat the oven to 350° F.

With an electric mixer beat the egg whites until they hold stiff peaks. Fold the meringue into the cooled turnip mixture and turn the pudding into a buttered 1½-quart baking dish. Bake the turnip pudding for 30 to 40 minutes, until a knife inserted in the center comes out clean. Makes 8–10 servings.

Spring Vegetables with Dill

2   *tablespoons butter*
12   *small white onions, peeled*
6   *new potatoes*
6   *carrots, scraped and cut into 1-inch*
     pieces
½   *cup chicken broth*
2   *tablespoons snipped fresh dill, or 1*
     teaspoon dried dill
1   *cup fresh peas or thawed frozen peas*
     salt and pepper

In a large skillet melt the butter over medium heat. Add the onions and sauté them for 5 minutes, or until they are slightly browned. Add the potatoes and carrots and toss them to coat them with butter. Stir in the chicken broth, bring it to a boil, and add the dill. Reduce the heat and simmer the vegetables, covered, for 15 minutes. Add the peas and cook the mixture, covered, for 10 to 15 minutes more, or until the vegetables are tender. Season the mixture with salt, if necessary, and pepper to taste. Turn the vegetables and the remaining cooking liquid into a bowl and serve them at once. Makes 6 servings.

Grilled Baby Vegetables

6   *baby artichokes, trimmed*
6   *small onions, trimmed and peeled*
6   *baby eggplants, trimmed*
6   *baby summer squash, trimmed*
6   *large mushrooms, trimmed*
½   *cup olive oil*
     salt and pepper

Prepare a charcoal grill or preheat the broiler.

Steam the artichokes over boiling water for 10 minutes, or until they are almost tender. Plunge the onions into boiling water and cook them for 5 minutes, or until they are just tender. Steam the eggplants and summer squash over boiling water for 5 minutes.

Thread the partly cooked vegetables and the mushrooms on skewers, brush them with olive oil, and grill them over hot coals or in the broiler for 8 to 10 minutes. Season them with salt and pepper to taste. Makes 6 servings.

Allerei

¾ teaspoon salt
3 carrots, cut in 2-inch pieces
¼ pound green beans, trimmed
1 cup sliced mushrooms or small whole
    mushrooms
8 asparagus spears, trimmed
1½ cups cauliflower florets
1 large kohlrabi, trimmed, peeled, and
    sliced
½ cup (1 stick) butter
2 tablespoons flour
   pepper

Bring a kettle of water to a boil and add the
salt. Plunge the carrots into the water, reduce
the heat, and simmer the carrots for 20
minutes, or until they are tender. With a
slotted spoon transfer the carrots to a colander.

Plunge the green beans into the boiling
water and cook them for 20 minutes, or until
they are tender. Transfer them to the colander.

In the same manner cook the mushrooms
for 1 minute, the asparagus for 10 minutes, the
cauliflower for 15 minutes, and the kohlrabi
for 25 minutes.

Measure out 1 cup of the cooking liquid and
set it aside.

In a large skillet melt the butter over
medium heat. Stir in the flour and cook the
roux for 5 minutes, stirring constantly. Add the
reserved cooking liquid and whisk the sauce
for 5 minutes, or until it is smooth and bubbly.
Season the sauce with pepper to taste, stir in
the vegetables, and cook the mixture, stirring
constantly, until the *Allerei* is heated through.
Makes 4 servings.

Sauerkraut-Potato Casserole

6 large unpeeled potatoes
¼ cup milk
   salt and pepper
6 tablespoons (¾ stick) butter, cut into
    small pieces
1 small onion, sliced
1 pound sauerkraut, rinsed and well
    drained
2 tablespoons grated Swiss cheese

Scrub the potatoes and cook them in water to
cover for 35 to 40 minutes, or until they are
tender. Submerge them in cold water until they
are just cool enough to handle. Slip off the
skins, put the potatoes in a large bowl, and
mash them with an electric mixer, adding
enough of the milk to make the mixture
smooth and fluffy. Season the potatoes with salt
and pepper to taste, stir in 2 tablespoons of the
butter, and set the bowl aside.

Preheat the oven to 350° F.

In a heavy skillet over medium heat melt 2
tablespoons of the remaining butter. Add the
onion and sauté it, stirring constantly, until it is
translucent. Stir in the sauerkraut, reduce the
heat to low, and simmer the mixture for 10
minutes.

Spoon half of the mashed potatoes into a
buttered 1½-quart casserole. Cover the
potatoes with the sauerkraut mixture and top
the casserole with the remaining mashed
potatoes. Spread the grated cheese over the top
layer and scatter the butter over the cheese.
Bake the casserole, covered, for 25 minutes.
Uncover the dish and bake the mixture for 10
minutes more. Makes 6–8 servings.

Zweibelkuchen (Onion Pie)

    6   tablespoons bacon drippings
 1¾   cups flour
    1   teaspoon baking powder
  ⅓   cup milk
    3   tablespoons butter
    8   large onions, sliced
 1⅓   cups sour cream
    3   eggs
  ½   teaspoon salt
    2   teaspoons caraway seeds
    5   slices bacon

Preheat the oven to 450° F.

In a large bowl stir the bacon drippings with a wooden spoon until they are smooth. Sift together 1¼ cup plus 2 tablespoons of the flour and the baking powder. Add the dry ingredients to the bacon drippings in batches, beating the mixture with a wooden spoon to blend the ingredients well. Stir in the milk in a thin stream until the dough forms a ball. Knead the dough a few times and roll it into a rectangle about 13 by 9 by 2 inches. Fit the dough onto a cookie sheet, crimping the edges to form a rim, and bake the shell for 10 to 12 minutes, or until it is slightly browned. Set the pie shell aside to cool slightly.

Reduce the oven temperature to 375° F.

In a large saucepan melt the butter over medium heat. Add the onions and cook them, stirring often, for 8 to 10 minutes, until they are soft. Stir in the remaining 6 tablespoons flour and cook the roux for 3 or 4 minutes, taking care not to let it brown. Add the sour cream, eggs, salt, and caraway seeds and simmer the mixture, stirring constantly, until it is smooth and bubbly. Turn the mixture into the pastry shell and lay the bacon strips across the top. Bake the onion pie for 50 to 60 minutes. Makes 8–10 servings.

Macédoine of Vegetables

  ½   teaspoon salt
    2   carrots, cut into 1-inch pieces
    1   cup green beans, cut into 1-inch pieces
    1   cup wax beans, cut into 1-inch pieces
    1   small zucchini, sliced
    6   asparagus spears, cut into 1-inch pieces
    1   cup cauliflower florets
    1   stalk broccoli, cut into 1-inch pieces
    3   tablespoons butter
  ¼   teaspoon pepper

Bring a large saucepan of water to a boil and add the salt. Plunge the carrots, green beans, and wax beans into the water, reduce the heat, and simmer the vegetables for 10 minutes. With a slotted spoon transfer them to a colander. Return the water to a boil, plunge the zucchini and asparagus into the saucepan, reduce the heat, and simmer the vegetables for 7 minutes. Transfer them to the colander. Repeat the process, parboiling the cauliflower for 7 minutes and then the broccoli for 7 minutes and draining them well.

In a large skillet melt the butter over medium heat. Add all of the parboiled vegetables and cook them, tossing often, for 10 minutes. Season the macédoine with the pepper. Makes 4–6 servings.

Red River Cabbage

4   *strips bacon*
8   *cups grated red cabbage*
1   *cup white vinegar*
4   *tablespoons sugar*
1   *teaspoon salt*

In a heavy kettle cook the bacon until it is crisp. Transfer it to paper towels to drain. Add about ½ cup of the red cabbage to the kettle and toss it to coat it with the bacon drippings. Repeat the procedure with the remaining red cabbage.

In a 2-cup measure combine the vinegar, sugar, and salt and pour the mixture over the cabbage. Cover the skillet and simmer the cabbage for 20 to 30 minutes, until it has reached the desired degree of doneness.

Turn the cabbage into a serving dish and crumble the bacon over it. Makes 8 servings.

Cabbage in White Wine

3   *tablespoons butter*
2   *medium-size onions, thinly sliced*
2   *tart apples, cored, peeled,*
       and sliced
½   *cup dry white wine*
½   *cup water*
6   *cups coarsely grated cabbage*
1   *teaspoon lemon juice*
       grated rind of 1 lemon
½   *teaspoon salt*
1   *teaspoon sugar*
½   *cup white wine*

In a large heavy kettle melt the butter over medium heat. Add the onions and sauté them for 5 minutes, or until they are soft. Reduce the heat to low, add the apples, and cook them for 10 minutes, or until they begin to soften. Pour in the wine and the water and cook the mixture, covered, for 10 minutes.

In a large bowl toss together the cabbage, lemon juice, lemon rind, salt, and sugar. Turn the mixture into the kettle and toss it lightly to mix it with the onions and apples. Cook the mixture, tightly covered, for 15 minutes. Add the wine and cook the cabbage, uncovered, for 10 minutes more. Makes 8 servings.

Sweet-and-Sour Cabbage

3   *slices bacon*
8   *cups chopped cabbage*
½   *medium onion, diced*
1   *tart apple, cored, peeled, and diced*
¼   *cup seedless green grapes*
2   *cups water*
½   *teaspoon salt*
¼   *teaspoon pepper*
1½   *tablespoons vinegar*
1   *tablespoon sugar*

In a large heavy skillet cook the bacon until it is crisp. Transfer it to paper towels to drain. To the skillet add the cabbage, tossing it well to coat it with the bacon drippings. Stir in the onion, apple, and grapes. Add the water and toss the ingredients together. Cook the mixture, partly covered, for 1 hour. Stir in the salt, pepper, vinegar, and sugar and cook the mixture over medium heat, stirring constantly, until most of the cooking liquid has evaporated. Turn the sweet-and-sour cabbage into a heated serving bowl and crumble the bacon over it. Makes 8–10 servings.

Rotkohl

8 cups grated red cabbage
1½ cups red wine vinegar
1½ teaspoons salt
½ cup sugar
2 tablespoons vegetable oil
1 medium-size onion, sliced
1 large tart apple, cored, peeled, and chopped
6 tablespoons chicken broth
6 cloves
1 small onion, peeled
1 bay leaf

In a large bowl thoroughly combine the cabbage, 1 cup of the vinegar, 1 teaspoon of the salt, and ¼ cup of the sugar. Set the mixture aside at room temperature for 15 minutes.

In a heavy kettle or a Dutch oven heat the oil over medium heat. Add the sliced onion and the apples and sauté them for 10 minutes, or until they are soft but not browned. Drain the cabbage well, turn it into the kettle, and toss it with the oil, onion, and apple. Add the remaining ½ teaspoon salt, ¼ cup sugar, and ½ cup vinegar and reduce the heat to low.

In a small saucepan heat the chicken broth. Stick the cloves into the small peeled onion and drop the onion into the broth. Add the bay leaf and simmer the broth over low heat for 5 minutes. Pour the broth, onion, and bay leaf into the kettle and toss the mixture well. Simmer the cabbage, covered, for 1 hour, stirring occasionally and adding water if necessary.

Correct the seasonings and serve the *Rotkohl* at once or refrigerate it for up to 3 days. Makes 10–12 servings.

Bacon-Wrapped Corn

8 ears sweet corn in the husk
8 strips bacon
butter
salt and pepper

Strip the husks away from the corn, but do not detach them. Remove the silk and soak the corn in cold water for 45 minutes. Wrap 1 bacon strip around each ear of corn and pull the husks back in place, twisting the ends together. Cook the corn over hot coals, turning every 5 minutes, for 15 to 20 minutes, or until the husks are charred.

Serve the corn with butter, salt, and pepper. Makes 8 servings.

Maple–Sweet Potato Puff

1½   *pounds sweet potatoes*
4   *egg yolks*
½   *cup maple syrup*
2   *tablespoons butter*
¼   *teaspoon nutmeg*
¾   *teaspoon salt*
4   *egg whites*
¼   *cup chopped salted peanuts or pecans*

Preheat the oven to 375° F. Scrub the potatoes, pierce the skins with a fork, and bake the potatoes for 40 to 45 minutes, or until they are tender. Set them aside until they are cool enough to handle.

Reduce the oven temperature to 350° F.

In a large bowl lightly beat the egg yolks. Stir in the syrup, butter, nutmeg, and ½ teaspoon of the salt. Peel the sweet potatoes, drop them into a large bowl, and mash them with an electric mixer until they are smooth. Beat the egg yolk mixture into the mashed potatoes.

In another bowl with the electric mixer beat the egg whites with the remaining ¼ teaspoon salt until they hold stiff peaks. Fold the egg whites into the mashed potato mixture and spoon the mixture into a greased 2-quart soufflé dish or a deep casserole. Scatter the nuts over the top and bake the puff for 45 to 50 minutes, until a knife inserted in the center comes out clean. Makes 6 servings.

Glazed Rutabaga and Apple Slices

½   *teaspoon salt*
1   *pound rutabagas, peeled and sliced*
2   *tart apples*
2   *tablespoons butter*
2   *tablespoons brown sugar*

Half fill a saucepan with water, bring the water to a boil, and add the salt. Plunge the rutabaga slices into the boiling water, reduce the heat, and cook the rutabaga for 25 minutes, or until it is almost tender.

Peel and core the apples and cut them into thick slices.

In a large skillet melt the butter over medium heat. Stir in the brown sugar and cook the glaze until it is syrupy. Add the rutabaga and apple slices and spoon the glaze over them. Cook the mixture until the rutabagas are tender and the apples are slightly soft. Makes 4 servings.

POULTRY AND GAME

*U*NTIL recently, chickens, ducks and geese were to be found in practically every American farmyard. And they have always been standard fare on American tables from coast to coast—roasted, broiled, baked, fricasseed, stewed and barbecued.

The cuisine of Germany has long been celebrated for its game dishes and over the centuries German cooks have perfected the art of keeping the meat tender and moist (often no mean feat). German immigrants to America brought with them treasured family recipes, very much aware that a good day's hunting often made a significant difference in the adequacy of a winter larder.

Roast Pheasant with Purple Plum Sauce

2 *pheasants*
2 *apples, peeled, cored, and quartered*
3 *tablespoons butter*
1 *cup dry vermouth*
1 *cup water*

SAUCE

1 *pound canned purple plums, pitted*
¼ *cup butter*
3 *tablespoons finely chopped onion*
¼ *cup fresh lemon juice*
¼ *cup brown sugar*
2 *tablespoons chili sauce*
1 *teaspoon Worcestershire sauce*
½ *teaspoon ground ginger*

Preheat the oven to 450° F.

Sprinkle the pheasants with salt and pepper and stuff them with the apples. In a heavy skillet melt the butter and brown the pheasants on all sides. Place the pheasants on a rack and roast them for 45 minutes, basting every 10 to 15 minutes with the vermouth mixed with the water, and the pan juices.

While the birds are roasting, make the sauce. Drain the plums and chop them coarsely, reserving the juice. In a heavy saucepan melt the butter and sauté the onions until they are golden. Stir in the remaining ingredients, the plums, and the plum juice. Simmer the sauce for 30 minutes, or until it is thickened.

Serve pheasants with sauce. Makes 4 servings.

Pennsylvania Dutch Chicken Fricassee

2 *tablespoons oil*
1 *stick (¼ pound) butter*
1 *5-pound chicken, cut up*
1 *large onion, sliced*
1 *cup sliced celery*
1 *cup sliced mushrooms*
2 *cups sliced carrots*
3 *cups chicken broth or water*
1 *bay leaf*
4 *tablespoons flour*
1 *cup heavy cream*
2 *tablespoons lemon juice*
  salt and pepper
  spaetzle or noodles

In a Dutch oven or a heavy kettle heat the oil and ½ stick (4 tablespoons) of the butter over medium-high heat. Add the chicken pieces, a few at a time, and brown them on all sides. Transfer the chicken to a platter and reduce the heat to medium. Add the onion, celery, mushrooms, and carrots to the kettle and sauté them, stirring often, for 8 to 10 minutes, or until they are soft and slightly browned. Return the chicken to the kettle and pour the broth or water around it. Add the bay leaf, bring the broth to a boil, and reduce the heat. Simmer the chicken and vegetables for 40 to 45 minutes, or until they are tender. Transfer the chicken to a heated platter and keep it warm.

Strain the broth into a saucepan and skim the fat from the surface. Bring the broth to a boil and reduce it to 1½ cups, or add water or chicken broth to make 1½ cups. In the Dutch oven or kettle over medium heat melt the remaining ½ stick butter. Stir in the flour and cook the roux for 3 minutes. Slowly add the cream and the hot cooking broth and cook the sauce, stirring constantly, for 5 minutes, until it is thickened and smooth. Add the lemon juice and season sauce with salt and pepper to taste.

Spoon the sauce over the chicken and serve the fricassee with spaetzle or noodles. Makes 6 servings.

Baked Martini Chicken

1 *2½-pound chicken, quartered*
1 *teaspoon salt*
¼ *teaspoon cayenne*
2 *cups gin*
1 *medium-size onion, sliced*
2 *carrots, sliced*
4 *shallots, minced*
3 *crushed juniper berries*
1 *cup sliced mushrooms*

Rub the chicken pieces with the salt and sprinkle them very lightly with the cayenne. Put them in a casserole and pour the gin over them. Cover the chicken with the onion, carrots, and shallots, add the juniper berries to the marinade, and refrigerate the chicken, covered, for 8 hours, or overnight, turning the pieces once.

Remove the chicken from the refrigerator and let it stand at room temperature for 20 minutes. Preheat the oven to 350° F.

Bake the chicken in the marinade, covered, for 35 minutes. Scatter the mushrooms over the chicken and cook the casserole, uncovered, for 25 minutes more, or until the chicken is done and the carrots are tender. Makes 4 servings.

Chicken Paprika

  4 tablespoons butter
  ½ cup chopped onion
  1 3-pound chicken, quartered
     salt
  2 tablespoons plus ½ teaspoon paprika
  1 tomato, peeled, seeded, and chopped
  1 cup chicken broth
  3 tablespoons flour
  ¼ cup heavy cream
  ½ cup sour cream
     buttered wide noodles

In a deep heavy skillet melt the butter over medium heat. Add the onion and sauté it for 10 minutes, or until it is soft and lightly browned. Add the chicken quarters, sprinkle them with salt to taste, and brown them on both sides. Stir 2 tablespoons of the paprika into the skillet, add the tomato, and pour in ½ cup of the chicken broth, stirring to combine the sauce well. Bring the mixture almost to a boil, reduce the heat to low, and simmer the sauce for about 5 minutes. Cover the skillet and cook the chicken, turning it once or twice, for 40 minutes. Transfer the chicken to a heated platter and keep it warm.

In a measuring cup combine the flour with about ¼ cup of the pan liquid. Stir the paste into the cooking liquid in the skillet and cook the sauce for 3 minutes, stirring briskly, until it is smooth and bubbly. Gradually add the remaining ½ cup chicken broth and simmer the sauce, stirring often, until it is thick and smooth. Stir in the heavy cream and the sour cream and cook the sauce, stirring briskly, until

the sauce is heated through, but take care not to let it boil.

Spoon the sauce over the chicken, dust it with the remaining ½ teaspoon paprika, and serve the dish with the buttered noodles. Makes 4 servings.

Grilled Chicken and Shrimp

  2 cups dry white wine
  1 cup light rum
  1 cup lemon juice
  ½ cup olive oil
  6 chicken breasts, halved
 16 jumbo shrimp, peeled, deveined, and
       butterflied
  1 lemon, thinly sliced
  6 cloves garlic
  4 sprigs fresh rosemary or thyme
     salt and pepper

In a large shallow dish or enameled pan combine the wine, rum, lemon juice, and olive oil. Place the chicken pieces and the shrimp in the mixture, turning them to coat them well, and let them marinate in the refrigerator for 2 to 4 hours.

Prepare a charcoal grill and when it is almost ready place the lemon slices, garlic, and herbs sprigs directly on the coals. Grill the chicken breasts, basting them often with the marinade and turning them occasionally, until they are almost done. Add the shrimp to the grill and cook them, turning once or twice, just until they are pink. Season the chicken and shrimp with salt and pepper to taste and serve them at once. Makes 8 servings.

Coq Au Riesling

1 cup flour
  salt and pepper
4 chicken breasts, halved
2 tablespoons vegetable oil
1 stick (½ cup) plus 3 tablespoons butter
¼ teaspoon nutmeg
1 teaspoon fresh or ¼ teaspoon dried
    thyme
1 leek, well washed
6 sprigs parsley
1 medium-size yellow onion stuck with 2
    whole cloves
⅓ cup cognac, heated
1⅓ cups Riesling or other dry white wine
2 slices salt pork, diced
12 mushroom caps
16 small white onions, peeled
2 tablespoons sugar
3 egg yolks
¾ cup heavy cream

In a shallow pan combine the flour with salt and pepper to taste. Dredge the chicken in the flour mixture until it is well coated. In a deep heavy skillet or a Dutch oven heat the oil and ½ stick (¼ cup) of the butter over medium-high heat. Add the chicken and brown it quickly on both sides. Add the nutmeg and thyme, the leek, one of the parsley sprigs, and the clove-studded onion. Pour the warm cognac over the chicken and ignite it. When the flames die down, add the wine and bring the cooking liquid to a boil. Reduce the heat and simmer the mixture, covered, for 10 to 15 minutes.

In a small skillet melt 1½ tablespoons of the remaining butter over medium heat. Add the salt pork and sauté it until it is golden. With a slotted spoon transfer the sautéed salt pork into the Dutch oven with the chicken and simmer the casserole for 10 minutes more.

To the skillet in which the salt pork was cooked add another 1½ tablespoons of the butter. Stir in the mushrooms and sauté them over medium heat until they are tender and slightly browned. Set the skillet aside and keep the mushrooms warm.

In a separate pan sauté the small white onions in the remaining ½ stick (¼ cup) butter for 5 minutes, or until they are slightly softened. Sprinkle them with the sugar, season them with salt to taste, and toss them to coat them with the glaze. Cover the pan and cook the onions over low heat for 10 minutes, or until they are tender.

Transfer the cooked chicken and salt pork to a heated platter and keep them warm.

Over medium-high heat reduce the cooking liquid in the Dutch oven to 1½ cups; keep the mixture warm over very low heat. In a bowl beat together the egg yolks and the cream; beat in about ¼ cup of the cooking liquid. Slowly stir the egg mixture into the Dutch oven and cook the sauce over low heat until it is smooth and creamy, taking care not to let it boil.

Arrange the mushrooms and the glazed onions around the chicken and garnish the platter with the remaining parsley sprigs. Serve the sauce in a gravy boat. Makes 8 servings.

Chicken with Grapes

4   *chicken breasts, halved*
½   *cup flour*
¼   *cup (½ stick) butter*
¼   *cup chopped onion*
1   *cup halved mushrooms*
⅔   *cup Sauterne*
1   *cup seedless green grapes*
    salt and pepper
⅓   *cup light cream*
4   *tablespoons chopped parsley*

Dredge the chicken in the flour until it is well coated. Heat the butter in a heavy skillet, add the chicken in batches, and lightly brown it over medium-high heat. Reduce the heat, transfer the chicken to a platter, and set it aside. In the butter remaining in the skillet, sauté the onion over medium-low heat for 2 or 3 minutes, stirring often, until it is slightly softened. Stir in the mushrooms and cook the mixture, tossing occasionally, for 10 minutes, or until the vegetables are tender.

Return the chicken to the pan, add the Sauterne, and cook the mixture, covered, over medium-low heat, stirring often, for 20 to 25 minutes, or until the chicken is tender and the juices run clear. Add the grapes and simmer the mixture for 5 minutes more, until the grapes are heated through. With a slotted spoon transfer the chicken to a heated platter, season it with salt and pepper to taste, and arrange the grapes around it. Stir the cream into the cooking liquid and heat the sauce through, but take care not to let it boil. Spoon the sauce over the chicken and garnish the platter with the parsley. Makes 8 servings.

Grilled Marinated Chicken

¼   *teaspoon cayenne*
1   *teaspoon paprika*
2   *teaspoons sugar*
1   *cup water*
2   *tablespoons vinegar*
1   *tablespoon Worcestershire sauce*
1   *teaspoon Dijon mustard*
1   *medium onion, chopped*
1   *clove garlic, minced*
1   *2½-pound frying chicken,*
    cut up
1   *teaspoon salt*

In a saucepan combine the cayenne, paprika, and sugar. Stir in the water, vinegar, Worcestershire sauce, and mustard and bring the mixture to a boil. Add the onion and garlic, reduce the heat, and simmer the marinade for 15 minutes, or until it is slightly reduced. Let the marinade cool for 10 minutes.

Rub the chicken pieces with the salt and place them in a single layer in a large shallow dish or pan. Pour the cooled marinade over the chicken and refrigerate the mixture for 4 to 8 hours, turning the chicken three or four times.

Preheat the oven to 350° F. or prepare a charcoal grill. Bake the chicken, basting often with the marinade, for 1 hour, or grill it over hot coals, until it is tender and the juices run clear. Makes 8 servings.

Chicken Pot Pie

 4   cups diced peeled potatoes
 7   tablespoons butter
 2   large onions, chopped
 ½   pound mushrooms, thinly sliced
 5   tablespoons all-purpose flour
 1½ cups chicken stock or broth
 2½ cups plus 1 tablespoon milk
     salt and pepper
 1   cup heavy cream
 1½ cups cooked peas
 1½ cups cooked sliced carrots
 5   cups diced cooked chicken
 2   unbaked 9-inch pie shells about 2 inches
       deep
     pastry to cover two 9-inch pies
 1   egg

In a large saucepan cook the potatoes in lightly salted water to cover for 10 to 15 minutes, or until they are almost tender. Drain them well and transfer them to a large bowl.

In a large skillet over medium heat melt 3 tablespoons of the butter. Add the onions and sauté them for 5 minutes, or until they are slightly softened. Add the mushrooms and cook the mixture, tossing often, for 10 minutes more, or until the mushrooms are slightly browned and the onions are translucent. With a slotted spoon transfer the mushrooms and onions to the bowl and toss them with the potatoes.

In the same skillet melt the remaining 4 tablespoons butter over medium-low heat. Stir in the flour and cook the roux for about 2 minutes, stirring constantly and taking care not to let it brown. Gradually stir in the chicken stock and the 2½ cups milk and cook the sauce, stirring, until it is thickened and bubbly. Reduce the heat and season the sauce with salt and pepper to taste. Add the cream, stir in the peas and carrots, and heat the sauce through.

Preheat the oven to 400° F.

Toss the chicken with the potatoes, onions, and mushrooms. Pour the sauce over the potato mixture and combine the ingredients well. Divide the filling between the two pie shells, cover each shell with a pastry crust, and cut several vents in the top crusts to allow steam to escape. In a small bowl beat the egg with the remaining 1 tablespoon milk and brush the mixture over the pies. Place the pies on a large cookie sheet and bake them for 25 to 30 minutes, or until they are golden brown. Let the pies cool on a rack for 10 to 15 minutes.

To freeze an unbaked chicken pie, place the pie, uncovered, in the freezer for 1 hour. Wrap the frozen pie in foil and return it to the freezer. To cook a frozen pie, place it in a preheated 400° F. oven and bake it for 1 hour, or thaw the pie and bake it at 400° F. for 25 to 30 minutes.

To freeze a baked chicken pie, let the pie cool completely and place it, uncovered, in the freezer for 1 hour. Wrap the frozen pie in foil and return it to the freezer. Before serving, thaw the pie, preheat the oven to 350° F., and heat the pie for 35 to 40 minutes, or until it is hot and bubbly. Makes 2 pies, 6 servings.

Chicken with Caraway Biscuits

1   *stick (½ cup) butter*
1   *3-pound chicken, cut up*
¼ *teaspoon pepper*
1   *teaspoon salt*
2   *cups plus 3 tablespoons flour*
3   *cups chicken broth*
3   *teaspoons baking powder*
¼ *cup shortening*
3   *tablespoons caraway seeds*
⅔ *cup milk*

Preheat the oven to 350° F.

In a deep heavy skillet melt the butter over medium heat. Add the chicken in batches and brown it well on all sides. Season the chicken with the pepper and ½ teaspoon of the salt and transfer it to a large casserole or a deep baking dish. Stir 3 tablespoons of the flour into the drippings in the skillet and cook the roux, stirring, for 2 to 3 minutes, taking care not to let it brown. Gradually add the broth, stirring constantly, until the gravy is smooth and bubbly. Pour the gravy into the casserole and bake the chicken, covered, for 1 hour and 15 minutes, adding water or broth if the gravy becomes too thick.

Into a large bowl sift together the remaining 2 cups flour, the baking powder, and the remaining ½ teaspoon salt. Cut in the shortening until the mixture is mealy. Stir in the caraway seeds. Make a well in the center of the mixture and add the milk, stirring until the dough clumps together and adheres to the spoon. (Add 2 to 3 tablespoons more milk if the dough is too hard.) Turn the dough onto a floured surface, knead it gently 10 or 12 times, and roll or pat it out ½ inch thick. Cut out biscuits with a cutter dipped in flour. Arrange the biscuits on top of the hot chicken and gravy and bake the casserole for 12 to 15 minutes, until the biscuits are crisp and golden brown. Makes 6–8 servings.

Chicken with Artichokes

1   *2½- to 3-pound frying chicken,*
     cut up
2   *celery stalks, leaves included*
1   *large carrot, quartered*
1   *medium-size onion, peeled and*
     quartered
1   *bay leaf*
¾ *teaspoon salt*
3   *peppercorns*
2   *9-ounce packages frozen artichoke*
     hearts, cooked and drained
6   *tablespoons butter*
½ *pound mushrooms, sliced*
¼ *cup flour*
2   *cups chicken stock*
½ *teaspoon nutmeg*
3   *cups grated Cheddar cheese*
½ *cup fine dry bread crumbs*
½ *teaspoon savory*
½ *teaspoon thyme*

In a large heavy saucepan or a kettle combine the chicken, celery, carrot, onion, bay leaf, salt, and peppercorns. Cover the chicken with water and bring the water to a boil. Reduce the heat and simmer the chicken, covered, for 45 minutes to 1 hour, until it is tender. Turn off the heat and let the chicken cool in the broth. Transfer the chicken to a platter.

Remove the skin and bones from the chicken and cut the meat into bite-size pieces. Put the chicken in a 3-quart casserole, add the artichoke hearts, and set the casserole aside.

In a large saucepan melt 4 tablespoons of the butter over medium heat. Add the mushrooms and sauté them, stirring often, for 8 to 10 minutes, until they are tender and slightly browned. With a slotted spoon transfer them to the casserole.

Preheat the oven to 350° F.

Stir the flour into the butter remaining in the saucepan. Cook the roux over medium heat, stirring constantly, for 2 to 3 minutes, taking care not to let it brown. Gradually add the chicken broth, stirring, and cook the sauce until it is smooth and thickened. Add the nutmeg and the cheese and stir the mixture until the cheese is melted and hot. Pour the sauce over the chicken and artichokes.

In a small bowl combine the bread crumbs with the savory and thyme, sprinkle the mixture over the cheese sauce, and top the casserole with the remaining 2 tablespoons butter. Bake the dish, uncovered, for 30 minutes.

Just before serving, run the casserole under the broiler for 2 to 3 minutes, or until the bread crumbs are browned and the cheese is bubbly. Makes 8 servings.

Winter Chicken and Potato Casserole

1⅓	*cups flour*
	salt and pepper
2	*chickens, cut up*
6	*tablespoons vegetable oil*
2	*medium-size onions, chopped*
16	*large mushrooms, sliced*
4	*cups chicken broth*
1	*teaspoon chopped fresh thyme, or ¼ teaspoon dried*
3	*tablespoons chopped parsley*
8–12	*new potatoes, peeled*
16–32	*baby carrots*
1	*cup thickly sliced celery*
6	*strips bacon, cooked and crumbled*

Put the flour in a paper or plastic bag and season it with salt and pepper to taste. Add the chicken pieces, two at a time, and shake them in the flour until they are well coated. Set the chicken aside and reserve 3 tablespoons of the flour.

In a large heavy skillet heat the oil. Add the chicken pieces in batches and brown them on all sides over medium-high heat. Transfer the chicken to a platter.

Preheat the oven to 375° F.

Add the onions and mushrooms to the skillet and sauté them for 10 minutes, or until the onion is translucent and the mushrooms are lightly browned. Sprinkle the reserved flour over the vegetables and cook the roux, stirring, for 2 to 3 minutes, taking care not to let it brown. Gradually stir in the broth and cook the sauce, stirring, until it is thickened and bubbly. Stir in the thyme and parsley, add more salt and pepper if desired, and set the sauce aside.

In a large casserole combine the chicken, potatoes, carrots, celery, and the sauce with the mushrooms and onions. Bake the casserole for 1 hour to 1 hour and 15 minutes, or until the chicken and vegetables are tender. Scatter the crumbled bacon over the casserole and serve it at once. Makes 8 servings.

Traditional Roast Duck

2	*4–5 pound ducklings*
2	*cups sliced carrots*
2	*medium yellow onions, sliced*
1	*cup sliced celery*
1	*large parsley sprig*
1	*bay leaf*
1/8	*teaspoon thyme*
	salt and pepper to taste
4	*cups water*
1	*lemon, halved*
1/2	*cup celery leaves*
1	*tablespoon cold butter, cut into bits*

Preheat oven to 450° F.

Cut the wing tips and necks off the ducks. In a large heavy saucepan combine the wing tips, necks, giblets (reserving the livers), half the carrots and onions, the celery, parsley, bay leaf, thyme, salt and pepper to taste, and the water. Bring the stock to a boil, skim any froth that rises to the surface, and simmer the stock while duck is roasting. Let stock reduce to 1½ cups.

Rub the ducks inside and out with the cut sides of the lemon. Salt the ducks lightly and stuff the cavities with some of the onion and the celery leaves. With a fork prick the skin around the thighs, backs, and lower breasts. In a large roasting pan, place the ducks breast side up and scatter the remaining onions and carrots around them.

Put the ducks in the oven and reduce the heat to 350° F. After 15 minutes turn the ducks on their sides and remove any accumulated fat with a bulb baster. Thirty minutes later, turn them on their other sides and remove the fat from the pan. After another 30 minutes, turn the ducks breast side up. Cook another 15 minutes. The ducks are done when the juice runs pale yellow from a pricked thigh.

Remove the ducks to a serving platter and keep them warm while you make the gravy. Skim the fat from the roasting pan and add the stock. Over medium heat boil the gravy, mashing the cooked vegetables, until it is reduced by half. Remove the pan from the heat and whisk in the cold butter, bit by bit, to finish the gravy. Serve the ducks with the gravy. Makes 4 servings.

SAUCE

1½	*cups water*
3/4	*cup orange juice*
1½	*cups sugar*
1	*pound fresh or frozen raw cranberries*

In a large heavy saucepan bring the water, orange juice and sugar to a boil, stirring constantly. Boil the mixture, uncovered, for 5 minutes without stirring. Add the cranberries, cover and simmer 5 to 7 minutes or until the skins burst. Serve the cranberries warm or cold.. Makes 1 quart.

Roast Duck with Melon

2 4-pound ducklings
   salt
1½ medium-size cantaloupes
½ medium-size honeydew melon
3 ounces melon liqueur
¼ teaspoon cayenne
1 teaspoon dry mustard
1 tablespoon butter

Preheat the oven to 350° F.

Sprinkle the ducklings with salt to taste, place them side by side in a roasting pan, and roast them, basting several times with the pan drippings, for 1 hour to 1 hour and 15 minutes, or until they are tender and the skin is crisp and browned.

Scoop out 12 melon balls from the cantaloupe and 12 from the honeydew and set the balls aside. Remove the rest of the flesh from the melons and purée it in a blender or a food processor fitted with steel blade.

Transfer the ducklings to a heated platter and keep them warm. Pour off all of the fat from the roasting pan, deglaze the pan with the melon liqueur, and place it over medium heat. Stir in the melon purée and simmer the sauce until it is slightly thickened. Season the sauce with cayenne, mustard, and salt to taste.

In a small skillet melt the butter over medium heat, add the melon balls, and sauté them, tossing often, until they are heated through.

Pour the sauce over the ducklings and garnish the platter with the sautéed melon balls. Makes 6–8 servings.

Rolf's Yuletide Goose

1 young goose (about 10–12 pounds)
2 tablespoons coarse salt
3 cloves garlic, minced
8 tablespoons (1 stick) butter
6 medium yellow onions, chopped
8 Granny Smith apples, quartered
1 pound prunes
6 oranges, quartered
3 bay leaves
1 teaspoon basil
4 tablespoons light brown sugar
1 quart Burgundy wine
4 quarts water
1 cup Grand Marnier
1 tablespoon cornstarch mixed with ½ cup
   cold water
4 ounces lingonberry jelly

Preheat the oven to 375° F.

Rub the goose inside and out with the salt and garlic. Prick it all over with a sharp fork and spread it with the butter. Place the goose in a very large roasting pan surrounded by the onions, apples, prunes, and oranges. Add the bay leaves and basil and sprinkle the brown sugar over the fruits. Pour the Burgundy and water over all.

Roast the goose 25 minutes to the pound, basting as often as possible. Thirty minutes before the bird is done, pour Grand Marnier over the entire bird and baste.

Remove the bird from the pan. Remove the solids from the pan with a slotted spoon. Set the pan over medium heat and stir in the cornstarch and water. Add the lingonberry jelly and cook briefly until the sauce has thickened. Stir well. Makes 4 servings.

Roast Goose with Sausage-Sauerkraut Stuffing

2   *pounds bulk sausage*
2   *medium-size onions, chopped*
2   *cloves garlic, minced*
7   *cups sauerkraut, rinsed and drained*
1   *10-pound goose or turkey*
1   *cup chicken broth*
½   *cup apple brandy*
20   *spiced apple rings*
20   *parsley sprigs*

Sauté the sausage in a large skillet, breaking it up into small pieces. When it begins to change color, add the onions and garlic and cook the mixture for 10 minutes, or until the onion is translucent and golden. Drain off the fat and add the sauerkraut, stirring well to combine it with the sausage. Simmer the stuffing, covered, for 30 minutes.

Preheat the oven to 350° F.

Stuff the sausage-sauerkraut mixture into the cavity of the goose and truss the fowl. Prick the skin all over with a fork and place the goose on a rack in a shallow roasting pan. Pour the broth and brandy over it, and roast it for 2½ hours to 3 hours and 20 minutes (15 to 20 minutes per pound), until it is tender and well browned, basting it often with the cooking liquid. Prick the skin in several places with a fork or the tip of a sharp knife and let the goose rest for about 10 minutes until some of the fat has escaped.

Transfer the goose to a heated serving platter and garnish it with the spiced apple rings and parsley sprigs. Makes 8–10 servings.

Country-Style Roast Turkey with Chestnut Stuffing

10   *cups day-old toasted white bread cubes*
2   *large onions, chopped*
1½   *cups chopped celery*
1   *clove garlic, crushed*
2   *cups chopped roasted chestnuts*
1   *teaspoon sweet marjoram*
1   *teaspoon thyme*
1½   *cups (3 sticks) butter, melted*
1   *cup hot water*
    salt and pepper
1   *12-pound turkey*
½   *cup yellow cornmeal*

Preheat the oven to 325° F.

In a large bowl toss together the bread cubes, onions, celery, garlic, and chestnuts. Stir in the marjoram, thyme, 1 cup of the melted butter, and just enough of the hot water to moisten the mixture well. Season the stuffing with salt and pepper to taste. Pack the stuffing into the cavity of the turkey and truss the bird. Brush the outside of the turkey with ¼ cup of the remaining melted butter and sprinkle it with the cornmeal. Sprinkle the bird lightly with salt and pepper and roast it for 4½ hours, basting often with the pan liquids and the remaining ¼ cup melted butter. The turkey is fully cooked when the drumsticks are soft and can be twisted easily or when a meat thermometer inserted in the thickest part of the breast registers 195° F. Makes 16–20 servings.

Quail with Cherries

8   *quail*
    salt and pepper
½   *cup (1 stick) butter*
½   *cup brandy*
½   *cup red currant jelly*
½   *cup Port*
    juice of 1 orange
    rind of 1 orange
1   *can pitted Bing cherries in their own*
      juice
1   *teaspoon cinnamon*
½   *teaspoon ground cloves*

Preheat the oven to 350° F.

Rub the quail with salt and pepper to taste. In a large flameproof casserole melt the butter over medium heat. Add the quail and sauté them, turning them occasionally, for 15 to 20 minutes, or until they are lightly browned. Put the casserole in the oven and roast the quail, covered, for 10 minutes. Transfer the birds to a platter.

Over medium heat add the brandy to the cooking liquid in the casserole, stirring well to scrape up the brown bits from the pan. Stir in the currant jelly, the Port, and the orange juice and cook the sauce, stirring, until it is heated through and the jelly is melted. Add the orange rind and the cherries with their juice and stir in the cinnamon and cloves. Heat the mixture to a simmer, reduce the heat to low, and return the quail to the casserole. Cook the quail in the sauce, turning them occasionally, for 10 minutes, or until the sauce is bubbly and the quail are heated through.

Transfer the quail to a heated platter, spoon about ¼ cup of the sauce and cherries over each bird, and serve the remaining sauce in a gravy boat. Makes 8 servings.

Roast Turkey with Sauerkraut

3   *tablespoons vegetable oil*
1   *large onion, chopped*
7   *cups (about 3½ pounds) sauerkraut,*
      drained
1   *tablespoon paprika*
2   *teaspoons caraway seeds*
1   *8-10 pound turkey*
    salt and pepper

Heat the oil in a deep heavy kettle, add the onion, and sauté it over medium heat, stirring often, for 5 to 8 minutes, or until it is golden. Add the sauerkraut, paprika, and caraway seeds and cook the mixture, stirring often, until it is well combined and heated through.

Preheat the oven to 350° F.

Stuff the cavity of the turkey with the sauerkraut mixture and reserve the remainder. Truss the turkey and sprinkle it lightly with salt and pepper. Place it on a rack in a shallow roasting pan and roast it for 1 hour and 30 minutes. Transfer the turkey to a rack and pour off the fat from the drippings in the pan. Add the reserved sauerkraut mixture to the roasting pan and set the turkey on top of the mixture. Roast the turkey for 2 to 2½ hours more, covering it lightly with foil if it browns too fast.

Transfer the turkey to a platter, let it cool for 15 minutes, and serve it surrounded by the sauerkraut mixture. Makes 8–10 servings.

Pheasant in Green Peppercorn Sauce

4   tablespoons (½ stick) butter
1   pheasant, quartered
    salt and pepper
2   tablespoons minced onion
½   cup dry white wine
1   cup heavy cream
2   teaspoons crushed green peppercorns
2   teaspoons whole green peppercorns
½   teaspoon tarragon
12 cherry tomatoes, trimmed

In a large heavy skillet melt the butter over medium heat. Add the pheasant quarters and sauté them until they are golden. Transfer the pheasant to a platter, season it with salt and pepper to taste, and stir the onion into the butter remaining in the skillet. Sauté the onion, stirring often, for 5 minutes, or until it is translucent and slightly browned. Pour in the wine and bring it to a simmer, stirring to scrape up the browned bits from the pan. Return the pheasant to the skillet, reduce the heat to low, and cook the mixture, covered, for 30 minutes, or until the pheasant is tender. Transfer the pheasant to a heated platter and keep it warm.

Stir the cream into the wine sauce and heat it through, taking care not to let it boil. Add the peppercorns, crushed and whole, and the tarragon and season the sauce with salt and pepper to taste.

Pour the hot sauce over the pheasant and garnish the platter with the cherry tomatoes. Makes 4 servings.

Roast Partridge

4   teaspoons minced garlic
¼   teaspoon thyme
¼   teaspoon tarragon
⅛   teaspoon rosemary
    salt and pepper
    juice of 1 lemon
6   partridges
½   cup (1 stick) butter
½   cup minced shallots
1   cup vermouth
⅓   cup Riesling

In a small bowl combine 2 teaspoons of the minced garlic with the thyme, tarragon, rosemary, and salt and pepper to taste. Stir in the lemon juice and rub the cavities of the partridges with the mixture.

In a large heavy skillet over medium-high heat, melt ¼ cup (½ stick) of the butter. Add the partridges and brown them quickly on all sides. Transfer them to a roasting pan and set them aside.

Preheat the oven to 400° F.

In the same skillet melt the remaining ¼ cup (½ stick) butter over medium heat. Add the shallots and the remaining 2 teaspoons garlic and sauté them until they are tender and slightly browned. Stir in the vermouth and the Riesling and bring the sauce almost to a simmer, stirring constantly and scraping up the brown bits from the pan. Pour the sauce over the partridges and roast the birds in the oven for 15 to 20 minutes, or until they are tender. Makes 6 servings.

Partridge Pie

12 *partridges*
2   *quarts water*
6   *sprigs parsley*
1   *medium-size onion, peeled*
3   *whole cloves*
    salt and pepper
2   *tablespoons butter*
2   *tablespoons flour*
    pastry for two 9-inch pies
2   *cups diced cooked potatoes*

Halve the partridges lengthwise, put them in a Dutch oven or a large kettle, and add the water. Bring the water to a boil and skim off the foam. Reduce the heat, add the parsley, onion, cloves, and salt and pepper to taste, and simmer the partridges for 25 to 35 minutes, or until they are tender.

Transfer the partridges to a cutting board and let them cool. Strain the cooking liquid and set it aside. In a large skillet melt the butter over medium heat. Add the flour and cook the roux, stirring constantly, for 2 to 3 minutes. Stir in 1 cup of the reserved cooking broth and cook the sauce until it is smooth and bubbly. Add 1 to 2 more cups of broth and cook the sauce until it reaches the desired consistency. Keep the sauce warm over very low heat.

Pull the skin from the partridges, cut the flesh away from the bone, and break it into bite-size pieces.

Preheat the oven to 350° F.

Line two 9-inch pie tins with pastry, pricking it well. Place a layer of partridge meat in each pie shell. Add about ¼ cup of the potatoes and moisten the filling with a little of the gravy. Continue to fill the shells in layers, moistening the filling with more of the gravy. Place a top crust on each of the pies, cut vents through which steam can escape, and bake the partridge pies for 20 minutes, or until they are browned and bubbly. Makes 12 servings.

Partridge with Lentils

1   *pound dried lentils*
10 *cups water*
2   *teaspoons salt*
2   *cloves garlic, minced*
    juice of 1 lemon
½   *teaspoon pepper*
4   *partridges or Rock Cornish hens*
¼   *pound salt pork or bacon, diced*
2   *large onions, minced*
1   *carrot, scraped and diced*
1   *celery stalk, chopped*
2   *tablespoons tomato purée*
1   *cup dry red wine*
1   *cup beef broth*
1   *teaspoon red wine vinegar*

In a large enameled or stainless steel kettle combine the lentils with the water and 1 teaspoon of the salt. Bring the water to a boil, reduce the heat, and simmer the lentils for 40 minutes, or until they are tender. Drain the lentils well, reserving 1 cup of the broth. Spoon the lentils onto a heated platter and keep them warm.

In a bowl mash the garlic and lemon juice

with the remaining 1 teaspoon salt and the pepper. Tie the wings of each partridge together and rub the birds inside and out with the garlic mixture.

Preheat the oven to 400° F.

Put the diced salt pork or bacon in a Dutch oven and heat it until it begins to melt. Add the onions, carrot, and celery and sauté the vegetables over medium heat until they are soft and lightly browned. Stir in the tomato purée, wine, and beef broth, heat the mixture through, and turn off the heat. Roll the partridges or hens in the tomato mixture, coating them completely, and place them breast side up in a deep casserole. Pour the remaining tomato mixture around the birds and bake them, covered, for 45 minutes, basting occasionally with the pan juices. Reduce the oven temperature to 350° F., turn the birds breast side down, and roast them, covered, for 15 minutes more, basting once or twice. Add water or more broth if necessary.

Split the partridges, place them on the lentils, and keep them warm.

Pour the cooking liquid from the roasting pan into a saucepan. Skim off the fat and heat the liquid through. Stir in the reserved lentil broth, bring the sauce to a boil, and add the vinegar. Reduce the heat and simmer the sauce for 5 minutes, until it is slightly thickened. Pour about ½ cup of the sauce over the partridges and serve the remaining sauce in a gravy boat. Makes 4–8 servings.

Venison Chili

2	*cups canned tomatoes in their own juice*
½	*cup chopped onions*
½	*cup chopped celery*
½	*cup green pepper, chopped*
½	*cup chili powder*
5	*cloves garlic, crushed*
2	*teaspoons cumin*
2	*teaspoons oregano*
½	*cup (1 stick) butter*
1	*pound ground lean pork*
2½	*pounds ground venison*
2	*15-ounce cans kidney beans*
2	*teaspoons salt*
½	*teaspoon pepper*
¾	*cup water*

Put the tomatoes and their juice in a large saucepan. Bring the juice to a simmer and cook the tomatoes over low heat for 5 minutes. Add the onions, celery, green pepper, chili powder, garlic, cumin and oregano and cook the mixture, stirring often, for 10 minutes, or until the vegetables are tender.

In a large heavy kettle melt the butter over medium-high heat. Add the pork and venison and sauté both meats, stirring them together, for 15 minutes, or until they are browned. Stir in the tomato mixture and the kidney beans and simmer the meats, stirring often, for 10 minutes. Season the meats with the salt and pepper, stir in the water, and cook the mixture, covered, for 1 hour, stirring often and adding more water if necessary. Remove the cover and cook the meat for 1 hour more. Makes 8–10 servings.

Canadian Hare with Burgundy

4	cups dry white wine
12½	cups water
6	bay leaves
1	tablespoon peppercorns
3	hares, cut up
½	cup flour
2	teaspoons salt
1	teaspoon white pepper
½	teaspoon minced garlic
8	tablespoons vegetable oil
4	cups red Burgundy
1	large onion, thinly sliced
24	small white onions, peeled
½	pound mushrooms, thinly sliced
3	tablespoons cornstarch

In a large enameled or stainless steel saucepan combine the white wine, 8 cups of the water, the bay leaves, and the peppercorns. Place the hare portions in the marinade, turning them to coat well, and marinate them in the refrigerator for 8 hours or overnight, turning occasionally.

Preheat the oven to 400° F.

In a shallow pan or dish combine the flour, salt, white pepper, and garlic. Dredge the hares in the flour mixture. Heat 4 tablespoons of the oil in a large heavy skillet over medium heat, add the hare pieces, a few at a time, and brown them quickly on all sides, adding more oil to the skillet when needed. Transfer the browned hare portions to paper towels to drain.

In a large glass or enameled casserole combine the Burgundy, 4 cups of the remaining water, and the sliced onion. Add the hare and bake the casserole, covered, for 1 hour and 30 minutes.

Half fill a large saucepan with water, bring the water to a boil, and plunge in the small white onions. Reduce the heat and simmer the onions for 10 minutes, or until they are tender. Drain them well and set them aside.

Transfer the hare to a heated platter and keep it warm. Strain the cooking liquid from the casserole into a deep saucepan, bring it to a boil, and cook it over high heat until it is reduced by about half. Stir the onions and the mushrooms into the sauce and simmer the mixture over low heat for 10 minutes, or until the mushrooms are tender.

In a measuring cup combine the cornstarch with the remaining ½ cup water. Stir the paste into the gravy and cook the sauce, stirring constantly, until it is thickened, smooth, and bubbly. Pour about ½ cup of the sauce over the hares and serve the rest in a gravy boat. Makes 12 servings.

Hasenpfeffer

2½	cups vinegar
2½	cups water
½	cup sugar
1	medium-size onion, sliced
1	teaspoon salt
¼	teaspoon pepper
1	teaspoon pickling spices
1	2½- to 3-pound rabbit, cut up
1	cup flour
4	tablespoons vegetable oil

In a dish or enameled pan combine the vinegar, water, sugar, onion, salt, pepper, and pickling spices. Place the rabbit pieces in the marinade, turn them to coat them well, and marinate them in the refrigerator, turning occasionally, for 24 hours.

Drain the rabbit, reserving the marinade, pat it dry, and dredge it in the flour, reserving 3 tablespoons of the flour. Strain the marinade and reserve it.

Heat the oil in a large heavy skillet over medium-high heat. Add the rabbit and brown it quickly on all sides. Gradually pour in the reserved marinade and bring it to a boil. Reduce the heat and simmer the rabbit for 1 hour, or until it is tender.

Transfer the rabbit to a heated platter and keep it warm. In a measuring cup add about ¼ cup of the cooking liquid to the reserved 3 tablespoons flour. Stir the mixture until it becomes a paste and stir into the cooking liquid in the skillet. Cook gravy over medium heat, stirring constantly, until smooth, bubbly, and thickened. Serve with rabbit. Makes 4 servings.

Venison Paprika

    1   cup flour
        Salt and pepper
    ½   cup (1 stick) butter
    3   pounds venison, cut into 1-inch cubes
    1   cup sliced celery
    2   medium onions, peeled and quartered
    2   teaspoons paprika
    2   cups beef broth
    2   cups sour cream
        Buttered spaetzle or noodles

In a large shallow pan combine the flour with salt and pepper to taste and dredge the venison in the mixture.

In a Dutch oven melt the butter over medium heat, add the venison, and brown it on all sides. Add the celery, onions, and 1 teaspoon of the paprika and cook the mixture, stirring, for 5 minutes, or until the vegetables are slightly soft. Stir in the beef broth, bring it to a boil, and reduce the heat to low. Cover the pan and simmer the venison for 1 hour, or until it is tender.

Transfer the venison to a heated platter and keep it warm. Stir the sour cream into the pan juices and heat the sauce through, but do not let it boil. Spoon the sauce over the meat and sprinkle it with the remaining teaspoon of paprika. Serve the venison with the spaetzle or noodles. Makes 6 servings.

Saddle of Venison (Rehrücken)

    1   teaspoon salt
    ½   teaspoon pepper
    4   juniper berries, crushed
    1   saddle of venison
    6   thin strips bacon
    2   cups beef broth

Preheat the oven to 350° F.

In a small bowl combine the salt, pepper, and crushed juniper berries and rub the mixture over the venison. Put the venison in a large greased roasting pan and lay the bacon strips over it. Pour 1 cup of the broth into the pan and roast the saddle of venison for 1 hour, basting it frequently with the pan juices and adding more broth if necessary. Makes 6 servings.

Venison Ragout (Rehpfeffer)

4   *tablespoons (½ stick) butter*
1   *large carrot, sliced*
1   *medium-size onion, sliced*
2   *stalks celery, leaves included, chopped*
1   *clove garlic, minced*
½   *teaspoon thyme*
1   *small bay leaf*
6   *cloves*
1   *teaspoon salt*
½   *teaspoon pepper*
1   *cup dry red wine*
1   *cup water*
3   *pounds venison, cut into 1-inch cubes*
3   *tablespoons flour*
2   *cups beef broth*
3   *strips bacon*
½   *cup tomato purée*
1   *cup sour cream (optional)*

In a large heavy skillet melt 2 tablespoons of the butter over medium heat. Add the carrot, onion, celery, and garlic and sauté the *mirepoix* until the vegetables are soft. Stir in the thyme, bay leaf, cloves, salt, and pepper. Pour in the wine and the water and heat the mixture to a boil. Reduce the heat and simmer the *mirepoix* for 10 minutes. Turn off the heat and let the *mirepoix* cool for 10 minutes.

Put the venison in a large shallow dish or enameled pan and pour the *mirepoix* over it. Marinate the venison, covered and refrigerated, for 24 hours.

Preheat the oven to 350° F.

Drain the meat and pat it dry, reserving the marinade. In a heavy flameproof casserole over medium-high heat, melt the remaining 2 tablespoons butter. Add the venison, in batches, and brown it quickly on all sides. Sprinkle the meat with the flour and pour the beef broth over it. Strain the marinade and pour it over the venison. Bake the venison, covered, for 1 hour, or until it is almost tender. Uncover the casserole and cook the meat for 30 minutes more, or until it is very tender.

Transfer the venison to a heated platter and keep it warm.

In a skillet cook the bacon until it is crisp. Drain it well and crumble it over the venison. Stir the tomato purée into the cooking liquid in the casserole and season the sauce with salt and pepper to taste. Stir in the sour cream, if desired. Makes 6 servings.

Game Goulash

6   *strips bacon*
3   *medium-size onions, chopped*
3   *pounds flank or shoulder of venison,*
     hare, or rabbit, cut in 1-inch cubes
1½   *cups dry red wine*
3   *teaspoons paprika*
     salt and pepper
3   *tablespoons flour*

In a large heavy skillet cook the bacon until it is crisp. Transfer it to paper towels to drain. To the bacon drippings in the skillet add the onions and sauté them over medium heat for 10 minutes, or until they are soft and slightly browned. Add the meat and brown it well on all sides. Pour in the wine and stir the mixture well, scraping up the brown bits from the pan. Sprinkle the paprika over the meat and season it with salt and pepper to taste. Reduce the heat to low and cook the goulash, covered, for 30 minutes.

Transfer the meat to a heated platter, crumble the bacon over it, and keep it warm.

In a measuring cup stir together the flour and about ¼ cup of the cooking liquid. Pour the paste into the skillet and cook the sauce over medium heat, stirring, until it is thickened and bubbly. Pour some of the sauce over the meat and serve the remainder in a gravy boat. Makes 6 servings.

Roast Elk with Lingonberry Sauce

1   *4-pound elk roast*
2   *medium-size onions, peeled and quartered*
6   *carrots, scraped and cut into 1-inch pieces*
6   *celery stalks, cut into 1-inch pieces*
2   *bay leaves*
    salt and pepper
2–3 *quarts water or water and beef broth combined*
1   *7-ounce jar lingonberries in syrup*
4   *tablespoons red currant jelly*
1   *tablespoon Worcestershire sauce*
2   *tablespoons lemon juice*
    hot pepper sauce

Preheat the oven to 300° F.

Put the roast in a deep roasting pan with the onions, carrots, celery, and bay leaves. Season the meat and vegetables with salt and pepper to taste and pour the water or broth into the pan. Bake the roast, covered, for 5 to 6 hours, until the meat is tender.

In a small saucepan combine the lingonberries, with their syrup, the currant jelly, Worcestershire sauce, and lemon juice. Season the mixture with hot pepper sauce to taste and bring it to a boil, stirring often. Reduce the heat and simmer the sauce for 5 minutes.

Transfer the elk roast to a heated platter, pour the lingonberry sauce over it, and serve it at once. Makes 8 servings.

POTATOES, NOODLES, DUMPLINGS AND RICE

Potatoes served at breakfast
At dinner served again;
Potatoes served at supper
Forever and Amen!

*T*HIS ditty is attributed to a nineteenth century Pennsylvania Dutch farm worker. It reveals—despite a mild note of weariness—the historically important role of the adored potato. Today, even in the light of our new consciousness of calories and other aspects of healthy eating, the potato—rich in vitamins and minerals—is still one of the main dietary staples of German American cuisine. Dumplings are another German American culinary passion, often served as accompaniments for soups and stews, and even prepared for dessert.

Potato Kugel

⅓ cup matzo meal or flour
1 teaspoon baking powder
1 teaspoon salt
3 eggs, beaten
5 large potatoes

Preheat the oven to 400° F. Butter a shallow baking dish and set it in the oven for 10 minutes.

In a large bowl sift together the matzo meal or flour, the baking powder, and the salt. Beat in the eggs, one at a time, and stir the mixture until it is smooth. Peel and finely grate the potatoes and drain them well. Fold them into the egg mixture until they are well incorporated.

Pour the potato mixture into the hot baking dish and spread it out with a wooden spoon. Bake the *Kugel* for 50 to 60 minutes, until the potatoes are tender and crusty. Makes 4 servings.

Note: For a *Kugel* that is lighter in texture and color, substitute one large cooked and mashed potato for one of the grated potatoes and decrease the amount of matzo meal or flour to ¼ cup.

German Pan-Fried Potatoes

6   *medium-size potatoes*
1   *large onion*
2   *teaspoons paprika*
½   *teaspoon salt*
¼   *teaspoon pepper*
4   *tablespoons bacon drippings or butter*

Peel the potatoes and the onion, cut them into thin slices and drain them on paper towels. In a small bowl combine the paprika, salt, and pepper; sprinkle the mixture over the potatoes and onions.

In a heavy skillet heat the bacon drippings or butter over medium-high heat. Add the potatoes and onions and fry them, turning them often with a wide spatula, for 25 to 30 minutes, until they are tender and browned. Makes 6–8 servings.

Potato Balls

8–10   *medium-size potatoes*
2   *eggs, lightly beaten*
1   *cup fine bread crumbs*
2   *teaspoons salt*
½   *teaspoon pepper*
½   *cup flour*

Cook the potatoes in boiling water to cover for 35 to 45 minutes, or until they are tender. Submerge them in cold water until they are cool enough to handle. Peel, quarter, and mash the potatoes and refrigerate them for at least 30 minutes.

In a large bowl combine the potatoes with the eggs, bread crumbs, salt, pepper, and ¼ cup of the flour and stir the mixture until it is smooth and easy to handle, adding more flour if the potato mixture is too runny. Form the potato mixture into spheres the size of golf balls and roll the potato balls in the remaining flour.

Half fill a large saucepan with water and bring the water to a fast simmer. Drop the potato balls, three or four at a time, into the simmering water. The balls will sink to the bottom of the pan and remain there for 5 to 8 minutes, until they are almost fully cooked. After they have risen to the surface, cook them for 3 minutes more. Drain them, transfer them to a heated platter, and keep them warm while the remaining balls are cooked. Serve the potato balls with roast meat or sauerbraten. Makes 6–8 servings.

Fried Potatoes

6   *tablespoons vegetable oil*
4   *cups sliced cooked potatoes*
    salt and pepper

In a large heavy skillet heat the oil over medium-high heat. Add the potatoes and reduce the heat to medium-low. Fry the potatoes, turning them frequently with a wide spatula, until they are tender and well browned. Transfer the potatoes to paper towels to drain and sprinkle them with salt and pepper to taste. Makes 4–6 servings.

German Potato Pancakes

4   large Idaho potatoes
3   large eggs, lightly beaten
1   teaspoon salt
½   teaspoon nutmeg
6   tablespoons shortening

Peel the potatoes, drop them into a bowl of cold water, and let them stand for 1 hour. Grate the potatoes coarsely and drain them on paper towels. In a large bowl combine the potatoes, eggs, salt, and nutmeg.

In a large heavy skillet melt 2 tablespoons of the shortening over medium-high heat. Spoon in enough of the potato mixture to cover the bottom of the skillet and press the mixture down with a wide spatula. Cook the pancake for 20 to 25 minutes, or until the edges are lacy and the underside of the pancake is browned. Turn the pancake and cook it for 5 to 10 minutes more, until the other side is browned. Repeat the procedure until all of the potato mixture has been cooked. Serve the potato pancakes with butter and syrup. Makes 4–6 servings.

Potato Pancakes

6   medium-size potatoes
4   cups ice water
1   medium-size onion
2   eggs, lightly beaten
1   teaspoon salt
¼   teaspoon pepper
½   teaspoon baking soda
6   tablespoons vegetable oil or bacon
      drippings
4   cups applesauce

Peel the potatoes, drop them into the ice water, and let them stand for 1 to 2 hours. Grate the potatoes and drain them on paper towels. Peel and grate the onion and drain it on paper towels. In a bowl combine the potatoes, the onion, and the beaten eggs. Stir in the salt, pepper, and baking soda and combine the mixture well.

In a large heavy skillet heat 4 tablespoons of the oil or bacon drippings over medium heat. Drop the potato mixture by the spoonful, in batches, into the hot oil and cook the pancakes, turning them once, until they are golden brown on both sides. Repeat the procedure with the remainder of the potato mixture, adding more oil when necessary.

Serve the hot potato pancakes with the applesauce. Makes 6 servings.

Potato and Apple Pancakes

6   medium-size potatoes
2   eggs, lightly beaten
½   cup flour
1   teaspoon salt
¼   teaspoon pepper
2   tablespoons grated onion
1   tart apple, cored, peeled,
      and grated
6   tablespoons lard

Peel the potatoes, drop them into a bowl of cold water, and let them stand for 1 hour. Grate the potatoes and drain them on paper towels. In a large bowl combine the potatoes, eggs, flour, salt, pepper, onion, and apple.

In a large heavy skillet melt 2 tablespoons of the lard over medium-high heat. Spoon about one fourth of the potato mixture into the skillet and press it down with a wide spatula. Cook the pancake for 20 to 25 minutes, until the underside is browned. Turn the pancake and cook it for 5 to 10 minutes more, until the other side is browned and the potatoes are tender. Transfer the pancake to paper towels to drain and keep it warm, but do not cover it.

Add more lard to the skillet and repeat the procedure until all of the potato mixture has been cooked. Makes 4–6 servings.

Hashed Brown Potatoes

4   medium-size potatoes
1/3 cup minced onion
     Salt and pepper
4   tablespoons bacon drippings or vegetable oil

Half fill a saucepan with water, add the potatoes, and bring the water to a boil. Reduce the heat and cook the potatoes for 25 to 30 minutes, or until they are almost tender. Submerge the potatoes in cold water until they are cool enough to handle. Slip off the skins and grate the potatoes coarsely. In a large bowl combine the potatoes with the onion and salt and pepper to taste. Stir the mixture well.

In a large heavy skillet heat the bacon drippings or oil over medium-high heat. Spread the potatoes in a single layer on the bottom of the skillet and press them flat with a wide spatula. Reduce the heat to low and cook the potatoes for 20 to 25 minutes, until the underside of the layer is golden brown. With the spatula cut the potato layer into four wedges, turn the wedges over, and press them down with the spatula. Cook the potatoes for 5 to 10 minutes more, or until the other side is golden. Makes 4 servings.

Scalloped Potatoes

4   medium-size potatoes, peeled and sliced 1/4-inch thick
3   tablespoons flour
4   tablespoons (1/2 stick) butter, cut into small pieces
     Salt and pepper
1 1/2 cups milk

Preheat the oven to 350° F.

Butter a 1 1/2-quart casserole and cover the bottom of the casserole with a layer of potatoes. Sprinkle the potatoes with flour, scatter a few pieces of butter over them, and season them with salt and pepper to taste. Repeat the procedure until all of the potatoes have been used and top the casserole with a few dots of butter. Pour milk into the casserole until it almost covers the potatoes. Bake the potatoes for 1 hour, or until they are tender. Makes 4 servings.

Rohe Kartoffelklosse (Dumplings Made from Raw Potatoes)

7   medium-size potatoes
4   cups cold water
1   tablespoon lemon juice
1   tablespoon butter
2   eggs
1   slice day-old bread
¾   cup flour
1   cup day-old white bread crumbs
1   teaspoon salt

Cook one of the potatoes in boiling water to cover for 40 to 45 minutes, or until it is tender. When the potato is cool enough to handle, peel it and mash it until it is smooth.

In a saucepan combine the cold water with the lemon juice. Peel the remaining raw potatoes, grate them directly into the water, and let stand for 10 minutes. Drain potatoes on paper towels, pressing out the excess moisture.

Half fill the saucepan with fresh water and bring the water to a fast simmer.

In a small saucepan melt the butter over medium-high heat. In a shallow dish beat one of the eggs with a fork. Dip the slice of bread into the egg and fry it quickly in the hot butter, turning once, until it is well browned on both sides. Drain the fried bread on paper towels and cut it into 12 cubes.

In a large saucepan combine the mashed potato and the grated potatoes with ½ cup of the flour, the bread crumbs, and the salt. In a small bowl lightly beat the remaining egg, stir it into the potato mixture, and combine the dough well. If the mixture is runny or sticky, add 1 tablespoon more of the flour. Turn the mixture out onto a floured surface and knead it 10 to 12 times, adding the remaining flour, 1 tablespoon at a time, if necessary, until the dough is soft and manageable. Roll about 1 tablespoon of the mixture into a ball and drop it into the simmering water. If the dumpling falls apart, add more flour to remaining dough. Shape the dough into 12 two-inch balls.

Force one cube of fried bread into the center of each ball and seal the potato mixture around it. Cook the dumplings in the simmering water, in batches, for 10 minutes, or until they rise to the surface. Transfer them with a slotted spoon to a heated platter and keep them warm.

Serve the potato dumplings with meat and gravy. Makes 12 dumplings.

Gekochte Kartoffelklosse (Dumplings Made from Cooked Potatoes)

6   medium-size potatoes
3   tablespoons butter, goose or chicken fat
1   cup day-old bread crumbs
8   cups beef or chicken broth
2   eggs, beaten
1   teaspoon salt
1   cup flour
½   cup melted butter

Cook the potatoes in boiling water to cover for 40 to 45 minutes, or until they are tender.

In a small skillet heat the butter or fat over

medium-high heat. Add the bread crumbs and sauté them, tossing often, for 8 minutes, or until they are browned. Set them aside to cool.

In a kettle or a large saucepan bring the broth to a fast simmer.

When the potatoes are cool enough to handle, peel them and mash them thoroughly. Stir in the eggs, the salt, and about ½ cup of the flour and combine the mixture well. If the dough is runny or sticky, add more of the flour until the mixture is manageable. Test the mixture by dropping a small ball of it into the simmering water; if it falls short, add more flour to the dough. Shape the dough into 2- or 3-inch balls, force about ¼ teaspoon fried bread crumbs into the center of each ball, and press the potato mixture closed around the filling. Cook the dumplings in the simmering broth, a few at a time, for 10 minutes, or until they rise to the surface. Transfer the dumplings with a slotted spoon to a heated serving dish and keep them warm.

Spoon the melted butter over the dumplings and sprinkle them with the remaining fried bread crumbs. Makes 8–12 dumplings.

Potato Dumplings

5	*Idaho potatoes*
1½	*cups flour*
1	*egg*
1	*teaspoon salt*
⅛	*teaspoon white pepper*
1	*teaspoon grated onion*
½	*teaspoon marjoram*
¼	*cup small croutons*
8	*cups water*

3	*tablespoons butter*
1	*tablespoon fine bread crumbs*

Cook the potatoes in water to cover for 45 to 55 minutes, or until they are tender. Drain them, cool them in cold water, pat them dry, and refrigerate them, covered, overnight.

Peel the potatoes and grate them into a large bowl. Combine them with 1 cup of the flour, the egg, and ½ teaspoon of the salt. Stir in the pepper, onion, and marjoram, blending the mixture well. Add all or part of the remaining ½ cup flour, a little at a time, until the mixture holds together.

Turn the dough out onto a floured surface and shape it into 2-inch balls. Flatten each ball, place 3 or 4 croutons in the center, and fold the dough around the croutons, pressing together the loose edges and reshaping the dumpling into a ball.

In a large saucepan or kettle bring the water to a boil and add the remaining ½ teaspoon salt. Drop the dumplings into the water and cook them for 8 to 10 minutes, until they are light and fluffy. With a slotted spoon transfer the dumplings to a heated platter and keep them warm.

In a small skillet melt the butter over medium-high heat. Add the bread crumbs and sauté them, stirring often, until they are soft and browned. Pour the crumbs and melted butter over the dumplings and serve the dish at once. Makes 6 servings.

Note: For a spicy variation of the potato dumplings, add ½ teaspoon nutmeg to the dough.

Bayerische Leberknodel (Bavarian Liver Dumplings)

4   soft white rolls, quartered
1   pound ground liver
3   eggs
1   medium-size onion, minced
2   tablespoons minced parsley
¼   teaspoon marjoram
    grated rind of ½ lemon
    salt and pepper
3   cups beef broth
2   cups fine bread crumbs
2   tablespoons flour
    sauerkraut
    mashed potatoes

Put the rolls in a large bowl, cover them with lukewarm water, and let them soak for 10 minutes. Drain them on paper towels, pressing down on them to extract the excess water. Return the rolls to the bowl and break them up with a fork. Stir in the liver, eggs, and onion and season the mixture with the parsley, marjoram, lemon rind, and salt and pepper to taste. Set the mixture aside for 10 minutes.

In a large saucepan or kettle bring the broth to a fast simmer.

Work the bread crumbs into the liver mixture until they are well incorporated. Turn the mixture out onto a floured surface, knead it 5 or 6 times, and shape it into 1-inch balls. Drop the dumplings, in batches, into the simmering broth and cook them for 10 minutes, or until they rise to the surface. Transfer the dumplings with a slotted spoon to a heated platter and keep them warm.

In a measuring cup combine the flour with about ¼ cup of the cooking broth, pour the paste into the broth in the kettle, and cook the sauce, stirring constantly, until it is thickened and smooth. Pour the sauce over the liver dumplings and serve them with the sauerkraut and mashed potatoes. Makes 4 servings.

Chicken Liver Dumplings

¼   pound ground chicken livers
¾   pound ground beef
1   egg, lightly beaten
1½   cups bread crumbs
2   tablespoons chopped parsley
1   teaspoon salt
½   teaspoon white pepper
½   teaspoon thyme
6   cups chicken broth
⅓   cup chopped celery
⅓   cup chopped onion
⅓   cup peeled, seeded, and chopped tomato

In a large bowl combine the chicken livers and the beef. Add the egg, bread crumbs, and 1 tablespoon of the parsley. Season the mixture with the salt, pepper, and thyme and stir the batter until it is well combined. Refrigerate the mixture, covered, for 1 hour.

In a soup kettle combine the chicken broth, celery, onion, and tomato. Bring the broth to a boil.

Form the liver-beef mixture into 1-inch balls and drop the balls, in batches, into the broth. Cook them, stirring occasionally, for 10 to 15 minutes, or until they are plump. Transfer the dumplings with a slotted spoon to a heated platter and garnish them with the remaining parsley. Makes 6 servings.

Dampfnudeln (Steamed Yeast Dumplings)

1	envelope active dry yeast
¼	cup warm water
¾	cup milk
¾	cup (1½ sticks) butter
¼	cup sugar
1	teaspoon salt
3	cups flour

In a small dish dissolve the yeast in the warm water.

In a saucepan combine ¼ cup of the milk, ¼ cup (½ stick) of the butter, the sugar, and the salt. Bring the mixture to a boil, remove it from the heat, and let it cool to lukewarm.

Sift 2½ cups of the flour into a large bowl, make a well in the center, and pour in the yeast mixture. Add the cooled milk mixture and stir the dough until the ingredients are well blended. Turn the dough out onto a floured surface and knead it until it is smooth. Loosely cover the dough with a towel and let it rise in warm place for 1½ hours, or until it has doubled in volume. Punch the dough down, recover it with the towel, and let it rise again for about 30 minutes. With well-buttered hands tear off pieces of dough and roll them into 1-inch balls.

Pour the remaining ½ cup milk into a large heavy pot or a Dutch oven. Add the remaining ½ cup (1 stick) butter and heat the mixture until the milk is hot and the butter is melted. Drop the balls of dough into the pot, lay a cloth over top of pot, and cover it with the lid. Bring the liquid to a boil, immediately reduce the heat to very low, and cook the dumplings very slowly for about 30 minutes, or until the butter begins to crackle, which means the milk has been completely absorbed.

Serve the *Dampfnudeln* with meat. Makes 10–12 dumplings.

Spaetzle

2	eggs
¼	cup milk
⅓	cup water
½	teaspoon salt
⅛	teaspoon pepper
¼	teaspoon nutmeg
1¾	cups flour
8	cups beef broth or consommé

In a large bowl beat the eggs. Add the milk, water, salt, pepper, and nutmeg and combine the mixture well. Add the flour, a little at a time, beating after each addition until the batter is smooth.

In a saucepan bring the broth to a boil, reduce the heat to low, and keep the broth at a simmer. Set a colander into the hot broth and press the batter through with the back of a wooden spoon, if necessary, or mill the batter into the broth using a spaetzle mill. Simmer the batter in the broth for 10 to 12 minutes, or until the spaetzle is cooked through. Makes 6–8 servings.

Plum Dumplings

1 cup flour
½ teaspoon baking powder
2 large eggs, well beaten
1 teaspoon salt
½ pound very ripe blue
   plums, halved and
   stoned
8 cups water
3 tablespoons butter
½ cup bread crumbs

In a large bowl sift together the flour and baking powder. Stir in the eggs and ¼ teaspoon of the salt and beat the mixture well. Refrigerate the dough for 20 minutes. Turn the dough out onto a floured surface and roll it into a cylinder about 3 inches in diameter. Cut the cylinder into ½-inch slices. Press each slice into a flat circle large enough to encase half a plum. Set a plum half in each circle, fold the dough around it, and press the loose edges firmly together.

In a kettle or a large saucepan bring the water to a boil and add the remaining ¾ teaspoon salt. Drop the plum dumplings, in batches, into the boiling water and cook them until they are puffy and light. With a slotted spoon transfer the dumplings to a heated platter, cover them with paper towels, and keep them warm.

In a small skillet melt the butter over medium-high heat. Add the bread crumbs and sauté them, stirring often, until they are soft and browned.

Remove the paper towels from the platter, pour the crumbs and melted butter over the dumplings, and serve them at once with meat, poultry, or game. Makes 10–12 dumplings.

Apple Dumplings

2 cups flour
2½ teaspoons baking powder
½ teaspoon salt
⅔ cup shortening
½ cup milk
6 tart apples, cored, peeled, and halved
2 cups brown sugar
2 cups water
¼ cup (½ stick) butter
½ teaspoon cinnamon

Preheat the oven to 350° F.

Into a large bowl sift together the flour, baking powder, and salt. Cut in the shortening until the mixture is smooth and stir in enough of the milk to make the dough manageable. Turn the dough out onto a floured surface and knead it 5 or 6 times. Roll or pat the dough out flat and cut it into 12 squares. Place an apple half on each square, dampen the edges of the dough, and press the dough closed around the apple to form a ball. Set the dumplings in a large casserole.

In a bowl combine the brown sugar, water, butter, and cinnamon. Pour the sauce over the dumplings and bake them for 30 minutes until the apples are soft and the dough is golden brown. Makes 12 dumplings.

Amish Apple-Cranberry Dumplings

2 cups water
½ teaspoon cinnamon
½ teaspoon ground cloves
2 cups plus 2 tablespoons sugar
½ cup (1 stick) butter, cut into small pieces
2 cups flour
1 teaspoon salt
1 tablespoon baking powder
½ cup shortening
¾ cup milk
4 cups peeled and grated tart apples
1 cup cooked whole cranberries, drained,
      or 1 cup whole cranberry sauce,
      drained
½ cup chopped walnuts
1 teaspoon grated orange rind

In a large saucepan combine the water, cinnamon, cloves, and 2 cups of the sugar. Bring the water to a boil, reduce the heat, and simmer the mixture for 5 minutes, or until the sugar is dissolved. Remove the syrup from the heat, add the butter, and stir the mixture until the butter is melted. Set the syrup aside.

Preheat the oven to 425° F.

Into a large bowl sift together the flour, salt, baking powder, and the remaining 2 tablespoons sugar. Cut in the shortening until the mixture is well blended. Gradually stir in enough of the milk to make a soft dough. Turn the mixture out onto a floured surface and roll it into an 18- by 12-inch rectangle. Spread the apples, cranberries, walnuts, and orange rind over the rectangle, roll the dough up jelly-roll fashion, and cut it into slices 1 inch thick. Arrange the slices in a single layer in a 13- by 9- by 2-inch baking pan. Pour the syrup over the slices and bake the Amish dumplings for 40 minutes. Makes 8–10 servings.

Schleifen Nudeln (Hand-Rolled Noodles)

2 eggs
2 cups sifted flour
2 tablespoons water
¼ cup onion greens, more if desired,
      chopped

Beat the eggs until foamy and gradually add the water and the flour to make a dough which will roll out. This quantity should give two biscuit-sized balls. Instead of rolling out the dough, slice off small pieces, about 1 inch in length, on the floured board. (I slice off some ten pieces at a time). Take one piece in the palm of your floured hands, quickly roll it back and forth, and flip it on a floured board or piece of paper. Repeat the procedure with the remaining dough pieces. Leave board to dry 30 to 45 minutes. Occasionally, change position of noodles with a spoon or your hands. (Both ends of the noodle come to a point).

Bring 2 to 3 quarts of salted water to a full boil, add the noodles, and boil them till they are done. Drain most of the water, leaving enough that you can easily stir the noodles in the liquid. Add 1 to 3 tablespoons flour and ¼ cup onion greens. Reheat the noodles thoroughly, stirring occasionally.

Egg Noodles

4   *eggs*
2   *tablespoons milk*
    *enough flour to make a dough that is not
    sticky*

Beat the eggs and add the milk and the flour.
Roll the dough very thin on floured board. Let
dough dry until slightly hard. When the dough
is dry, roll it up jelly-roll fashion and cut it into
thin, or wider strips, as desired. Place the strips
on a cookie sheet and dry the strips some
more. Noodles can be made the day before
using. Cook them in salted water until just
tender. Serve them with gravy, or with bread
crumbs or cubes that have been browned in
butter.

Wild Rice Pilaf
with Almonds

12   *ounces wild rice, washed and drained*
½   *cup (1 stick) butter*
1   *large onion, minced*
1   *cup slivered almonds*
2   *16-ounce cans beef consommé*
2   *cups water*
½   *teaspoon salt*
⅛   *teaspoon pepper*

Pour the rice into a bowl, cover it with water,
and let it soak overnight. Drain the rice well
and set it aside.
    Preheat the oven to 350° F.

In a flameproof casserole melt the butter
over medium heat. Add the onion and the
almonds and sauté them, stirring often, for 10
minutes, until the onion is soft and the
almonds are browned. Add the rice and stir it
to coat it with the butter. Pour in the
consommé and water, stir in the salt and
pepper, and bring the mixture to a simmer,
stirring occasionally. Transfer the casserole to
the oven and bake the rice pilaf, covered, for
35 minutes. Remove the lid and cook the
mixture for 15 to 20 minutes more, or until the
rice is tender. Makes 6 servings.

German Rice and Cabbage

4   *strips lean bacon*
2   *medium-size onions, chopped*
2   *garlic cloves, minced*
1   *8-ounce can tomato sauce*
1   *cup chicken broth*
2   *cups shredded cabbage*
½   *teaspoon crushed caraway seeds*
     salt
     hot red pepper flakes
3   *cups cooked rice*
¼   *cup grated Emmenthal or Gruyère cheese*

In a heavy kettle or a Dutch oven cook the
bacon until it is crisp. Transfer it to paper
towels to drain. Pour the bacon drippings into
a measuring cup, let the solids settle, and
measure off and reserve 4 tablespoons, or add
melted butter to make 4 tablespoons.
    Return the reserved bacon drippings to the
kettle and heat them over medium heat. Add

the onions and garlic and cook them, stirring often, until they are soft but not brown. Stir in the tomato sauce, chicken broth, and cabbage. Sprinkle the mixture with the caraway seeds and season it with salt and red pepper to taste. Crumble the bacon into the kettle and simmer the cabbage, covered, for 15 minutes, or until it is tender. Stir in the rice and cook the mixture, covered, until most of the liquid has been absorbed. Transfer the rice and cabbage to a heated serving dish and sprinkle the cheese on top. Makes 4–6 servings.

Wild Rice and Vegetables

½   cup (1 stick) butter
¼   cup minced onion
¼   cup minced celery
½   cup sliced mushrooms
2   cups wild rice, washed and drained
½   teaspoon salt
2   cups beef broth
2   cups chicken broth
¼   cup dry sherry
½   cup chopped parsley

In a skillet melt the butter over medium heat. Add the onion, celery, and mushrooms and sauté them for 10 minutes, stirring often, until they are tender. Add the rice, stirring it to coat

it well, and season the mixture with the salt. Pour in the beef broth, chicken broth, and sherry and bring the mixture to a simmer. Cover the pan and reduce the heat to low. Simmer the rice for 55 to 65 minutes, or until the rice is tender.

Spoon the rice and vegetables into a serving dish and fold in the chopped parsley. Makes 4 servings.

Rice with Scallions

1½   cups rice
⅔   cup salad oil
¼   cup tarragon vinegar
1   clove garlic, minced
1   teaspoon mustard
    salt
    hot pepper sauce
½   cup sliced scallions

Cook the rice according to package directions. Set it aside and let it cool almost to room temperature.

In a jar with a tight lid combine the oil, vinegar, garlic, mustard, and salt and hot pepper sauce to taste. Shake the mixture well and pour it over the rice. Add the scallions and toss the mixture very well. Makes 6 servings.

MEAT

*T*HERE is an old Pennsylvania Dutch saying, "Better a louse in the kraut than no meat at all!" And, judging from the wealth of meat recipes in Pennsylvania Dutch cooking, these and other German Americans maintained the tradition of serving, and enjoying, a variety of meat dishes.

In Germany, where pasture land has always been scarce, pork has been the most popular meat. German immigrants to this country in the eighteenth and nineteenth centuries, however, found pasture land readily available and beef dishes quickly became a large part of German American cuisine.

Typically, the meat is pot-roasted, braised or simmered in a saucepan. Not only is this the most economical way to cook meat, but the all-essential gravy this technique produces becomes the perfect accompaniment for the much-loved dumpling, potatoes or noodles.

Choucroute Garnie

3	*pounds sauerkraut*
1/3	*cup lard, goose fat, or chicken fat*
3	*onions, coarsely chopped*
2	*cups Riesling wine*
1½	*cups chicken broth*
1	*pound lean bacon*
2	*pounds smoked pork chops*
1	*teaspoon pepper*
6–8	*crushed juniper berries*
2	*bay leaves*
2	*cloves garlic, crushed*
2	*whole cloves*
2	*pounds potatoes, peeled*
6	*bratwurst, mettwurst, or weisswurst*
6	*knockwurst*
1	*pound smoked sausage links*

Preheat the oven to 350° F.

Rinse the sauerkraut, drain it thoroughly, and set it aside. Melt the fat in a large Dutch oven, add the onions, and sauté them over medium heat until they are limp but not brown. Add the wine and broth and stir to blend. Simmer the mixture over low heat.

In a heavy skillet cook the bacon until it is about half done; transfer the bacon to paper towels to drain. Add the pork chops to the skillet and brown them lightly. Transfer the chops and bacon to the Dutch oven. Add the sauerkraut, pepper, juniper berries, bay leaves, garlic, and cloves. Be sure the meat is covered with the sauerkraut mixture. Cook the mixture over low heat for 1½ hours.

In a large saucepan cook the potatoes in water to cover for 20 minutes, or until they are tender.

In another saucepan simmer the wursts and the smoked sausages gently in water to cover for 10 to 15 minutes, taking care not to overcook them and handling them gently so that the skins do not burst.

Drain the sauerkraut, remove the bay leaves and cloves, and spread the mixture on a large heated platter. Arrange the meats and potatoes on top of and around the sauerkraut. Makes 8–10 servings.

Charcoal Grilled Brats in Beer

2   tablespoons butter
4   medium-size yellow onions, sliced
8   bratwurst
2   12-ounce bottles beer
     frankfurter buns
     mustard

Prepare a charcoal grill.

In a heavy skillet melt the butter. Add the onions and sauté them over medium heat until they are tender and golden, about 10 minutes. Place the bratwurst on top of the onions and pour the beer over them. Simmer the wurst, covered, for 15 minutes, turning occasionally. Remove the bratwurst from the skillet and keep them warm.

Over high heat cook the beer and onions, stirring often, until the cooking liquid is greatly reduced and the mixture reaches a spreadable consistency. Spoon the onion sauce into a small serving dish and set it aside, keeping it warm if desired.

Place the bratwurst over glowing charcoal and grill them, turning often, until they are browned and crisp. Serve them on frankfurter buns and pass the onion sauce and mustard. Makes 4–8 servings.

Midwest Scrapple

¼   cup minced onion
1   pound ground beef
½   pound ground pork
1½   teaspoons sage
⅛   teaspoon cayenne
1½   teaspoons salt
½   teaspoon pepper
3½   cups water
1   cup cornmeal
     flour
     oil for frying

In a large saucepan combine the first eight ingredients. Bring the mixture to a boil and simmer it gently for 20 minutes. Gradually stir in the cornmeal and cook the scrapple, stirring, until it is thickened. Pour it into a 5-x-9-inch loaf pan and chill it for several hours.

Cut the scrapple into slices about ½ inch thick. Dust them with flour, and fry them in oil until they are lightly browned. Makes 12 slices.

Grandma's Scrapple

3 *cups water*
1 *cup cornmeal*
½ *cup buckwheat flour*
1½ *pounds ground pork*
¼ *cup chopped onions*
1 *tablespoon each chopped fresh parsley and chives*
1 *teaspoon sage*
¼ *teaspoon thyme*
1 *clove garlic, minced*
1½ *cups chicken broth*
salt and pepper
flour
butter for frying

Mix 1 cup of the water with the cornmeal and buckwheat flour and set the mixture aside.

In a large heavy saucepan combine the pork with the onions, herbs, garlic, and chicken broth. Add the remaining 2 cups of water and salt and pepper to taste. Combine the mixture well and bring it to a boil. Add the cornmeal mixture slowly, stirring constantly. Lower the heat and simmer the scrapple, uncovered, for 20 minutes, stirring occasionally.

Rinse a 5- x 9-inch loaf pan with cold water. Pack the scrapple into the pan, press down to compress it, and let it cool completely. When it is firm, turn the loaf out of the pan, wrap it in plastic, cover it with foil, and refrigerate it for several hours or overnight.

Cut the scrapple into ¼-inch slices, dust them lightly with flour, and fry them in butter until they are crisp. Serve the fried scrapple with maple syrup or honey or as a breakfast meat with fried or scrambled eggs.

The loaf can be divided into 2 or 4 parts, and each portion can be wrapped and frozen until needed. Makes 20–25 slices.

Wild Rice with Sausage

2 *cups wild rice*
1 *pound bulk sausage*
1 *pound mushrooms*
2 *medium-size onions*
¼ *cup flour*
½ *cup heavy cream*
2½ *cups chicken broth*
½ *teaspoon oregano*
⅛ *teaspoon thyme*
⅛ *teaspoon marjoram*
¼ *teaspoon salt*
⅛ *teaspoon pepper*
¼ *cup chopped parsley*

Cook the wild rice according to package instructions. Drain it well and transfer to a large bowl.

In a large heavy skillet thoroughly cook the sausage over medium heat, breaking it up into small chunks. With a slotted spoon transfer it to paper towels. When it is well drained, put it in the bowl with the wild rice. To the same skillet add the mushrooms and onions and sauté them for 10 minutes, or until they are tender. Add them to the rice and sausage.

Preheat the oven to 350° F.

In a small saucepan mix the flour with the cream. Add the chicken broth and cook the mixture over medium heat , stirring, until it is smooth and thickened. Stir in the oregano, thyme, marjoram, salt, and pepper. Pour the sauce over the rice and sausage and toss the mixture until it is well combined. Turn the mixture into a large casserole and bake it for 25 to 30 minutes, until it is bubbly. Sprinkle the parsley around the rim of the casserole. Makes 4–6 servings.

Sausage Links in Cornmeal Pudding

1   *pound sausage links*
2   *tablespoons water*
2   *cups milk*
1/2   *cup yellow cornmeal*
1/2   *teaspoon salt*
4   *eggs, well beaten*

Place the sausages and water in a cold skillet. Cover the skillet tightly and cook the sausages slowly for 5 minutes.

Preheat the oven to 350° F.

Heat the milk in a double boiler or a heavy saucepan. Add the cornmeal, salt and eggs and cook the mixture slowly, stirring to blend the ingredients. Pour the cornmeal mixture into a greased 11¾- x 7¼-inch baking dish and arrange the sausages side by side in two rows across the top. Bake the casserole for 40 to 50 minutes, or until the top is golden brown. Makes 4–6 servings.

Peasant Pork Stew

4   *tablespoons vegetable oil or bacon drippings*
2   *pounds pork shoulder, cut into 1½-inch cubes*
3   *medium-size white onions, sliced*
6   *tablespoons butter*
3   *potatoes, peeled and sliced*
2   *carrots, julienned*
1   *cup shredded white cabbage*
1½   *teaspoons caraway seeds salt and pepper*
1   *cup strong beef stock or broth*

Heat the oil or bacon drippings in a heavy skillet, add the pork cubes, and brown them on all sides over medium-high heat. Remove the pork from the skillet and set it aside.

In another skillet sauté the onions in the butter until they are golden. Remove the onions from the skillet and set them aside, reserving the butter in which they were cooked.

Preheat oven to 375° F.

In a shallow baking dish arrange half the potato slices. Cover them with alternating layers of meat, onions, carrots, and cabbage, sprinkling each layer with caraway seeds and salt and pepper to taste. Make a top layer of potatoes and pour over them the reserved butter drippings. Add the stock or broth, put the stew in the oven, and bake it, covered, for 1 hour. Uncover the stew and bake it for another 30 minutes, allowing the top layer of potatoes to brown. Serve the stew in the baking dish. Makes 8 servings.

Austrian Pot Roast

2 tablespoons oil
4½ pounds boneless loin of pork
1 cup chopped onion
1 cup chopped carrot
½ teaspoon salt
1 teaspoon paprika
¼ teaspoon pepper
1 cup chicken broth
2 tablespoons flour
¼ cup sour cream
1 tablespoon chopped parsley
2 teaspoons caraway seeds
1 teaspoon capers
Parsley sprigs

Heat the oil in a large Dutch oven or heavy kettle. Add the pork loin and brown it on all sides over medium-high heat. Remove the pork and set it aside.

Preheat the oven to 350° F.

Sauté the onion and carrot in the same pot until they are golden. Stir in the salt, paprika, pepper, and chicken broth. Return the pork to the kettle and bring the liquid to a boil. Cover the pot tightly, put it in the oven, and cook the pork, basting occasionally with the cooking liquid, for 2½ hours, or until the meat is thoroughly cooked and tender.

Transfer the pork to a heated platter and let it stand for about 15 minutes before slicing. Strain the cooking liquids into a saucepan, pressing down hard on the vegetables before discarding them. Skim the strained liquid. Combine the flour and 1 tablespoon of the cooking liquid to make a smooth paste and stir the paste into the liquid in the saucepan. Cook the gravy for about one minute, stirring constantly, until it is thickened and bubbly. Adjust the seasoning, adding more salt if necessary. Slowly blend in the sour cream. Add the chopped parsley, caraway seeds, and capers. Heat the sauce through, but do not let it boil.

Cut the pork into slices ¼ to ½ inch thick. Drizzle some of the gravy over the slices and serve the remainder in a gravy boat. Garnish the pork with parsley sprigs. Makes 6–8 servings.

Spareribs with Apples and Sauerkraut

4½ pounds pork spareribs
   salt and pepper
2 tablespoons oil
2 teaspoons minced garlic
2 pounds onions, sliced
4 tart apples, cored, peeled, and sliced
2 tablespoons brown sugar or maple syrup
2 pounds sauerkraut, rinsed and drained
3 cups dry white wine
1–2 cups chicken broth
2 whole cloves
1 bay leaf
12 juniper berries
1 teaspoon peppercorns
2 teaspoons thyme
2 teaspoons marjoram
2 tablespoons chopped parsley

Place the ribs in a large pot, cover them with

cold water, and bring the water to a boil; reduce the heat and simmer the meat for 10 minutes. Drain the ribs and cut them into 2-rib portions. Sprinkle them with salt and pepper to taste and set them aside.

In a large Dutch oven heat the oil over medium heat. Add the garlic and onions and sauté them until they are soft but not brown. Add the ribs, reduce the heat to low, and cook the meat and onions for 10 to 15 minutes, stirring occasionally.

Preheat the oven to 325° F.

Add the apples and brown sugar or maple syrup to the Dutch oven and sauté the mixture for 5 minutes. Add the sauerkraut, wine, and 1½ cups of the chicken broth. Make a bouquet garni by placing all of the remaining ingredients in a cheesecloth pouch. Add the bouquet garni to the Dutch oven and bake the dish, covered, for 2 hours, checking during the last 30 minutes to see if more broth is needed. Serve the mixture on a heated platter. Makes 6–8 servings.

Pork Loin Stuffed with Apricots and Raisins

- *1   3-pound rolled pork loin*
  salt and pepper
- *1½   cups fresh bread crumbs*
- *½   cup chopped raisins*
- *2   tablespoons chopped dried apricots*
- *⅓   cup orange juice*
- *1   egg, lightly beaten*
- *½   teaspoon thyme*

dash cinnamon
Apricot Sauce (recipe follows)

Unroll the pork loin, place it fat side down, and sprinkle it lightly with salt and pepper.

Preheat the oven to 325° F.

In a bowl combine the bread crumbs, raisins, apricots, orange juice, egg, thyme, and cinnamon. Spread the mixture evenly over the meat. Roll up the pork loin and tie it firmly with string. Place the meat on a rack in a roasting pan and roast it for 2 hours, or until a meat thermometer reaches 160° F. During the last 30 minutes of roasting, brush the meat several times with Apricot Sauce. Slice the pork loin thick and serve it with warm Apricot Sauce. Makes 6–8 servings.

Apricot Sauce

- *1   cup apricot jam*
- *½   cup water*
- *½   cup unsalted butter, cut into chunks*
- *½   teaspoon cinnamon*
- *¼   teaspoon ground cloves*

In a small saucepan combine the jam with the water. Stir the sauce over low heat until it is well combined and add the butter, cinnamon, and cloves. Cook the mixture until the butter is melted and the sauce begins to bubble. In a food processor or blender, purée the mixture until it is smooth. This sauce can also be used to glaze ham or chicken, or it may be served, warm or chilled, over ice cream or cake. Makes about 1¾ cups sauce.

Pork Loin Hunter Style

1   *3-pound boneless pork loin*
    salt and pepper
2   *cups dry white wine*
1   *tablespoon oil*
2   *bay leaves*
½   *medium-size onion, sliced*
2   *cloves garlic, chopped*
6   *peppercorns, crushed*
1   *teaspoon juniper berries, crushed*
½   *cup plus 3 tablespoons flour*
3   *tablespoons butter*
2   *cups fresh cranberries*
½   *cup plus 3 tablespoons water*
½   *cup sugar*

Trim most of the fat from the meat. Sprinkle the roast lightly with salt and pepper, roll it up, and tie it firmly with string.

In a stainless steel, glass, or enameled bowl (do not use aluminum) combine the wine, oil, bay leaves, onion, garlic, peppercorns, and juniper berries. Place the meat in the marinade and refrigerate it, covered, for 24 hours, turning occasionally.

Strain and reserve the marinade. Pat the meat dry and dredge it lightly in the ½ cup flour. Heat the butter in a Dutch oven, add the meat fat side down, and brown it well on all sides over medium-high heat. Lower the heat and add the strained marinade. Partially cover the pot and cook the meat slowly, turning and basting it occasionally, for 1½ to 2 hours, or until it can be pierced easily with a fork.

Wash the cranberries. In a small saucepan bring the ½ cup water to a boil and add the cranberries and sugar. Cook the berries for 7 to 10 minutes, or until the skins burst. Skim off the foam. Set the berries aside, but keep them warm.

Transfer the cooked pork to a cutting board and keep warm. Skim the fat from the cooking liquid. Dissolve the remaining 3 tablespoons flour in the 3 tablespoons water and add the paste to the cooking liquid. Cook the gravy over low heat until it is smooth, scraping up the brown bits from the bottom of the pan. Serve the pork, sliced, with the cranberries and gravy as accompaniments. Makes 6–8 servings.

Pork Loin with Juniper Berries

20   *juniper berries*
1   *bay leaf*
1½   *teaspoons salt*
1   *teaspoon sugar*
¾   *teaspoon ground ginger*
½   *teaspoon pepper*
1   *whole allspice*
1   *clove garlic, crushed*
1   *tablespoon white wine*
1   *tablespoon olive oil*
1   *3-pound rolled pork loin*
2   *tablespoons bacon drippings*
18   *small white onions*
18   *new potatoes, peeled*
2   *large cooking apples, peeled, cored, and*
    cut into sixths

Place the juniper berries, bay leaf, salt, sugar, ginger, pepper, and allspice in a blender. Add the garlic, wine, and olive oil and and blend until the spices are evenly ground. Spread the spice mixture over the outside of the pork loin and refrigerate the meat, in a large covered bowl, for 2 days, turning every 12 hours.

Preheat the oven to 325° F.

Wipe the excess marinade from the roast. In a large skillet heat the bacon drippings. Add the meat and brown it on all sides over medium-high heat. Transfer the pork loin to a baking dish, reserving the drippings in the skillet, and roast it in the oven, covered, for 1 hour, basting occasionally with its own juice.

Cut an X in the root end of each onion. In a small saucepan blanch the onions in boiling salted water for 1 minute; drain and peel them. In a large saucepan blanch the potatoes for one minute; drain them and pat them dry. In the skillet, quickly brown the potatoes and onions over medium-high heat. Arrange them around the roast in the baking dish, baste the meat and vegetables with the pan juices, and bake the dish, covered, for an additional 30 minutes. Add the apples and bake for another 20 minutes.

Transfer the pork to a heated platter and arrange vegetables around it. Makes 6 servings.

Swabian Pork Chops

6 *strips bacon*
4 *loin pork chops*
4 *large potatoes, peeled and
    thinly sliced*
1 *large onion, sliced ¼ inch thick
    salt and pepper*
2 *cloves garlic, minced*

1 *cup dry white wine
    chopped parsley*

Preheat the oven to 300° F.

Cook the bacon in a skillet and drain it on paper towels. Brown the chops in the bacon drippings and set them aside.

Arrange half the potatoes in a deep casserole or Dutch oven. Top the potatoes with half the onion slices and season with salt and pepper to taste. Crumble three of the bacon strips over the potatoes and onions. Add the pork chops in a single layer. Arrange the remaining potatoes and onion slices over the chops and sprinkle with salt and pepper. Mix the garlic with the wine, pour it into the casserole, and crumble the remaining bacon over the top. Cover the casserole with a double thickness of foil, then with the lid, and bake it for 1¼ hours. Serve the casserole garnished with parsley. Makes 4 servings.

Pan-Fried Weisswurst

1 *12-ounce bottle of beer*
4 *weisswurst*
2 *tablespoons butter*

In a large saucepan bring the beer to a simmer. Add the weisswurst and simmer gently for 15 minutes.

In a skillet melt the butter. Gently remove the parboiled weisswurst, taking care not to break their delicate casings. Add weisswurst to the skillet and fry just until brown. Serve with Düsseldorf mustard. Makes 2 servings.

German Ham Loaf

2 *pounds ground ham*
1 *pound ground pork or veal*
1 *teaspoon dry mustard*
  pepper
2 *tablespoons minced parsley*
2 *eggs, lightly beaten*
3/4 *cup milk*
1 *cup saltine crumbs*

Preheat the oven to 325° F.

Mix the ham and pork or veal together. Add the remaining ingredients and mix well. Place the meat mixture in a loaf pan and set the loaf pan in a pan of hot water. Bake the ham loaf for 1½ to 2 hours. Makes 6 servings.

Cottage Schnitzel

2 *pounds pork tenderloin*
2 *large eggs*
1/2 *cup plus 2 tablespoons flour*
2 *tablespoons grated Parmesan cheese*
1/2 *cup milk*
1/2 *teaspoon salt*
1/4 *teaspoon white pepper*
  pinch nutmeg
1 *tablespoon chopped parsley*
6 *tablespoons butter*
2 *tablespoons lemon juice*

Thoroughly trim the fat from the tenderloin, slice the pork ¼ inch thick, and flatten the medallions slightly with a meat mallet or the blunt side of a cleaver until each one is about 3 inches across.

In a large mixing bowl lightly beat the eggs. Add the 2 tablespoons flour and beat to combine. Add the cheese, milk, salt, pepper, nutmeg, and parsley and beat the mixture until it is smooth.

Dredge the pork medallions in the remaining ½ cup flour and dip them in the batter. Melt the butter in a heavy skillet, add the pork medallions, and sauté them over medium-high heat until they are golden brown on both sides. Transfer the pork to a heated platter. Add the lemon juice to the skillet and cook it briefly over high heat, scraping to loosen the brown bits. Pour the pan juices over the pork and serve at once. Makes 4 servings.

Pork Schnitzel with Sour Cream

6 *pork cutlets (about 1½ pounds), cut ½ inch thick*
1/4 *cup plus 1 tablespoon flour*
  salt and pepper
1 *egg, beaten*
2 *tablespoons milk*
3/4 *cup fine dry bread crumbs*
1 *teaspoon paprika*
3 *tablespoons vegetable oil*
3/4 *cup chicken stock or broth*
1/2 *teaspoon dried dill weed*
1 *teaspoon minced onion*
1/2 *cup sour cream*
  lemon wedges

Pound the pork cutlets to ¼- to ⅛-inch thickness. Slit the edges of the cutlets to prevent curling.

Put the ¼ cup flour into a large paper or plastic bag and season it with salt and pepper to taste. Combine the egg and milk in a shallow bowl. In a separate bowl mix the bread crumbs with the paprika. Shake the cutlets in the flour, dip them into the egg mixture, then dredge them in the bread crumbs. Place the cutlets on a cookie sheet in a single layer, cover them lightly with wax paper, and refrigerate them overnight.

Heat the oil in a large skillet. Add the cutlets and sauté them over medium-high heat for 6 to 8 minutes on each side, or until they are golden brown. Transfer the cutlets to a heated platter and keep them warm.

Pour the chicken stock into the skillet and stir, scraping to loosen the brown bits. Thoroughly mix the dill weed and minced onion into the sour cream; add the remaining 1 tablespoon flour and mix well. Stir the sour cream mixture into the chicken stock. Cook and stir the sauce over medium heat until it thickens, but do not let it boil. Garnish the cutlets with lemon wedges and serve them with the sour cream sauce. Makes 6 servings.

Bavarian Beef Boiled in Beer

5   *pounds beef rump or flank in one piece*
    salt and pepper
6   *strips bacon, lightly cooked*
2   *large white onions, sliced ½-inch thick*
    and separated into rings
3   *carrots, sliced*
2   *turnips, sliced*
2   *cloves garlic, minced*
8   *juniper berries, crushed*
3   *black peppercorns*
2   *bay leaves, crumbled*
2   *12-ounce bottles beer*
2   *tablespoons butter*
2   *tablespoons flour*

Pound the beef flat with a wooden mallet and rub it well with salt and pepper. Lay the bacon in a deep flameproof casserole or a Dutch oven and place the beef on top of it. Spread the onions, carrots, and turnips around the meat. Add the garlic, crushed juniper berries, peppercorns, and bay leaves. Pour the beer over the meat and vegetables. Bring the liquid to a boil over high heat. Lower the heat and simmer the meat, covered, for 2 to 2½ hours, until it is tender. Remove the casserole from the heat, drain off the broth, reserving 2 cups, and keep the meat warm.

In a heavy saucepan over low heat, melt the butter and blend in the flour. Cook the roux until it is brown and smooth. Add the reserved broth, stirring constantly. Bring the sauce to a boil, lower the heat, and simmer the gravy gently for 20 minutes. Season the sauce with salt and pepper to taste and serve it with the meat. Makes 8–10 servings.

Souse

    4 *pig knuckles, feet, jowls, or other pork*
       parts
    1 *quart chicken stock or broth*
  4–5 *peppercorns, cracked*
    2 *tablespoons grated onion*
   ½   *cup minced parsley*
       salt and pepper
10–20 *fresh spinach leaves*
    4 *cups bite-size raw carrots, green beans,*
       and cauliflower

In a large pot cook the pig knuckles in the stock with the peppercorns. Bring the stock to a boil, reduce the heat, and cook the meat for 1 hour, or until it is tender. Remove the pig knuckles from the pot, reserving the stock, and cut the meat off the bone. Strain the stock and refrigerate the meat and the stock separately.

Remove the fat from the cold stock and chop the meat. In a large pot over high heat reduce the stock to 3 cups, add the meat, onion, and parsley. Remove the meat with a slotted spoon. Season it with salt and pepper to taste, press it into a loaf pan, and pour ½ cup of the stock over it, reserving the rest of the stock for another use. Cover the surface of the meat with wax paper, put a weight on top of it, and refrigerate it for several hours until it is firm. Turn the loaf out onto a bed of fresh spinach leaves and arrange the raw vegetables around it. Makes 8 servings.

Pork Roast with Dill Sauce

    1 *fresh pork shoulder with the skin left on*
       Salt
       Ground ginger
   ⅓   *cup fresh dill leaves*
       Freshly ground black pepper
    1 *cup dry white wine*

SAUCE

    2 *tablespoons butter*
    1 *tablespoon all-purpose flour*
   ½   *cup degreased drippings from roasting*
       pan
   ½   *cup heavy cream*
   ¼   *cup minced dill leaves*
    1 *teaspoon ground ginger*
       salt and freshly ground black pepper

Preheat the oven to 350° F.

Slash the pork skin in a fine diamond pattern. Rub the surface with salt and ground ginger. Make deep cuts in the pork with a sharp knife. Stuff the slits with the dill leaves. Salt and pepper the surfaces of the roast. Place the pork in a roasting pan, pour in the wine, and roast it 25 minutes per pound. DO NOT BASTE.

To prepare the sauce, melt the butter in a saucepan, stir in the flour, and cook the roux until it is golden brown. Pour in the degreased cooking liquid and cream. When thickened, stir in the dill, ginger, and salt and pepper to taste. Serve the sauce in a separate dish. Makes 6–8 servings.

Tex-Mex Spiced Pot Roast

2   cloves garlic, minced
1½ teaspoons salt
1   5-pound rump of beef
3   tablespoons salad oil
3   medium onions, sliced
4   teaspoons chili powder
½   teaspoon ground cumin
½   teaspoon chopped coriander
⅓   cup tomato paste
1   17-ounce can whole tomatoes
1   beef bouillon cube
2   cups white rice
1   cup canned red kidney beans, heated
2   avocados, sliced, for garnish

Mix together garlic and salt. With a sharp knife, cut several small holes in the meat and fill them with the garlic mixture. Heat the oil in a Dutch oven and brown the meat on all sides. Add spices, seasonings, and tomato paste. Drain the tomatoes, reserving the juice, and set the tomatoes aside. If necessary, add water to the juice to make 1¼ cups. Add the bouillon cube to the tomato juice and heat to dissolve. Add this to the meat, cover and simmer for 2¼ hours, or until the meat is almost tender. Add the tomatoes and simmer another 15 minutes, or until the meat is tender and the tomatoes are heated through. Adjust seasonings. Toss the rice with the kidney beans. Transfer the meat to a heated platter. Pour the juices over the meat, surround it with the rice and kidney bean mixture, and garnish with the avocado slices. Makes 10–12 servings.

Beer Brisket

3–4 pounds beef brisket
     salt and pepper
1   onion, sliced
¼   cup chili sauce
2   tablespoons brown sugar
1   clove garlic, minced
1   12-ounce bottle beer
2   tablespoons flour
½   cup water

Preheat the oven to 350° F.

Trim the excess fat from the brisket and season the meat with salt and pepper to taste. Place the beef in a 9-x-13-inch baking dish and cover it with onion slices.

In a bowl combine the chili sauce, brown sugar, garlic, and beer and pour the mixture over the meat. Cover the baking dish tightly with foil and bake the meat for 3½ hours. Uncover the dish and bake the brisket for another 30 minutes, basting occasionally with the cooking liquid. Transfer the meat to a heated platter and keep it warm. Skim the excess fat from the pan liquid, strain it, and add enough water to make 1 cup. Pour the liquid into a small saucepan. Blend the flour and water; add the paste to the liquid, and cook the gravy over medium heat, stirring constantly, until it is thickened and bubbly. Slice the meat against the grain, pour about ¼ cup gravy over the slices, and serve the rest of the gravy as an accompaniment. Makes 6–8 servings.

Swabian Pot Roast

2   *tablespoons oil*
1   *3½-pound rump roast*
1½ *cups chopped onion*
½   *teaspoon salt*
3   *anchovies, chopped*
¼   *cup vinegar*
2   *tablespoons light corn syrup*
16 *peppercorns*
2   *teaspoons allspice*
2   *bay leaves*
2   *cups beef stock or broth*

Heat the oil in a large Dutch oven. Put the beef into the pot and brown it on all sides over medium-high heat. Lower the heat, add all of the remaining ingredients, and simmer the pot roast, covered, over medium heat for 4 to 5 hours, adding water if necessary. Serve the beef with buttered noodles or spaetzle. Makes 6–8 servings.

Hofbrau Steak

¾   *cup (1½ sticks) plus 4 tablespoons butter*
2   *pounds sirloin steak, ½ inch thick, cut into serving-size portions*
½   *cup lemon juice*
4   *teaspoons minced garlic*

Melt the 4 tablespoons butter in a large heavy skillet. Add the steak portions and cook them over medium-high heat for 2 to 3 minutes on each side, or until almost cooked to taste. Add

the lemon juice, garlic, and the ¾ cup butter to the pan and cook the meat until the butter is melted. Transfer the steak to a platter and pour the sauce over it or serve the sauce on the side. Makes 6–8 servings.

Vienna Steaks

2   *pounds beef top round steak, about ½ inch thick*
½   *cup plus 3 tablespoons flour salt and pepper*
4   *strips bacon, chopped*
1½ *cups chopped onion*
½   *cup chopped carrot*
1   *clove garlic, minced*
3   *cups beef stock or broth*
¼   *cup white wine vinegar*
2   *tablespoons minced parsley*
3   *bay leaves*
⅛   *teaspoon thyme*
⅛   *teaspoon allspice*
1   *thin strip lemon peel*
¾   *cup heavy cream*
1   *teaspoon lemon juice*

Cut the beef into 6 serving-size portions. Dredge the meat in the ½ cup flour seasoned with salt and pepper to taste and set it aside.

Fry the bacon in a large heavy skillet until it is cooked but not browned. Drain the bacon and set it aside.

Brown the beef on both sides in the same skillet over medium-high heat. Remove the meat from the skillet, keeping it warm, and lower the heat to medium. Add the onion, carrot, and garlic to the skillet and sauté them until they are soft but not browned, adding oil if needed. Stir in the remaining 3 tablespoons flour. Add the bacon, beef broth, and vinegar and stir to combine. Stir in the parsley, bay leaves, thyme, allspice, and lemon peel. Return the meat to the skillet and simmer it, covered, for 1 to 1½ hours, or until it is tender. Transfer the meat to a platter and keep it warm.

Strain the pan liquid and return it to the skillet. Over medium heat add the cream and lemon juice, heat the sauce through, and adjust the seasonings. Serve the sauce over the beef. Makes 6 servings.

Königsberger Klops

    3   tablespoons butter
    1   medium-size yellow onion, minced
    1   garlic clove, minced
  ¾   pound lean ground beef
  ¾   pound ground veal
  ¼   pound ground pork
    1   cup bread crumbs
    2   eggs, lightly beaten
        salt and pepper
    3   cups beef stock or broth
    1   bay leaf
    1   whole clove
    1   teaspoon black peppercorns
    2   tablespoons flour
  ¼   cup water
    2   tablespoons lemon juice
    1   cup dry white wine
    1   tablespoon capers
        buttered noodles or spaetzle
        chopped parsley

Melt the butter in a heavy kettle or Dutch oven, add the onion, and cook it over medium heat until it is soft but not brown. Add the garlic and cook, stirring, for a few minutes longer, until the garlic is soft.

Place the ground meats in a large bowl. Remove the onions and garlic from the kettle with a slotted spoon and spread them over the meat. Add the bread crumbs, eggs, and salt and pepper to taste. Combine the mixture until the ingredients are well blended. Shape the meat into 2-inch balls.

Pour the beef stock into the same heavy kettle or Dutch oven. Place the bay leaf, clove, and peppercorns on a square of cheesecloth, tie the ends together, and add the bouquet garni to the kettle. Bring the stock to a boil. With a slotted spoon transfer the meatballs to the kettle. Cook the meatballs, covered, over moderate heat for 30 minutes.

Transfer the meatballs to a heated platter and keep them warm. Remove the bouquet garni and skim the fat off the cooking liquid. Strain the liquid and return it to the kettle. Dissolve the flour in the water and add the mixture to the kettle. Cook the sauce, stirring constantly, over medium heat until it bubbles and begins to thicken. Add the lemon juice, wine, and capers and cook, stirring, until the sauce reaches the desired consistency. Adjust the seasonings, return the meatballs to the sauce, and cook just until heated through. Serve the *Königsberger Klops* with buttered noodles or spaetzle garnished with chopped parsley. Makes 6–8 servings.

Dot's Sauerbraten

1   *3-pound boneless rump roast*
½   *teaspoon salt*
½   *teaspoon pepper*
1   *onion, sliced*
5   *whole cloves*
2   *bay leaves*
6   *peppercorns*
6   *juniper berries*
1   *cup vinegar*
1½ *cups water*
1   *tablespoon oil*
1   *tablespoon flour*
1   *cup raisins*

Season the roast with the salt and pepper. Place the meat in a ceramic bowl with the onion, cloves, bay leaves, peppercorns, and juniper berries. Mix the vinegar with the water and add the mixture to the marinade. Place the meat in the marinade and refrigerate it, covered, for 2 to 3 days, turning it occasionally.

Remove the meat from the marinade and pat it dry. Heat the oil in a heavy kettle or Dutch oven and brown the meat well on all sides over medium-high heat. Strain the marinade and add it to the kettle. Bring it quickly to a boil and turn the heat to low. Simmer the meat, uncovered, for 1½ hours, or until it is tender. Transfer it to a heated platter and keep it warm.

Add enough cooking liquid to the flour to make a thick paste. Stir the paste into the kettle and whisk it into the cooking liquid. Simmer the gravy, stirring, until it is thickened. Add the raisins, heat the sauce through, and pour it over the meat. Makes 6 servings.

Classic Sauerbraten

MARINADE

2   *cups cider or red wine vinegar*
2   *cups water*
2   *medium onions, sliced*
8   *whole cloves*
4   *bay leaves, crumbled*
2   *teaspoons salt*
1   *teaspoon freshly cracked black pepper*
2   *tablespoons sugar*
1   *garlic clove, minced*

SAUERBRATEN

4–5 *pounds beef (sirloin tip, eye of round, or blade pot roast)*
½   *cup plus 6 tablespoons flour*
2   *tablespoons vegetable oil*
4   *tablespoons butter*
1   *tablespoon sugar*
8–10 *gingersnaps, crushed*

Combine the marinade ingredients in a saucepan and heat the liquid through, but do not let it boil. Place the meat in a large heatproof bowl and pour the hot marinade over it. Cover the bowl and marinate the meat in the refrigerator for 3 or 4 days, turning it once or twice a day.

Remove the meat from the bowl and pat it dry with paper towels. Strain and reserve the marinade. Dredge the beef lightly in the ½ cup flour. In a Dutch oven or heavy kettle, heat the oil and brown the meat on all sides. Add 2 cups marinade to the meat, reserving the rest. Bring to a boil, lower heat, and simmer gently 3 hours.

In a separate saucepan melt the butter; add the remaining 6 tablespoons flour and the sugar and stir until the roux is a rich brown. Add the remaining marinade, stirring until the sauce is smooth. Add the sauce to the Dutch oven and cook the sauerbraten for 1 hour longer, or until the meat is very tender.

Adjust the seasoning, if necessary. Transfer the meat to a platter and add the crushed gingersnaps to the sauce, whisking until the crumbs are completely incorporated. Serve the beef with the gravy.   Makes 10 servings.

Goulash with Sauerkraut

4 tablespoons beef suet or butter
2 pounds beef or veal, cut in 1½-inch squares
1½ cups sliced onions
1 clove garlic, chopped
1 cup chopped fresh tomatoes
salt and pepper
1 cup sour cream
2 teaspoons paprika
2 teaspoons caraway seeds
1 pound (about 2 cups) sauerkraut
2–3 teaspoons chopped parsley

Heat the suet or butter in a large heavy kettle or Dutch oven. Add the meat and brown it lightly over high heat. Lower the heat, add the onions, and cook them for 5 minutes. Add the garlic and tomatoes and salt and pepper to taste. Pour in enough water to barely cover the mixture. Cook the meat, covered, over low heat, stirring often, for about 45 minutes, or until it is nearly tender and the sauce is greatly reduced. Add the sour cream, paprika, and caraway seeds and simmer another 30 minutes. In a saucepan heat the sauerkraut.

Arrange alternate rows of goulash and sauerkraut on a heated platter. Sprinkle the top with parsley. Makes 6–8 servings.

Beef Carbonnade

¼ pound bacon, chopped
4 tablespoons oil or butter
2 pounds boneless chuck or bottom round, cubed
3 large onions, sliced thin
1 tablespoon sugar
1 tablespoon vinegar
2 12-ounce bottles dark beer
1½ tablespoons Dijon mustard
1 slice pumpernickel
1 bay leaf, crumbled
½ teaspoon thyme
½ teaspoon ground thyme
salt and pepper

In a Dutch oven or heavy pot cook the bacon until it is crisp; transfer it to paper towels to drain. Add the oil or butter to the bacon drippings and in it brown the meat on all sides over medium-high heat. Turn the heat to medium, add the onions, and cook them until they are soft but not browned. Add the sugar and vinegar and stir to combine. Stir in the beer and the reserved bacon. Spread the mustard on the pumpernickel and add the bread to the pot along with the bay leaf and thyme. Simmer the carbonnade, covered, for 1 hour, or until the meat is tender. Reduce the sauce over high heat to the desired consistency and adjust the seasonings. Slice the beef and serve it with the sauce. Makes 4–6 servings.

Beef Ragout with Basil

1   *pound tiny white onions,*
     peeled
1   *pound baby carrots*
4   *tablespoons butter*
2   *tablespoons bacon drippings*
3   *pounds lean round steak, cut into 2-inch*
     cubes
3   *tablespoons flour*
3/4   *cup burgundy*
2   *teaspoons chopped fresh basil or 1/2*
     teaspoon dried basil
2   *cloves garlic, minced*
1/2   *teaspoon oregano*
     salt and pepper
1   *tablespoon sugar*
3/4   *cup Madeira*
1/4   *cup brandy*
     chopped parsley

In a large saucepan parboil the onions and carrots in water to cover for 10 minutes, or until they are barely tender. Drain the liquid from the saucepan into a 2-cup measure and add water, if necessary, to make 2 cups. Set the liquid aside and refrigerate the vegetables.

In a large heavy skillet heat 2 tablespoons of the butter and the bacon drippings. Add the beef cubes and brown them well on all sides. Transfer the browned beef to a Dutch oven or a large casserole with a lid and keep it warm.

Preheat the oven to 300° F.

Add the flour to the drippings in the skillet and cook, stirring constantly, over medium heat until it begins to brown. Add the cooking liquid from the 2-cup measure, stirring until the sauce is smooth and thickened. Add the burgundy, the basil, garlic, and oregano. Season the sauce with salt and pepper to taste. Pour the sauce over the meat in the Dutch oven and cook the ragout in the oven for 3 hours, or until the meat is fork-tender.

Melt the remaining 2 tablespoons butter in a skillet and add the sugar, stirring until it is dissolved. Add the carrots and onions and cook them over medium heat until they are glazed and slightly brown. Transfer the carrots and onions to the Dutch oven and stir in the Madeira. Cover the ragout, return it to the oven, and cook it for another 30 minutes. Stir in the brandy a few minutes before removing the ragout from the oven. Arrange the meat and vegetables on a heated platter and garnish it with chopped parsley. Serve the gravy as an accompaniment. Makes 6–8 servings

Beef Rouladen

3   *tablespoons Dijon mustard*
1   *tablespoon horseradish*
4   *slices round steak (about 1/2 pound), 1/2*
     inch thick or less
     salt and pepper
8   *bacon strips, cooked*
2   *medium onions, minced*
1/4   *cup flour*
2–4   *tablespoons oil*
1   *cup water*
3   *tablespoons lemon juice*
     buttered spaetzle or noodles
     parsley sprigs

Mix together mustard and horseradish. Set aside.

Season the meat on one side with salt and pepper to taste and spread each portion lightly with the mustard-horseradish mixture. Top each slice with two strips of bacon and one-fourth of the onions. Roll up each portion, tucking in the loose ends, and secure it with string. Dredge the *Rouladen* in the flour.

Heat the oil in a heavy skillet, add the *Rouladen*, and brown them well on all sides. Add the water and lemon juice, cover the skillet, and simmer the *Rouladen* for 1½ hours, or until the meat is tender, adding water if necessary. Serve the *Rouladen* with spaetzle or noodles garnished with parsley sprigs. Makes 4 servings.

Bavarian Braised Beef

2	tablespoons cooking oil
2½	pounds lean beef, cut in one-inch cubes
3	cups sliced onions
2	cloves garlic, minced
½	cup beef consommé
1	tablespoon brown sugar
1	bay leaf
¼	teaspoon thyme
	salt and pepper
1	12-ounce bottle beer
	parsley sprigs
1½	tablespoons cornstarch
1½	tablespoons water

Heat the oil in a heavy skillet, add the beef, and brown it well on all sides. Remove the beef from the skillet and keep it warm. Add the onions to the skillet and cook them over medium heat until they are soft but not brown, about 10 minutes. Move the onions to one side of the skillet, add the garlic, and cook it, stirring, for about 30 seconds. Return the beef to the skillet and add the consommé, sugar, bay leaf, and thyme. Season the beef with salt and pepper to taste and pour the beer over it. Bring the pan liquid to a boil, cover the skillet, and simmer the beef gently until it is tender, about 2 hours. Transfer the meat to a heated platter, garnish it with parsley sprigs, and keep it warm.

Strain the pan liquid and return it to the skillet. Dissolve the cornstarch in the water, stir the paste into the cooking liquid, and cook the sauce over medium heat, stirring constantly, until it is smooth and thickened. Serve the braised beef with the sauce. Makes 6–8 servings.

Grilled Beer Burgers

1	tablespoon strong Dijon mustard
1	teaspoon chopped scallion
¼	teaspoon freshly cracked pepper
2	tablespoons beer or ale
1½	pounds ground beef
	salt

Prepare a charcoal grill or preheat the broiler.

Work the mustard, scallion, pepper, and ale into the ground meat, blending the ingredients well. Shape the beef into 6 patties and season them with salt to taste. Grill the burgers over glowing coals or in the broiler to the desired degree of doneness. Makes 6 servings.

Stuffed Beef Rolls

2½   *pounds top round steak*
       salt and pepper
3   *tablespoons flour*
4   *strips bacon*
4   *large onions, minced*
¼   *cup chopped parsley*
3   *tablespoons olive or corn oil*
1   *leek, white part only, thinly sliced*
1   *carrot, sliced*
1½   *cups beef stock or broth*
½   *cup sour cream*
3   *tablespoons tomato paste*

Slice the steak into 12 to 16 strips and pound the strips very thin. Season the meat strips with salt and pepper to taste, dust lightly with flour, and set aside.

In a large flameproof casserole cook the bacon and transfer it to paper towels to drain. Add about three-fourths of the onions to the bacon drippings and cook over medium heat until they are soft and golden but not brown. Add the parsley and stir to blend. With a slotted spoon transfer the onions and parsley to paper towels to drain.

Spread 1½ tablespoons of the onion-parsley mixture over the unfloured sides of the meat strips. Crumble the bacon and sprinkle it evenly over the meat. Roll up the beef strips and tie them with string.

Heat the oil in the casserole, add the beef rolls, and brown them over medium heat. Add the leek, carrots, and remaining onions and cook them over medium heat for about 8 minutes, until they are soft and slightly browned. Add the broth and bring it to a boil. Lower the heat and simmer the beef rolls gently for 1 to 1½ hours, adding more broth, or water, if necessary. Transfer the beef rolls to a heated platter and keep them warm. Skim the fat from the cooking liquid, add the sour cream and tomato paste, stirring to blend, and heat the sauce, stirring, until it is smooth and heated through. Pour some of the sauce over the meat and serve the rest in a gravy boat. Makes 6–8 servings.

Sauerbraten Loaves

1   *pound ground beef*
½   *cup dry bread crumbs*
⅓   *cup milk*
1   *egg, beaten*
¼   *cup finely chopped onion*
1   *teaspoon salt*
¼   *teaspoon dry mustard*
8   *small whole new potatoes*
½   *cup gingersnaps, crumbled*
½   *cup brown sugar*
1½   *cups water*
¼   *cup raisins*
3   *tablespoons lemon juice*
2   *beef bouillon cubes*

Preheat the oven to 350° F.

Combine the meat, bread crumbs, milk, egg, onion, salt, and mustard. Shape the mixture into 6 loaves and arrange the loaves in a baking dish so that they do not touch one another. Bake the beef loaves, uncovered, for 30 minutes.

In a large saucepan parboil the potatoes until they are almost tender, about 10 minutes. Drain them and set them aside. In another saucepan dissolve the gingersnap crumbs and brown sugar in the water. Add the raisins, lemon juice, and bouillon cubes and bring the sauce to a boil. Reduce the heat and cook the sauce gently until the bouillon cubes dissolve.

Arrange the potatoes around the beef loaves in the baking dish, pour the sauce over the meat and potatoes, return the dish to the oven, and bake the meal for another 30 minutes. Makes 6 servings.

Stuffed Cabbage

½ **pound ground pork or veal**
1 **pound lean ground beef**
   salt and pepper
1 **egg**
1 **tablespoon Worcestershire sauce**
2 **cloves garlic, minced**
½ **cup day-old pumpernickel crumbs**
½ **cup cooked rice**
12 **large cabbage leaves, steamed until barely tender**
2 **tablespoons butter**
1 **cup sliced carrots**
1 **cup chopped onion**
1 **bay leaf**
1 **teaspoon dried basil**
1 **tablespoon brown sugar**
1½ **cups canned Italian plum tomatoes with their juice**
1 **cup beef stock or broth**
1 **cup sour cream**
1 **tablespoon caraway seeds or dill seeds (optional)**

Combine the pork or veal with the beef and season the meat with salt and pepper to taste. Add the egg, Worcestershire sauce, garlic, pumpernickel crumbs, and rice and blend the filling well. Divide the mixture into 12 equal parts and place each portion in the hollow of a cabbage leaf. Rolls the leaves up tightly, tucking in any loose edges. In a shallow flameproof baking pan arrange the cabbage rolls close together in a single layer, seam side down, and set the dish aside.

Preheat the oven to 350° F.

In a heavy skillet melt the butter over medium heat and sauté the carrots and onion until they are soft but not brown. Add the bay leaf, basil, brown sugar, tomatoes, and beef stock. Bring the sauce to a boil, lower the heat, and simmer it for 5 minutes. Gently pour the sauce over the cabbage rolls, place the pan in the oven, and bake the stuffed cabbage, uncovered, for 45 minutes.

Using a slotted spoon, carefully transfer the cabbage rolls to a heated platter. Place the baking pan over high heat on top of the stove and reduce the sauce, scraping up any brown bits from the bottom. Pour the sauce over the cabbage rolls and top the rolls with sour cream sprinkled with caraway seeds or dill seeds, if desired. Makes 6 servings.

Beef Stew with Beer

3 pounds beef stew meat, cubed
⅔ cup flour
4 tablespoons butter
1 16-ounce can beer
¾ cup water
1 tablespoon brown sugar
3 large onions, sliced
2 carrots sliced
10 whole cloves
  salt and pepper
½ cup water
  cooked rice or noodles

Dredge the meat in the flour, reserving 4 tablespoons flour. In a large pot with a tight-fitting lid, heat the butter. Add the meat and brown it well on all sides. Pour the beer and water over the meat and stir in the brown sugar. Simmer the meat, covered, for 1¼ hours. Add the onions, carrots, cloves, and salt and pepper to taste and simmer the stew for another 45 minutes.

With a slotted spoon transfer the meat and vegetables to a heated platter and keep them warm. Strain the cooking liquid and return it to the pot. Dissolve the 4 tablespoons flour in the water. Gradually stir the paste into the cooking liquid and cook the sauce over medium heat, stirring constantly, for about 5 minutes, until it is smooth and bubbly. Serve the stew with the rice or noodles. Makes 6 servings.

Liver and Dumplings

1¾ cups flour
  Salt and pepper
1 pound calves' liver, cut into serving-size portions
¼ cup plus 2 tablespoons shortening
1 large onion, sliced and separated into rings
3 cups water
2 teaspoons baking powder
½ teaspoon salt
1 egg, beaten
⅓ cup milk

Season ½ cup of the flour with salt and pepper to taste and dredge the liver in the mixture. In a large, deep skillet, melt the ¼ cup shortening over medium-high heat, add the liver, and brown it on both sides. Remove the liver and set it aside. Cook the onion rings in the drippings until they are soft and slightly brown. Remove them and set them aside. Add ¼ cup of the remaining flour to the pan drippings and cook it, stirring constantly, for 3 minutes. Stir in the water and cook the gravy over medium heat, stirring constantly, until it is smooth and bubbly. Adjust the seasonings if necessary. Return the liver and onions to the skillet and cook the mixture over low heat for 10 minutes.

Sift the remaining 1 cup flour, the baking powder, and the ½ teaspoon salt together into a mixing bowl. Add the beaten egg, the milk, and the remaining 2 tablespoons shortening and mix well. Drop the batter by teaspoonfuls into the gravy in the skillet. Cover and cook for

5 minutes. Turn the dumplings with a slotted spoon and cook them for another 5 minutes. Arrange the liver and dumplings in a deep serving dish and pour the gravy over them. Makes 4 servings.

Sister Lettie's Veal Loaf

3   *pounds ground veal*
1/2 *pound ground pork*
1   *cup fine cracker crumbs*
1   *large onion, chopped*
1   *teaspoon celery seeds*
   salt and pepper
3   *eggs*
1   *cup milk*
2–3 *strips bacon*
2   *tablespoons flour*
1   *cup chicken broth*
2   *tablespoons heavy cream*

Preheat the oven to 225° F.

Place the meats, cracker crumbs, onion, and celery seeds in a large bowl and add salt and pepper to taste. In a small bowl, beat the eggs and milk together. Add the mixture to the meat and mix until all of the ingredients are well blended. Shape the mixture into a loaf, place it in a flameproof baking dish, and lay the bacon strips on top. Bake the veal loaf for 2 hours, basting frequently with the pan juices.

Carefully transfer the loaf to a heated platter and keep it warm. Place the baking pan over medium heat, add the flour, and cook it, stirring constantly, until it begins to brown. Gradually add the chicken broth, stirring until

the gravy is smooth and thickened. Stir in the cream and heat the sauce through without allowing it to boil. Serve the sauce in a gravy boat as an accompaniment to the veal loaf. Makes 6 servings.

Rolf's Veal Shank

1/2 *cup olive oil*
1   *3 1/2–4 pound veal shank*
1   *tablespoon coarse salt*
   pepper
2   *cloves garlic, chopped fine*
4   *onions, quartered*
12 *carrots, peeled and cut in 2 pieces*
6   *celery stalks, chopped*
1   *bay leaf*
1/8 *teaspoon oregano*
2   *quarts water*
1   *teaspoon paprika*
8   *ounces tomato sauce*

Preheat oven to 375° F.

Pour the olive oil in a roasting pan. Place the veal shank in the pan. Rub the shank with salt, pepper, and chopped garlic. Add the onions, carrots, celery, bay leaf, and oregano. Pour in the water and sprinkle the shank with paprika.

Roast the veal shank for 1 1/2 hours, basting frequently. Remove the shank and the vegetables to a serving platter and keep them warm. Add the tomato sauce to the pan juices and whisk to incorporate. Serve the veal shank with the vegetables and sauce. Makes 2 servings.

Weiner Schnitzel

4   large veal chops
2   eggs
2   tablespoons fresh lemon juice
1   cup bread crumbs
2   tablespoons freshly grated Parmesan
      cheese
¼   teaspoon thyme
¼   teaspoon paprika
      salt and pepper
3   tablespoons butter
      lemon wedges
      parsley sprigs

Bone the chops and pound the veal until it is very thin. Beat the eggs with the lemon juice and set the mixture aside. Combine the bread crumbs, cheese, thyme, paprika, and salt and pepper to taste. Dip the veal in the egg mixture and then in crumbs, coating them evenly. Place the meat on a cookie sheet in one layer, cover it with wax paper, and refrigerate it for at least one hour.

In a heavy skillet melt the butter over medium-high heat, add the veal, and sauté the slices for 7 to 10 minutes, until they are lightly browned on both sides. Transfer them to a heated platter and garnish them with lemon wedges and parsley sprigs. Makes 4 servings.

German Meatballs with Anchovy-Caper Sauce

2   tablespoons butter
1½ cups chopped onion
2   pounds ground veal
¼   pound ground pork
1¼ cups herb-seasoned bread crumbs
1   teaspoon grated lemon peel
4   teaspoons anchovy paste
½   teaspoon Worcestershire sauce
¼   cup chopped parsley
2   eggs, lightly beaten
      salt and pepper
3   cups beef stock or broth
1   cup dry white wine
3   tablespoons cornstarch
¼   cup water
½   cup capers
      buttered spaetzle or noodles
      parsley sprigs

Heat the butter in a small skillet, add the onion, and cook it over medium heat until it is soft but not brown. Set the skillet aside.

Place the veal and pork in a large bowl with the bread crumbs, lemon peel, 3 teaspoons of the anchovy paste, Worcestershire sauce, chopped parsley, eggs, and salt and pepper to taste. Add the cooked onion and mix the ingredients well. Shape the mixture into 2-inch meatballs and set them aside.

In a large kettle bring the beef stock and wine to a boil. Using a slotted spoon, ease the meatballs one by one into the boiling liquid. Return the broth to a boil, reduce the heat, and simmer the meatballs, covered, for 20 minutes. Remove the meatballs from the liquid and keep them warm.

Skim the fat from the cooking liquid. Dissolve the cornstarch in the water and add the paste to the cooking liquid, stirring constantly. Simmer the sauce, stirring, until it thickens. Add the capers and the remaining 1 teaspoon anchovy paste. Return the meatballs to the kettle and bring the sauce to a simmer and cook, stirring constantly, for 5 minutes. Serve the meatballs and gravy with spaetzle or noodles. Makes 4–6 servings.

Veal with Artichokes and Mushrooms

1 *pound veal scallopine*
3 *tablespoons flour*
1 *teaspoon salt*
1 *teaspoon white pepper*
1 *egg*
2 *tablespoons water*
5 *tablespoons butter*
1 *tablespoon olive oil*
2 *packages frozen artichoke hearts, thawed and drained well*
½ *pound mushrooms, thinly sliced*
2 *tablespoons finely chopped scallion*
1 *tablespoon lemon juice*
1 *tablespoon finely chopped parsley*

Cut the scallopine into 8 half-portions, place them between two sheets of wax paper, and pound them to a thickness of about ¼ inch. Stir together the flour, salt, and white pepper and dredge the veal in the mixture. Lightly beat the egg with water and brush it on both sides of the cutlets.

In a large skillet heat 2 tablespoons of the butter with the olive oil and in it sauté the veal strips over medium-high heat for 2 minutes on each side. Transfer the browned cutlets to a heated platter and keep them warm.

In a Dutch oven, heat the remaining 3 tablespoons butter, add the artichokes, and sauté them for 2 minutes. Add the mushrooms and scallion and cook them for 5 minutes, stirring frequently. Add the lemon juice and parsley and cook for 2 minutes more. Spoon the vegetables and cooking liquid over the cutlets and serve immediately. Makes 4 servings.

Country Roast Leg of Lamb

1 *leg of lamb, 6–7 pounds*
2 *tablespoons unsalted butter*
8 *short stalks freshly cut rosemary, or ½ teaspoon dried rosemary*
½ *teaspoon salt*
¼ *teaspoon pepper*
1 *tablespoon flour*

Preheat the oven to 250° F.

Wipe the leg of lamb well, remove the excess fat, and cut shallow slits across the leg. Melt the butter in a small saucepan or skillet, gather the fresh rosemary into a bunch, dip it into the butter, and brush butter over the entire surface of the lamb. If using dried rosemary, spread the butter over the lamb with a pastry brush. Season the meat with the salt and pepper and dredge it lightly in the flour. Place it on a rack in a baking pan, spread the fresh or dried rosemary on top, and roast the meat for 3 hours, basting frequently with the pan juices or extra melted butter. Makes 8–10 servings.

Lamb Paprika in Sour Cream Sauce

¼ cup flour
1 teaspoon paprika
  salt and pepper
1½ pounds boneless lamb, cubed
3 tablespoons vegetable oil
1 cup chopped onions
1 cup sliced celery
1 clove garlic, minced
1½ cups water
2 tablespoons horseradish
1 teaspoon caraway seeds
¼ pound mushrooms, sliced
⅔ cup sour cream
  buttered noodles or rice

In a large paper or plastic bag combine the flour and paprika and salt and pepper to taste. Place the lamb cubes in the bag, a few at a time, and shake until they are well coated with flour.

Heat the oil in a large heavy skillet and add the lamb cubes. Cook the meat over medium-high heat until it is browned on all sides. Remove the lamb from the skillet and set it aside. Place the onions, celery, and garlic in the same skillet, adding more oil if necessary. Sauté the vegetables over medium heat, stirring occasionally, until they are soft but not brown. Return the lamb to the skillet and add the water, horseradish, and caraway seeds, stirring gently to combine. Simmer the lamb for 45 minutes, or until it is tender, adding more water if necessary. Add the mushrooms to the skillet during the last 5 minutes of cooking time. Just before serving, stir in the sour cream and heat it through without allowing it to come to a simmer. Correct the seasoning, if necessary, and serve the lamb paprika over the noodles or rice. Makes 4–6 servings.

Tongue with Raisin Cranberry Sauce

1 pork tongue (about 3½ pounds)
1½ teaspoons minced onion
3 tablespoons butter
3 tablespoons flour
1½ cups chicken stock or broth
2 tablespoons raisins
⅓ cup Cranberry Sauce
1 bay leaf, crumbled

Place the tongue in a kettle with boiling water to cover and simmer it, covered, for 3 hours. Remove the kettle from the heat and let the tongue cool in the cooking liquid. Drain the tongue, remove the skin and fat, and cut the meat into slices about ⅜ inch thick.

In a heavy skillet cook the onion in the butter over medium heat until it is transparent. Sprinkle the flour into the skillet, blending it thoroughly into the butter and onion. Add the stock, a little at a time, and cook the gravy, stirring, until it thickens. Place the sliced tongue in the skillet and spoon the gravy over it. Add the raisins, cranberry sauce, and bay leaf. Simmer the meat and sauce, covered, for 30 minutes. Makes 6 servings.

SAUCES, RELISHES AND DRESSINGS

*P*ENNSYLVANIA Dutch cooks are renowned for *siesses und saueres*, sweets and sours. Sour sauces and tart fruit relishes are elements of earlier continental German cookery, but pickles and relishes prepared with sugar are a more recent, and more American, culinary development—the result of the general availability of cheap white sugar and the influence on German American cooks of the sweet relishes and preserves favored here by Anglo-American neighbors.

Düsseldorf Mustard

1   *cup chopped onion*
2   *cloves garlic*
2   *cups dry white wine*
½   *cup dry mustard*
2   *tablespoons honey*
1   *tablespoon vegetable oil*
2   *teaspoons salt*
¼   *teaspoon hot pepper sauce, or to taste*

Put the onion and garlic in a food processor or blender and purée them until smooth. Scrape the purée into a small saucepan, set it over medium heat, and gradually add the wine, stirring constantly. Bring the mixture to a boil, lower the heat, and simmer the sauce for 5 minutes, stirring often.

Put the dry mustard in a 2-cup measure, add about ½ cup of the wine mixture, and stir to blend well. Slowly pour the mustard mixture into the saucepan, beating constantly with a whisk until the sauce is very smooth. Gradually add the honey and then the oil, stirring until the mustard thickens. Stir in the salt and hot pepper sauce and cook the mustard, stirring often, until it reaches the desired consistency. Taste the mustard and add more salt or hot pepper sauce if desired. Let the Düsseldorf mustard cool, scrape it into a jar, and cover it tightly. Chill it for at least 2 days before serving. Makes 2 cups mustard.

Catsup

1 *cup white vinegar*
1½ *teaspoons cloves*
1 *teaspoon celery seeds*
3 *cinnamon sticks, broken in half*
8 *pounds vine-ripened tomatoes (about 25 medium-size tomatoes), washed, trimmed, and quartered*
2 *tablespoons grated onion*
½ *teaspoon cayenne*
⅔ *cup sugar*
4 *teaspoons dry mustard*
4 *teaspoons salt*

Pour the vinegar into a small saucepan; add the cloves, celery seeds, and cinnamon. Cover the saucepan, bring the vinegar to a boil, and turn off the heat. Let the spiced vinegar steep for at least 1 hour.

In a large enameled saucepan mash the tomatoes coarsely with a potato masher or the back of a wooden spoon. Stir in the onion and cayenne and bring the mixture to a boil. Lower the heat to medium and cook the tomatoes for 15 minutes, stirring often. Transfer the mixture to a food processor or blender and run the motor just until the tomatoes are puréed. Rinse out the saucepan to remove any seeds and skin and strain the tomato mixture through a sieve into the saucepan, pressing the mixture with the back of a wooden spoon to extract all of the juice. Stir the sugar and the dry mustard into the tomato purée. Cook the catsup over medium heat, stirring often, for 50 to 60 minutes, or until it is reduced by half.

Pour the spiced vinegar through a fine sieve into the saucepan. Stir in the salt and simmer the catsup, stirring often, for 30 minutes longer, or until it has reached the desired consistency. Taste the catsup and add more salt or sugar if desired. Pour the catsup into hot, sterilized jars and seal the jars immediately. Makes 2 pints catsup.

Apple Chutney

½ *stick (¼ cup) butter*
1 *medium-size onion, chopped*
1 *pound tart cooking apples*
⅔ *cup firmly packed brown sugar*
¼ *cup water*
¼ *cup vinegar*
½ *cup raisins*
¼ *cup diced green pepper*
¼ *cup diced sweet red pepper*
½ *teaspoon dry mustard*
½ *teaspoon salt*
⅛ *teaspoon hot pepper sauce*
½ *teaspoon ginger*
½ *teaspoon allspice*

In a 3-quart saucepan melt the butter over medium heat. Add the onion and cook it, stirring often, for 8 to 10 minutes, until it is soft but not browned.

Core, peel, and dice the apples. Add them to the skillet and cook them over medium heat for 15 minutes. Sprinkle the brown sugar over the apples, a little at a time, stirring until it is almost dissolved. Pour in the water and the vinegar, stir them in, and bring the cooking liquid to a simmer.

Stir the raisins, peppers, and mustard over the apples and season the chutney with the salt and hot pepper sauce. Add the ginger and allspice and stir to distribute the seasonings.

Bring the cooking liquid to a boil, stirring often. Reduce the heat to low and simmer the chutney, stirring often, for about 50 minutes, or until it has thickened and the apples are soft. Cool the chutney and store it in the refrigerator.

Serve the chutney with beef, lamb, or pork. Makes about 2¼ cups chutney.

Homemade Mustard

¼ cup dry mustard
1 tablespoon sugar
½ teaspoon salt
¼ cup white wine vinegar
⅓ cup dry white wine
3 egg yolks

In the top of a double boiler over medium heat, stir together the dry mustard, sugar, and salt. Slowly add the wine vinegar and the wine, whisking constantly, and let the mixture stand at room temperature for 2 hours.

In a bowl beat the egg yolks until they are creamy. Pour them into the mustard mixture and stir the mixture over hot but not boiling water. Cook, stirring often, for 10 minutes, or until the mustard has thickened to the desired consistency. Scrape the mustard into a jar, cover it tightly, and store it in the refrigerator. It will keep for up to a month. Makes 1 cup.

Cranberry-Orange Chutney

2 cups water
4 cups (1 pound) cranberries
4 medium-size oranges
½ cup orange juice
2 cups sugar
¾ cup raisins
¼ cup crystallized ginger, minced
¾ teaspoon curry powder
⅛ teaspoon hot pepper sauce, or to taste
1 cinnamon stick

In a large saucepan bring the water to a boil. Add the cranberries and simmer them for 5 minutes, or until they burst.

Peel the oranges, reserving the rind, and remove the white membrane. Cut the oranges crosswise into ¼-inch slices and quarter the slices. Cut the rind into thin slivers to measure about ¼ cup. Set the orange sections and rind aside.

Add the orange juice, sugar, and raisins to the cranberries and stir the mixture over medium heat until the sugar is dissolved. Add the ginger, curry powder, and hot pepper sauce and stir to distribute the seasonings. Stir in the cinnamon stick, orange sections, and orange rind and simmer the chutney for 15 minutes, or until the liquid is reduced and the mixture is about the consistency of pickle relish.

Serve the chutney, hot or cold, with poultry, game, or pork. The chutney can be stored, covered and refrigerated, for 6 weeks. Makes 5–6 cups chutney.

Sautéed Apple Slices

¾   *cup granulated sugar*
½   *cup brown sugar, firmly packed*
1   *teaspoon cinnamon*
12   *cooking apples*
½   *cup (1 stick) butter*

In a large mixing bowl combine the granulated sugar, brown sugar, and cinnamon.

Core, peel, and slice the apples. Stir them with the sugar and cinnamon until they are well coated.

In a large heavy skillet melt the butter over medium heat. Add the apples and the sugar-cinnamon mixture and stir well to coat the apples with melted butter. Cover the skillet and cook the mixture over medium heat, stirring occasionally, for 15 minutes. Uncover the skillet, increase the heat to medium-high, and cook the apples for another 5 minutes.

Serve the sautéed apples with pork, ham, scrapple, or poultry. Makes 12 condiment servings.

Baked Apple Slices

1   *10-ounce jar red currant jelly*
⅓   *cup sugar*
⅔   *cup water*
⅓   *cup lemon juice*
1   *teaspoon cinnamon*
¼   *teaspoon nutmeg*
⅛   *teaspoon ground cloves*
5   *pounds tart apples*

Preheat the oven to 350° F.

In a saucepan combine the jelly, sugar, and water. Cook the mixture over medium heat, stirring often, until the jelly is melted. Turn off the heat and stir in the lemon juice, cinnamon, nutmeg, and cloves. Set the mixture aside.

Core and peel the apples and slice them into a baking dish. Pour the jelly mixture over them and loosely cover the baking dish with foil. Bake the apples for 1¼ hours, or until they are soft.

Serve the apples, hot or chilled, as an accompaniment to pork, ham, fish, or chicken. Makes 8–10 condiment servings.

Shaker Applesauce

2   *pounds very tart green cooking apples*
2   *cups plus 2 tablespoons sweet cider*
2   *tablespoons cinnamon*
½   *teaspoon nutmeg*

Core and peel the apples and slice them into a saucepan. Add the cider and bring it to a simmer over medium heat. Stir in the cinnamon and nutmeg and cook the apples for 10 to 15 minutes, or until they are tender but not mushy. With a slotted spoon transfer the apple slices to a food processor or blender, reserving the cooking liquid. Process or blend the apples until they are puréed and scrape the purée into a serving dish.

Reduce the pan liquid over medium-high heat until it is very thick and syrupy; pour it over the apple purée and refrigerate the applesauce. Makes 4 cups applesauce.

Pennsylvania Dutch-Style Sautéed Peaches

6   *large ripe peaches*
¼   *cup (½ stick) butter*
½   *cup dark brown sugar*
1   *teaspoon lemon juice*

Peel, stone, and slice the peaches.

In a heavy skillet melt the butter over low heat. Add the brown sugar and lemon juice and stir the syrup over low heat until the sugar is melted. Spread the peach slices in the skillet, spoon some syrup over them, and cook them for about 15 minutes, turning once or twice, until they are tender but not mushy.

Serve the sautéed peaches, warm or chilled, with meat or fish, or spoon them over peach or vanilla ice cream. Makes 12 condiment servings.

Pear Relish

½   *cup vinegar*
1   *cup water*
1   *cup brown sugar*
4   *pounds ripe pears*
2   *large onions, chopped*
1½   *cups raisins*
1   *teaspoon nutmeg*
½   *teaspoon cloves*
1   *cinnamon stick*

In an enameled cooking pot stir together the vinegar, water, and brown sugar.

Halve the pears and remove the cores; peel the pears and chop them coarsely. Put the chopped pears into the cooking pot, add the onions and raisins, and stir in the nutmeg and cloves. Drop in the cinnamon stick and bring the liquid almost to a boil. Lower the heat and cook the relish, stirring frequently, until it reaches the consistency of applesauce.

Serve the pear relish, hot or chilled, with ham, pork, or poultry. Makes about 2 pints.

Turnip Relish

1   *cup coarsely grated turnip*
1   *cup coarsely grated white onion*
2   *tablespoons horseradish*
1   *clove garlic, minced*
⅓   *cup white wine vinegar*
¼   *teaspoon salt*
⅛   *teaspoon white pepper*
1   *teaspoon sugar*

In a saucepan combine the turnip, onion, horseradish, garlic, and vinegar. Bring the mixture to a boil and immediately reduce the heat to low. Add the salt, pepper, and sugar and cook the relish, stirring often, for 20 minutes.

Taste the mixture and add more salt, pepper, or sugar, if desired. Cook the relish for 5 minutes longer, transfer it to a serving dish, and chill it for at least 24 hours.

Serve the relish with cold meats or broiled fish. Makes about 2 cups relish.

Red Pepper Relish

2 *sweet red peppers, diced*
2 *green peppers, diced*
1 *onion, minced*
½ *cup vinegar*
¼ *cup sugar*
½ *teaspoon salt*
⅛ *teaspoon crushed red pepper*
1 *bay leaf*

Combine all of the ingredients in a saucepan. Cook the relish over medium heat, stirring occasionally, until it comes to a boil. Reduce the heat to low, cover the pan, and simmer the relish for 30 minutes, stirring occasionally. Remove the bay leaf, turn the relish into a serving dish, and chill it for 8 hours or overnight.

Serve the relish with beef, chicken, turkey, or broiled fish. Makes about 1½ cups relish.

Bread-and-Butter Pickles

4 *quarts medium-size cucumbers,*
  sliced
5 *large onions, sliced*
3 *large green peppers, sliced*
3 *cloves garlic, slightly crushed*
½ *cup kosher or pickling salt*
2 *quarts cracked ice*
5 *cups sugar*
5 *cups vinegar*
1½ *tablespoons ground cloves*
2 *tablespoons mustard seed*
2 *teaspoons celery seeds*

In a large enameled pot with a tight lid, combine the cucumbers, onions, peppers, garlic, salt, and ice. Let the mixture stand, covered, at room temperature for 3 hours.

Put the sugar, vinegar, cloves, mustard seeds, and celery seeds into a saucepan. Bring the vinegar to a boil, reduce the heat, and simmer the mixture, stirring, until the sugar is dissolved.

Drain off all of the liquid from the cucumbers, onions, and peppers and remove the garlic cloves. Pour the vinegar mixture over the vegetables, set the cooking pot over medium-high heat, and return the liquid almost to a boil. Turn off the heat.

Pack the vegetables into six hot, sterilized jars, leaving ½ inch headspace. Fill each jar to within ¼ inch of the top with cooking liquid. Seal the jars and process them in a hot-water bath for 20 minutes. Makes 6 pints pickles.

Sweet Pickles

25–30 *medium-size cucumbers, thinly sliced*
8 *large onions, chopped*
2 *large green peppers, chopped*
½ *cup kosher or pickling salt*
5 *cups cider vinegar*
5 *cups sugar*
2 *tablespoons mustard seeds*
1 *teaspoon turmeric*
½ *teaspoon ground cloves*

In a large bowl combine the cucumbers, onions, green peppers, and salt; let the mixture stand at room temperature for 3 hours. Drain off all the liquid.

In a large enameled pot combine the vinegar, sugar, mustard seeds, turmeric, and cloves. Bring the vinegar to a boil, lower the heat, and stir in the drained vegetables. Heat the vegetables thoroughly, but do not let the liquid come to a boil. Pack the mixture into hot, sterilized jars, leaving ¼ inch headspace. Seal the jars and process them in a hot-water bath for 20 minutes.

Dill Pickles

4   *pounds 4- to 5-inch cucumbers*
8   *tablespoons dill seed*
4   *teaspoons caraway seed*
2   *teaspoons minced garlic*
1   *teaspoon crushed red pepper*
2   *quarts water*
2   *cups vinegar*
½   *cup kosher or pickling salt*
¼   *teaspoon alum (available at most drugstores)*

Pack the cucumbers into four hot, sterilized quart jars, leaving ½ inch headroom. To each jar add 2 tablespoons dill seed, 1 teaspoon caraway seed, ½ teaspoon garlic, and ¼ teaspoon crushed pepper. In a large saucepan combine the water, vinegar, salt, and alum; bring the mixture to a boil and pour it into the jars so that it covers the cucumbers, allowing ¼ inch headspace. Seal the jars and process them in a boiling-water bath for 15 minutes. Let them stand at least 8 weeks. Makes 4 quarts pickles.

Green Tomato Relish

12   *green tomatoes, coarsely chopped*
 6   *medium-size onions, coarsely chopped*
 6   *green peppers, coarsely chopped*
 1   *small hot pepper, minced*
½   *cup kosher or pickling salt*
 1   *quart vinegar*
 3   *cups sugar*
 1   *tablespoon turmeric*
1¼   *tablespoons pickling spices*

In a large bowl combine the tomatoes, onions, green pepper, hot pepper, and salt. Barely cover the vegetables with water and let them stand at room temperature for 8 hours or overnight.

Turn the vegetables into a sieve, rinse them under running water, and let them drain for 5 minutes.

In a large enameled cooking pot bring the vinegar to a boil; reduce the heat to medium, add the sugar, and simmer the mixture, stirring constantly, until the sugar is dissolved. Stir in the turmeric and pickling spices. Add the vegetables to the pot and return the liquid to a boil. Turn off the heat and pack the mixture into six hot, sterilized pint jars, leaving ¼ inch headspace. Seal the jars and process them in a hot-water bath for 20 minutes. Makes 6 pints relish.

Watermelon Rind Pickles

6 *cups cubed and peeled watermelon*
   rind
2 *quarts water*
¼ *cup plus 2 teaspoons kosher or pickling*
   salt
2 *cups vinegar*
2 *cups sugar*
1 *tablespoon cloves*
3 *cinnamon sticks*

Put the watermelon rind in a large enameled or stainless steel cooking pot; add 1 quart of the water, or more if necessary, to cover the rind, and pour in the ¼ cup salt. Cover the pot and let the mixture stand at room temperature for 8 hours or overnight. Pour off the liquid, rinse the watermelon rind well, and drain it. Sprinkle the remaining 2 teaspoons salt over the rind and pour the remaining 1 quart water over it. Bring the water to a boil, reduce the heat, and simmer the watermelon rind for 15 to 20 minutes, or until it is just tender.

In a saucepan combine the vinegar, sugar, and cloves. Bring the vinegar to a boil, lower the heat, and simmer the mixture for 12 to 15 minutes.

Drain the watermelon rind, return it to the cooking pot, and pour the hot vinegar mixture over it. Cook the rind in the vinegar for 3 to 5 minutes, or until it is translucent.

With a slotted spoon remove the chunks of rind from the cooking liquid and pack them in three hot, sterilized pint jars, leaving ½ inch headroom. Add 1 cinnamon stick to each jar and ladle in enough boiling syrup to cover the rind, but leave ¼ inch headroom. Seal the jars immediately and process them for 10 minutes in a boiling-water bath. Makes 3 pints pickles.

Pickled Okra

7 *cloves garlic*
7 *fresh dill sprigs*
7 *small hot peppers*
3 *pounds small okra*
1 *quart distilled white vinegar*
1 *cup water*
½ *teaspoon kosher or pickling salt*

Place 1 garlic clove, 1 dill sprig, and 1 hot pepper in the bottom of each of seven hot, sterilized pint jars. Pack the jars with okra, leaving ½ inch headroom.

In a saucepan bring the vinegar and water to a boil. Add the salt, lower the heat, and simmer the liquid for 5 minutes; pour the hot mixture into the jars to cover the okra, but leave ¼ inch headroom. Seal the jars with warm, sterilized lids and process them in a boiling-water bath for 30 minutes. Makes 7 pints pickles.

Dill Sauce

1   *tablespoon butter*
3   *tablespoons snipped fresh dill*
1   *tablespoon flour*
1   *cup beef stock or broth*
    Juice of ½ lemon
½ *cup sour cream*
    Salt

In a saucepan melt the butter over medium heat. Add 1 tablespoon of the dill and sauté it for 2 to 3 minutes until it is limp. Add the flour and cook the roux, stirring constantly, for 3 to 4 minutes, taking care not to let it brown. Pour in the stock all at once and bring the sauce to a boil, stirring constantly. Add the lemon juice, lower the heat, and simmer the sauce for 5 minutes. Stir in the remaining dill and the sour cream and heat the mixture through, but do not let it boil. Taste the sauce and add salt, if desired.

Serve the dill sauce with steamed vegetables. Makes 1½ cups sauce.

Caper Sauce

2 tablespoons butter
¼ cup chopped onions
4 tablespoons flour
2 cups chicken broth
¼ cup chopped capers
1 tablespoon chopped parsley

In a saucepan melt the butter, add the onions, and sauté them until they are soft and golden, about 8 minutes. Stir in the flour and cook the roux for 5 minutes, taking care not to let it brown. Add the broth and cook the sauce, whisking constantly, for about 5 minutes, or until it is smooth and bubbly. Stir in the capers and parsley and cook the mixture, stirring, for 3 minutes more.

Serve the caper sauce with broiled or poached fish or shellfish. Makes about 2 cups sauce.

Barbecue Dipping Sauce

¾ cup vinegar
¾ cup catsup
¼ teaspoon crushed red pepper, or to taste
1 tablespoon brown sugar
¼ cup water
salt and pepper

In a saucepan combine all of the ingredients and bring the mixture to a simmer. Cook the sauce, stirring often, until the sugar is dissolved.

Serve the sauce, chilled or at room temperature, with beef or spareribs. Makes about 1¾ cups sauce.

Anchovy Mayonnaise

1 teaspoon lemon juice
1 teaspoon Dijon mustard
1 egg yolk
1 cup olive oil
2 tablespoons anchovy paste
salt and pepper

In a bowl combine the lemon juice and mustard. Add the egg yolk and beat the mixture with a whisk until it is smooth. Pour in the oil in a thin stream, whisking constantly until the sauce is creamy. Stir in the anchovy paste and season it to taste with salt and pepper.

Serve the sauce with cold meats or seafood. Makes about 1½ cups mayonnaise.

Mustard Sauce

2   egg yolks
2   tablespoons Dijon mustard
1   teaspoon dry mustard
1   teaspoon salt
⅛   teaspoon cayenne, or to taste
2   teaspoons tarragon vinegar
¾   cup vegetable oil
1   tablespoon sour cream
3   tablespoons heavy cream
1   tablespoon finely chopped shallots or
     scallions

In a mixing bowl, combine the egg yolks with
the Dijon mustard. Stir in the dry mustard,
salt, and cayenne and beat the sauce with a
whisk until it is very thick. Add the vinegar, a
little at a time, beating well after each addition.
Pour the oil into the sauce in a thin stream,
whisking constantly. Stir in the sour cream and
heavy cream. Fold the shallots or scallions into
the sauce.

Serve the mustard sauce with asparagus or
other green vegetables. Makes 2 cups sauce.

Horseradish Sauce

1   day-old white roll
2   cups chicken broth
1   tablespoon butter
2   tablespoons horseradish
½   cup heavy cream
     salt and pepper

Halve the roll crosswise and with a fork
separate the soft center from the crust. Break
the soft part of the roll into small chunks. Put
the bread chunks in a saucepan, add the
chicken broth, and cook the mixture over low
heat until it comes to a simmer. With a whisk,
beat the sauce until the chunks of bread are
dissolved. Add the butter, horseradish, and
cream and whisk the sauce vigorously until it is
creamy, taking care not to let it boil. Taste the
sauce and season it with salt and pepper. Serve
the horseradish sauce with boiled beef or
poached fish. Makes 2 cups sauce.

Green Tomato Mincemeat

2   cups green tomatoes, chopped
2   cups peeled and chopped apples
½   cup raisins or dried currants
1   cup brown sugar, firmly packed
1   tablespoon butter
3   tablespoons vinegar
1   teaspoon cinnamon
¼   teaspoon nutmeg
¼   teaspoon ground cloves
½   teaspoon salt
½   cup chopped pecans or walnuts

Combine all of the ingredients in a large
enameled saucepan. Bring the mixture to a
boil, lower the heat, and simmer it gently for
25 minutes, stirring often and adding water if
necessary. Transfer the relish to a bowl and
refrigerate it, covered, for 8 hours or
overnight.

Serve the relish with cold meats or broiled
fish. Makes about 2½ cups relish.

BREADS

B READ—whether it's made from wheat, rye, corn or barley flour—is really basic to German (and of course German American) cooking. To people of German descent everywhere bread is considered to be truly "the staff of life," imbued with religious significance and figuring prominently in folklore and legend. And for all American pioneer settlers from everywhere, bread was a mainstay of the family diet and the hearth—a brick oven heated by a log fire—was an essential piece of kitchen equipment in every home.

Though we begin with basic breads, German American baked delights include rolls, pretzels, biscuits and coffee cakes—sweet breads satisfying enough to conclude any meal of the day, any day.

Amish Rye Bread

1 package active dry yeast
1 tablespoon sugar
4¼ cups warm water
3 cups sifted rye flour
2 tablespoons salt
3 tablespoons caraway seeds
1 tablespoon melted shortening
9 cups all-purpose flour

Dissolve the yeast and the sugar in ¼ cup of the warm water and let the mixture stand in a warm place until it is frothy.

Pour the remaining 4 cups water into a large bowl. Stir in the rye flour, salt, caraway seeds, shortening, and yeast mixture and combine the ingredients until the sponge is the consistency of pancake batter. Let the sponge rise in the bowl in a warm place for 1 hour and 30 minutes, or until bubbles form on the surface.

Butter and flour two 8½- x 4½- x 2½-inch loaf pans.

Preheat the oven to 375° F.

Turn the sponge out onto a lightly floured surface and knead in enough of the all-purpose flour to make a firm dough. Knead the dough for 10 minutes more. Shape the dough into two loaves, put the loaves in the pans, and let them rise, loosely covered with cloth towels, until they are double in bulk. Bake the bread for 1 hour. Makes 2 loaves.

Rye Bread

1½ cups water
1 cup milk
2 tablespoons shortening
2 tablespoons dark brown sugar
2 teaspoons salt
2 packages active dry yeast
3 cups rye flour
3 cups sifted all-purpose flour

In a small saucepan bring 1 cup of the water to a boil; turn off the heat and stir in the milk. In a large bowl cream the shortening with the brown sugar and salt until the mixture is smooth. Add the water and milk, stir the mixture well, and let it cool to lukewarm.

In a small bowl combine ½ cup lukewarm water with the yeast and let the mixture rest for 5 minutes. Sift the rye flour into a large bowl and stir in the yeast mixture. Add the brown sugar mixture, a little at a time, to the flour mixture, stirring after each addition. Stir in enough of the all-purpose flour to make the dough manageable.

Turn the dough out onto a lightly floured surface and knead it for 1 or 2 minutes. Let it rest for 10 minutes and knead it again for 10 minutes, adding the remaining all-purpose flour as necessary. The dough will be sticky. Put the dough in a buttered bowl, cover it loosely with a cloth towel, and let it rise in a warm place for 1 hour to 1½ hours, or until it is almost double in bulk.

Butter two 8½- x 4½- x 2½-inch loaf pans.

Return the dough to the floured surface, punch it down, and shape it into two loaves.

Put the loaves in the pans, cover them loosely with cloth towels, and let the dough rise again until it is double in bulk.

Preheat the oven to 375° F. Bake the bread for 45 to 50 minutes. Turn the loaves out of the pans and let cool on racks. Makes 2 loaves.

Saffron Breads

3 1-gram packets saffron
1½ cups warm water
1 packet active dry yeast
½ cup scalded milk
¼ cup sugar
1 teaspoon salt
¼ cup butter
6 cups sifted all-purpose flour
1 teaspoon cardamom
½ cup finely chopped blanched almonds
½ cup raisins
   almonds and raisins to decorate
1 egg, lightly beaten

Preheat the oven to 250° F.

On a baking sheet that is free from grease, dry the saffron in the oven and pound it with a mortar until fine. In a large bowl proof the yeast in the warm water. In a small bowl mix the milk, sugar, salt, saffron, and butter together, stirring until the sugar has dissolved and the butter is melted.

Add the milk mixture to the dissolved yeast and stir in 3 cups of the flour and the cardamom. Beat the dough with a wooden spoon until it is smooth. Add the additional flour, almonds, and raisins until you have a soft, somewhat sticky dough. Turn the dough out onto a lightly floured board and knead 8 to 10 minutes, or until the dough is smooth and elastic, add as little additional flour as possible.

Form the dough into a ball, place it in a large greased bowl, turning the dough to coat it. Cover the dough with a clean cloth and let it rise until it is double in bulk, about 1 hour.

Punch the dough down, turn it out onto a lightly floured board, and let it rest 5 minutes. Knead the dough lightly for 2 minutes and divide the dough in half. Shape one half of the dough into a large round loaf, the other half into many small buns. These can be decorated with dough, raisins, and almonds. Place the decorated breads on a greased baking sheet, cover them, and let rise until double in bulk.

Preheat the oven to 400° F. Brush the breads with the beaten egg and bake the large loaf for 35 to 40 minutes, the smaller loaves for 20 minutes, or until they sound hollow when rapped with your knuckles. Makes 1 large loaf and 8–10 smaller loaves.

Herb Bread

2   *envelopes active dry yeast*
2   *tablespoons sugar*
1/4   *cup warm water*
6   *cups all-purpose flour*
1/2   *cup rolled oats*
1/4   *cup bran*
1/4   *cup powdered milk*
1   *cup wheat germ*
1/2   *teaspoon salt*
2   *tablespoons grated onion*
1/4   *teaspoon celery seeds*
1/4   *teaspoon sage*
1   *tablespoon minced parsley*
1   *teaspoon oregano*
1/2   *teaspoon thyme*
1/2   *teaspoon marjoram*
1/4   *teaspoon pepper*
2   *cups hot water*
1/4   *cup melted butter*
1   *egg*

Dissolve the yeast and the sugar in the warm water and let the mixture rest for 5 minutes.

In a large bowl combine 2 cups of the flour with the oats, bran, powdered milk, wheat germ, salt, and grated onion. Stir in the celery seeds, all of the herbs, and the pepper. Pour the hot water, the melted butter, and the yeast mixture over the dry ingredients and beat the dough with an electric mixer at medium speed for 2 minutes. Add 1 more cup of the flour and the egg and beat the mixture at high speed for 1 minute more. With a wooden spoon stir in enough of the remaining flour to make a stiff dough.

Turn the dough out onto a lightly floured surface and knead it for 10 minutes, adding more of the flour as necessary, until the dough is smooth and elastic. Roll the dough into a ball, put it in a bowl, and cover it with a cloth towel. Let the dough rise in a warm place for 20 minutes, or until it is double in bulk. Return the dough to the floured surface, punch it down, and shape it into two loaves. Put the loaves into buttered loaf pans and let them rise for 1 to 2 hours, until they are double in bulk.

Preheat the oven to 400° F. and bake the bread for 20 to 30 minutes. Makes 2 loaves.

Medieval Beer Bread

3   envelopes active dry yeast
½   cup lukewarm water
1½ cups beer at room temperature
2   tablespoons sugar
2   teaspoons salt
1   egg, lightly beaten
½   cup whole wheat flour
5   cups unbleached flour
2   tablespoons milk

In a large bowl dissolve the yeast in the lukewarm water and let the mixture rest for 5 minutes. Stir in the beer, sugar, salt, and egg. Add the whole wheat flour and 4 cups of the unbleached flour and stir the mixture with a wooden spoon until it becomes a sticky dough.

Turn the dough out onto a floured surface and knead in the remaining 1 cup unbleached flour, a little at a time, until the dough is smooth and elastic. Knead the dough for about 10 minutes more, until blisters form on the surface or until the dough springs back when touched.

Place the dough in a lightly buttered bowl, turn it to coat it with butter, and cover it loosely with a cloth towel. Let the dough rise in a warm place for about 1 hour, or until it is double in bulk. Punch the dough down and divide it into two round loaves. Make four parallel slashes in the top of each loaf and let the dough rise in a warm place, covered loosely with towels, for 30 to 45 minutes.

Preheat the oven to 375° F. Brush the tops of the loaves with the milk and bake them for 30 minutes. Makes 2 round loaves.

Westphalian Ham Bread

2½ teaspoons active dry yeast
¾   cup warm water
    Pinch sugar
2   large eggs, lightly beaten
2   teaspoons fennel seeds
1   teaspoon salt
¾   cup whole wheat flour
2¾ cups all-purpose flour
2   tablespoons olive oil
1   cup minced onion
¾   pound thinly sliced Westphalian ham, diced
1   egg yolk
1   tablespoon cold water

In a large bowl dissolve the yeast in ¼ cup of the warm water with a pinch of sugar. Let the mixture stand for 15 minutes, or until it is foamy. Stir in the remaining ½ cup warm water, the 2 eggs, the fennel seeds, and the salt. Add the whole wheat flour, stirring it into the yeast mixture with a wooden spoon. Stir in enough all-purpose flour to make a soft dough.

Turn the dough out onto a floured surface and knead it for 10 minutes, or until it is smooth and elastic, adding more of the all-purpose flour, if necessary. Roll the dough into a large ball, put it in a buttered bowl, and turn it to coat it with butter. Let it rise in a warm place, loosely covered with a cloth towel, for 1 hour and 30 minutes, or until double in bulk.

In a small skillet heat the oil over medium heat. Add the onion and sauté it for about 10 minutes, or until it is tender and golden. With a slotted spoon transfer the onion to paper towels to drain and cool.

Return the dough to the floured surface and punch it down. Knead in the onion and the diced ham, shape the dough into a round loaf, and place it on a baking sheet. Let the dough rise again in a warm place for 30 to 45 minutes, or until it is double in bulk.

Preheat the oven to 350° F. Beat the egg yolk with the cold water until the mixture is smooth. Brush the egg wash over the top of the loaf and bake the bread for 35 minutes, or until it sounds hollow when tapped with the knuckles. Makes 1 loaf.

Whole Wheat Prune Bread

 2 *cups sifted all-purpose flour*
1½ *cups whole wheat flour*
 1 *teaspoon baking soda*
 ½ *teaspoon baking powder*
 1 *teaspoon salt*
 1 *egg*
 1 *cup sugar*
 1 *cup buttermilk*
 ½ *cup prune juice*
 2 *tablespoons shortening, melted*
 1 *cup cooked prunes, pitted, chopped, and drained*
 ¾ *cup chopped walnuts*

Preheat the oven to 350° F. and butter an 8½- x 4½- x 2½-inch loaf pan.

Into a large bowl sift together the all-purpose flour, whole wheat flour, baking soda, baking powder, and salt. In a separate bowl beat the egg until it is smooth. Stir in the sugar, buttermilk, prune juice, and melted shortening. Fold in the prunes and the nuts and turn the mixture into the dry ingredients, stirring just until the batter is evenly moistened. Pour the batter into the loaf pan and bake the bread for 1 hour and 20 minutes, or until the top of the loaf is browned and the sides have pulled away from the pan. Turn the bread out onto a rack and let it cool for 10 to 15 minutes before slicing. Makes 10–12 servings.

Black Walnut Bread

 3 *cups all-purpose flour*
4½ *teaspoons baking powder*
 ½ *cup sugar*
 1 *teaspoon salt*
 1 *cup chopped black walnuts*
 2 *eggs*
 1 *cup milk*
 ¼ *cup (½ stick) butter, melted*

Preheat the oven to 350° F. and butter an 8½- x 4½- x 2½-inch loaf pan.

Into a large bowl sift together the flour, baking powder, sugar, and salt. Stir in the nuts. In a separate bowl beat the eggs until they are smooth. Add the milk and the melted butter, stirring well to combine the ingredients. Add the mixture to the dry ingredients and stir the batter just until the flour is evenly moistened. (The batter will be lumpy.) Spoon the mixture into the loaf pan and bake the bread for 1 hour, or until it is lightly browned and a tester inserted in the center comes out dry. Turn the bread out onto a rack and let it cool for 10 to 15 minutes before serving. Makes 10–12 servings.

Whole Wheat Oatmeal Bread

2½ cups milk
¼ cup firmly packed brown sugar
¼ cup (½ stick) butter
2 teaspoons salt
2 cups all-purpose flour
4 cups whole wheat flour
2 packages active dry yeast dissolved in ¼
     cup warm water
1 cup old-fashioned or quick-cooking oats
2 tablespoons melted shortening

In a saucepan combine the milk, brown sugar, butter, and salt. Heat the mixture to lukewarm, but do not let it boil. Pour the mixture into a large bowl, add 1 cup of the all-purpose flour and 1 cup of the whole wheat flour and beat the mixture with an electric mixer or about 300 vigorous strokes with a wooden spoon. Add 1 more cup all-purpose flour, 1 more cup whole wheat flour, and the yeast mixture and beat the batter for 2 minutes more. Stir in the oats, the remaining whole wheat flour, and enough of the all-purpose flour to make a stiff dough.

Turn the dough out onto a lightly floured surface and knead it for 10 minutes, adding more of the all-purpose flour, if necessary, until it is smooth and elastic. Put the dough in a buttered bowl and brush it lightly with the melted shortening. Cover it loosely with a cloth towel and let it rise in a warm place for 1 hour, or until it is double in bulk.

Butter two 8½- x 4½- x 2½-inch loaf pans.

Return the dough to the floured surface, punch it down, and shape it into two loaves. Place the loaves in the pans and let them rise again for 1 hour, or until they are nearly double in bulk.

Preheat the oven to 400° F. and bake the loaves for 30 to 35 minutes, or until they are lightly browned. Makes 2 loaves.

Anadama Bread

1 package active dry yeast
½ cup warm water
2 cups water
½ cup light molasses
¼ cup (½ stick) butter
½ cup yellow cornmeal
5 cups unbleached flour
1½ teaspoons salt

Dissolve the yeast in the ½ cup warm water and let the mixture rest for 10 minutes.

In a saucepan combine the 2 cups water, the molasses, and the butter. Bring the water to a boil, add the cornmeal, and cook the mixture for 2½ minutes, stirring constantly. Remove the saucepan from the heat and let the mixture cool to 120° F.

In a large bowl combine 2 cups of the flour with the salt. Gradually add the cornmeal mixture, beating the batter with an electric mixer at low speed. Stir the yeast mixture, add it to the bowl, and beat the batter for 2 minutes at medium speed, or until it is thick. Stir in enough of the remaining flour to make a soft dough.

Turn the dough out onto a lightly floured surface and knead it for 10 minutes, adding more of the flour, if necessary, until the dough is smooth and elastic. Put the dough in a buttered bowl, turn it to butter the surface, and cover the bowl lightly with wax paper and a cloth towel. Let the dough rise in a warm place for 1 hour, or until it is double in bulk. Return it to the floured surface, punch it down, and divide it in half. Let the dough rest, covered with a cloth towel, for 10 to 15 minutes.

Butter two 9- x 5-inch loaf pans. Shape the dough into two loaves, put them in the pans, and let the dough rise again, covered with a damp cloth, for about 1 hour, or until it is double in bulk.

Preheat the oven to 400° F. Bake the bread for 30 to 40 minutes, until it is lightly browned. Let the loaves cool completely before slicing. Makes 2 loaves.

Pecan Bread

2½ *cups sifted all-purpose flour*
½ *cup sugar*
1 *teaspoon salt*
2 *teaspoons baking powder*
2 *cups pecans, chopped*
2 *eggs*
1 *cup milk*

Preheat the oven to 350° F. and butter an 8½- x 4½- x 2½-inch loaf pan.

Into a large bowl sift together the flour, sugar, salt, and baking powder. Stir in the pecans. In a separate bowl beat the eggs until they are smooth and thick. Stir in the milk and

add the mixture to the dry ingredients, stirring just until the batter is evenly moistened. Pour the batter into the loaf pan and bake the bread for 1 hour, or until it is well browned and a tester inserted in the center comes out clean. Turn the bread out onto a rack and let it cool. Makes 10–12 servings.

Almond Anise Bread

2½ *cups all-purpose flour*
2 *teaspoons baking powder*
½ *teaspoon salt*
½ *cup (1 stick) butter, softened and cut into small pieces*
1 *cup sugar*
5 *eggs*
¼ *teaspoon almond extract*
1 *teaspoon anise seed*
⅔ *cup toasted chopped almonds*

Preheat the oven to 350° F. and butter an 8½- x 4½- x 2½-inch loaf pan.

Into a large bowl sift together the flour, baking powder, and salt. In a separate bowl cream the butter and the sugar until the mixture is light. Add the eggs, one at a time, stirring after each addition until the mixture is well combined. Stir in the almond extract and add the dry ingredients, about ½ cup at a time, stirring just until they are moistened. Fold in the anise seed and the almonds and turn the batter into the loaf pan. Bake the bread for 1 hour, or until the top is lightly browned and a tested inserted in the center comes out clean. Makes 10–12 servings.

Anise Bread

1   package active dry yeast
¼   cup warm water
2   cups milk
¼   pound (1 stick) butter
6   tablespoons sugar
1   teaspoon salt
2   large eggs
8   cups all-purpose flour
2   tablespoons anise seeds
3   tablespoons sesame seeds (optional)

In a small dish dissolve the yeast in the warm water. Let the mixture stand for 5 minutes, or until it is foamy.

In a saucepan scald the milk. Pour the hot milk into a large bowl and add the butter, stirring until it is melted. Stir in the 6 tablespoons sugar and the salt. Let the mixture cool.

In two small bowls beat the eggs separately until they are smooth. Set them aside.

Stir 1 cup of the flour into the milk mixture. Add yeast and its liquid and stir in one of the beaten eggs and the anise seeds. Add enough of the remaining flour to form a stiff dough.

Turn the dough out onto a lightly floured surface and knead it for 8 to 10 minutes, until it is smooth and elastic, adding more of the flour, if necessary. Place the dough in a buttered bowl, cover it loosely with a cloth towel, and turn it to coat it with butter. Let it rise in a warm place for 1 hour and 30 minutes, or until it is double in bulk.

Return the dough to the floured surface, punch it down, and knead it again for about 2 minutes. Shape the dough into two braided loaves and put the loaves on a baking sheet, or form two 9-inch loaves and place them in two buttered 9- × -5-inch loaf pans. Brush the tops of the loaves with the remaining beaten egg and sprinkle them with the sesame seeds, if desired. Let the loaves rise for 30 to 45 minutes, or until they are double in bulk.

Preheat the oven to 350° F. and bake the loaves for 30 to 40 minutes, or until they are well browned. Makes 2 braided loaves.

Sweet Bread

1   package active dry yeast
¼   cup warm water
¾   cup milk
4   tablespoons (½ stick) butter
3   eggs
¾   cup plus 1 tablespoon cold water
½   teaspoon salt
½   cup sugar
7   cups all-purpose flour

In a large mixing bowl dissolve the yeast in the warm water and let the mixture rest until it is frothy. In a small saucepan scald the milk. Turn off the heat, add the butter, and stir it until it is melted. Pour the milk and melted butter into the yeast and let the mixture cool.

In another bowl beat two of the eggs until they are smooth. Add ¾ cup of the cold water, salt, and sugar and beat the mixture until it is well combined. Turn the egg mixture into the cooled yeast mixture and stir the batter until it is smooth. Add 5 cups of the flour and combine the dough until the flour is evenly moistened. Add more of the flour, a little at a time, until dough is smooth and manageable.

Turn the dough out onto a lightly floured surface and knead it until it is smooth and elastic. Roll it into a large ball and put it into a bowl. Loosely cover the dough with a cloth towel and let it rise for 1 hour and 30 minutes, or until it is double in bulk.

Preheat the oven to 350° F. Butter three bread pans and dust them with flour. Beat together the remaining egg and the remaining 1 tablespoon cold water; set the egg wash aside.

Return the dough to the floured surface, punch it down, and divide it into three parts. Form each portion into a loaf and place the loaves in the bread pans. Brush the tops of the loaves with the egg wash and bake them for 1 hour, or until they are golden brown. Makes 3 loaves.

Moravian Sugar Coffee Bread

  1   *package active dry yeast*
 1/3 *cup plus 1/2 teaspoon granulated sugar*
  1   *cup warm water*
  3   *cups sifted unbleached flour*
  2   *tablespoons powdered skim milk*
  3   *tablespoons powdered mashed potatoes, or 6 tablespoons potato flakes*
 3/4 *teaspoon salt*
  2   *large eggs at room temperature*
  1   *cup (2 sticks) butter, softened*
  1   *tablespoon light cream or half-and-half*
 2/3 *cup firmly packed brown sugar*
  1   *teaspoon cinnamon*

In a large bowl combine the yeast with 1/2 teaspoon of the granulated sugar and the water and let the mixture rest for 5 minutes, or until it is frothy and the yeast is dissolved. Stir in 2 cups of the flour, the powdered milk, the potatoes, and the salt. Add the eggs, the remaining 1/3 cup granulated sugar, and 1/2 cup (1 stick) of the butter and beat the mixture with an electric mixer at medium speed for 5 minutes. Add enough of the remaining flour, 1 tablespoon at a time, to make a soft, manageable dough. Loosely cover the bowl with a cloth towel and let the dough rise in a warm place for about 1 hour and 30 minutes, until it is double in bulk.

Turn the dough out onto a lightly floured surface, punch it down, and return it to the bowl. Let it rise in a warm place for about 45 minutes, until it is double in bulk.

Butter a 17- x 11- x 1-inch baking pan. Turn the dough into the pan and spread it evenly over the bottom. Loosely cover the pan with a cloth towel and let the dough rise again for 1 hour.

Preheat the oven to 375° F.

Melt the remaining 1/2 cup (1 stick) butter in a small saucepan and set it aside. Brush the dough with the cream or half-and-half. In a measuring cup combine the brown sugar with the cinnamon and sprinkle the mixture evenly over the dough. With one finger make shallow indentations in the dough 1 inch apart. Pour the melted butter over the dough and bake the sweet bread for 20 to 25 minutes. Makes 20 servings.

Graham Crescents

1⅓   *cups grated Swiss cheese*
¼   *cup plain yogurt*
2   *cups whole wheat flour*
2½   *teaspoons baking powder*
¼   *teaspoon salt*
3   *tablespoons butter*
¾   *cup plus 1½ teaspoons water*

Preheat the oven to 450° F. and grease a baking sheet.

To make the filling, combine ½ cup of the grated cheese with 3 tablespoons of yogurt in a small bowl. Set aside while making the dough.

In a large bowl combine the whole wheat flour, baking powder, and salt. Add ⅔ cup grated cheese and the butter and blend into the dry ingredients, with a pastry blender or your fingertips, until the mixture resembles a very coarse meal. Add ¾ cup water and stir with a fork until the ingredients are just mixed. On a lightly floured board, turn the dough out and knead for 2 or 3 turns.

Divide the dough into fourths. Roll out each piece into a 6-inch round and cut each round into four wedges. Place a teaspoon of the reserved cheese and yogurt filling near the wide rounded edge of each wedge. Roll up the dough from the filling side and pinch the pointed tips together to form a crescent.

Place the crescents about 2 inches apart on the baking sheet. In a small bowl combine the remaining yogurt with the 1½ teaspoons water and brush this mixture over the crescents. Sprinkle the crescents with the remaining cheese and bake them for 15 minutes. Serve the crescents warm. Makes 16 crescents.

Hard Rolls

1   *package active dry yeast*
1½   *cups warm water*
1   *tablespoon salt*
3½   *cups all-purpose flour*
¼   *cup cornmeal*
¼   *cup cold water*
4–5   *ice cubes*

In a large bowl dissolve the yeast in ¼ cup of the warm water and let it rest for 5 minutes.

Stir the remaining 1¼ cups warm water into the yeast mixture. Add the salt and 3 cups of the flour, stirring to moisten the flour evenly. Turn the dough out onto a lightly floured surface and knead it for 10 minutes, adding more flour as necessary, until it is smooth and elastic. Shape the dough into a large ball and put it in an *unbuttered* bowl, cover it loosely with a cloth towel, and let it rise in a warm place until it is double in bulk.

Return the dough to the floured surface and punch it down. Pull off pieces of dough slightly larger than golf balls and shape them into spheres, pinching any loose ends together at the bottom.

Sprinkle a baking sheet lightly with cornmeal and arrange the dough balls on it about 1 inch apart. Loosely cover them with a cloth towel and let them rise again until they double in bulk.

Preheat the oven to 450° F.

Brush the dough with the cold water and toss the ice cubes on the floor of the oven. Bake the rolls for 15 minutes, or until they are browned. Makes 18 rolls.

Variations: Just before baking brush the rolls with an egg white beaten with 1 tablespoon cold water and sprinkle them liberally with sesame seeds or poppy seeds. For Whole Wheat Hard Rolls, use ½ cup whole wheat flour in place of ½ cup of the white flour.

Sweet Potato Rolls

1   *large yam, peeled and cut into chunks*
1   *package active dry yeast*
1   *teaspoon salt*
3   *tablespoons sugar*
1   *tablespoon butter*
1   *cup milk*
4½ *cups sifted all-purpose flour*

In a saucepan cook the yam in water to cover for 15 to 20 minutes, or until it is tender. Drain it, reserving ¼ cup of the cooking water. Let the cooking broth cool, put it in a cup or a small dish, and dissolve the yeast in it.

Transfer the yam to a large bowl and mash it well. Beat in the salt, sugar, and butter.

In a saucepan heat the milk, skim off any skim that forms on the surface, and stir the milk into the yam mixture. Set the mixture aside, let it cool to lukewarm, and add the yeast and the liquid in which it was dissolved. Stir in the flour, 1 cup at a time, until the mixture becomes a dough that is dense enough to knead.

Turn the dough out onto a floured surface and knead it for 10 minutes, or until it is smooth and elastic. Put the dough in a buttered bowl and turn it to coat it with butter. Cover the bowl with a cloth towel and let the dough rise in a warm place for 1 hour, or until it is double in bulk.

Butter 20 muffin tins.

Return the dough to the floured surface and punch it down. Pull off pieces the size of golf balls and place one ball in each muffin tin. Set the muffin tins in a warm place and let the dough rise again, loosely covered with a cloth towel, for 30 minutes, or until it is double in bulk. Preheat the oven to 425° F. Bake the rolls for 13 to 15 minutes. Makes about 20 rolls.

Parker House Rolls

2 *cups milk*
4 *tablespoons (½ stick) butter*
3 *tablespoons sugar*
2 *teaspoons sugar*
2 *packets dry yeast*
4 *tablespoons warm water*
6 *cups all-purpose flour*
4 *tablespoons (½ stick) butter, melted*

In a saucepan over low heat beat the milk and add the butter, sugar, and salt. Stir until the butter is melted. Remove the pan from the heat. Dissolve the yeast in the warm water and stir it into the milk. Stir in the flour. Knead the dough until it is smooth and elastic. Cover the dough and let it rise until it is double in bulk. Punch down the dough and roll it into a rectangle ¼ inch thick.

Cut the dough into rounds with a large biscuit cutter. Brush the tops with melted butter. Make a crease across the center of each roll with the back of a knife. Fold the rolls over. Place the rolls on a baking sheet about one inch apart. Cover the bowl and let the rolls rise until they are double in bulk.

Preheat the oven to 400° F. Bake the rolls for 30 minutes. Makes 24 rolls.

Buttermilk Biscuits

2   cups all-purpose flour
1   teaspoon baking powder
¼   teaspoon baking soda
1   teaspoon salt
5   tablespoons shortening
¾   cup buttermilk

Preheat the oven to 450° F.

In a large bowl sift together the flour, baking powder, baking soda, and salt. Cut in the shortening until the mixture resembles coarse crumbs. Make a well in the center. Pour in the buttermilk and mix the dough with a fork until it holds together. Turn it out onto a floured surface and knead it about 10 times. Roll out the dough ½ inch thick and cut it into rounds with a floured 2-inch biscuit cutter. Arrange the rounds on an ungreased cookie sheet about 1 inch apart for crusty biscuits, or close together for softer biscuits, and bake the rounds for 12 to 15 minutes, or until they are golden brown. Transfer the biscuits to a plate and serve them at once. Makes 18 biscuits.

Sour Cream Biscuits

2   cups all-purpose flour
2   teaspoons baking powder
½   teaspoon baking soda
1   teaspoon salt
5   tablespoons butter
½   cup sour cream
½   cup milk
1   scallion, sliced (optional)

Preheat the oven to 375° F.

Sift the flour, baking powder, baking soda, and salt together into a large bowl. Cut in the butter until the mixture resembles coarse crumbs. In a separate bowl combine the sour cream and the milk. Add the scallion, if desired. Turn the sour cream mixture into the dry ingredients all at once, stirring just until the flour is evenly moistened. Turn the dough out onto a lightly floured surface and knead it 8 to 10 times, until it is smooth. Roll the dough out ½ inch thick and cut it into rounds with a floured 2½-inch biscuit cutter. Place the rounds on an ungreased baking sheet and bake them for 15 minutes, or until they are lightly browned. Transfer the biscuits to a plate and serve them at once. Makes 12 biscuits.

Potato Biscuits

½   cup hot milk
2   tablespoons shortening
2   tablespoons sugar
½   cup warm mashed potatoes
1   teaspoon salt
3¼ cups all-purpose flour
1   package active dry yeast
½   cup warm water

In a large bowl combine the milk, shortening, sugar, potatoes, salt, and ¼ cup of the flour. Let the mixture cool to lukewarm.

In a small dish dissolve the yeast in the warm water and let the mixture rest for 5 minutes.

Stir the yeast mixture into the potato mixture and beat the dough vigorously. Loosely cover the bowl with a cloth towel and let the dough rise in a warm place until it is light and bubbly. Stir the dough, add the remaining 3 cups flour, and combine the mixture well. Cover the bowl and let the dough rise again until it is double in bulk.

Turn the dough out onto a lightly floured surface and pat it out to a thickness of ¼ inch. Cut the dough into 2-inch rounds with a floured cutter and place the rounds about 1 inch apart on a buttered baking sheet. Cover the baking sheet with a cloth towel and let the dough rise for 30 minutes, or until it is almost double in bulk.

Preheat the oven to 425° F. and bake the biscuits for about 15 minutes, or until they are lightly browned. Makes about 15 biscuits.

Philadelphia Sticky Buns

1	*package active dry yeast*
¼	*cup lukewarm water*
1	*cup milk*
4½	*cups sifted all-purpose flour*
10	*tablespoons (1¼ sticks) butter, melted*
6	*tablespoons granulated sugar*
2	*egg yolks, well beaten*
1	*teaspoon salt*
	grated rind of 1 lemon
1	*teaspoon cinnamon*
½	*cup currants*
¾	*cup brown sugar*

In a large bowl dissolve the yeast in the lukewarm water and let the mixture rest for 5 minutes, until it is frothy.

In a saucepan scald the milk, remove it from the heat, and let it cool to lukewarm.

Pour the cooled milk into the yeast mixture, add 1½ cups of the flour, and beat the mixture vigorously until it is smooth. Loosely cover the bowl with a cloth towel and let it stand in a warm place until the mixture is light or until dimples appear on the surface. To the dough add 4 tablespoons of the melted butter, 4 tablespoons of the granulated sugar, the egg yolks, the salt, and the lemon rind. Combine the mixture well and stir in enough of the remaining flour to make a smooth dough. Knead the dough in the bowl until it is smooth and elastic. Cover the bowl with a cloth towel and let the dough rise in a warm place for several hours, until it is double in bulk.

Turn the dough out onto a lightly floured surface, punch it down, and roll it out into a ¾-inch-thick rectangle. (Because the dough will be elastic and will tend to spring back, this step will take time and patience.) Brush the surface of the dough with 2 tablespoons of the remaining melted butter and sprinkle it with the remaining 2 tablespoons granulated sugar, the cinnamon, and the currants. Roll dough up jelly-roll fashion and cut it in 1-inch-thick slices.

In a heavy skillet combine the brown sugar with the remaining 4 tablespoons melted butter, spreading the mixture over the bottom of the pan. Arrange the dough rolls on the brown sugar mixture, spacing them evenly, and let the dough rise again in a warm place until it is double in bulk.

Preheat the oven to 350° F. Bake the sticky buns in the skillet for 30 minutes, or until they are well browned. Invert the skillet over a rack to dislodge the buns and serve the buns while they are hot. Makes 12 buns.

Moravian Love Feast Buns

1 large potato, peeled and cut into 1-inch
   chunks
1 package active dry yeast
¼ cup warm water
½ cup (1 stick) butter, melted
1 cup sugar
1 teaspoon salt
2 eggs, well beaten
5 cups all-purpose flour
½ cup light cream, or ½ cup melted butter

Cook the potato in water to cover for 15 to 20 minutes, or until it is tender. Drain the potato, reserving ½ cup of the cooking liquid. Mash it until it is smooth and measure out ½ cup of mashed potato, setting the rest aside for another use.

Dissolve the yeast in the warm water and let the mixture rest until it is frothy.

In a large bowl combine the reserved ½ cup mashed potato with the reserved cooking liquid and the butter, sugar, salt, and eggs. Stir in the yeast and cover the bowl loosely with a cloth towel. Let the mixture rise in a warm place until it looks spongy. Add 4 cups of the flour and stir the mixture, adding more of the flour if necessary, until it becomes a soft, elastic dough. Loosely cover the dough with the towel and let it rise in a warm place until it is double in size.

Turn the dough out onto a lightly floured surface and punch it down. Knead the dough until it is smooth and elastic. Pull off 2-inch chunks of dough and pat them into buns about 3 inches in diameter. Arrange the buns on a buttered baking sheet, cover them with a cloth towel, and let them rise in a warm place until they are almost double in bulk.

Preheat the oven to 375° F. and bake the buns for 15 minutes, or until they begin to look browned. Brush the buns with the cream or melted butter and bake them for 10 to 15 minutes more. Let the buns cool for at least 20 minutes before serving. Makes 12 buns.

Hot Cross Buns

2 packages active dry yeast
¼ cup warm water
½ cup milk, scalded
½ cup (1 stick) butter
⅓ cup granulated sugar
1 teaspoon salt
½ teaspoon cinnamon
4 cups sifted all-purpose flour
3 eggs, beaten
1 cup raisins
1 cup chopped candied mixed fruits

½ cup melted butter
⅓ cup sifted confectioners' sugar
1 egg white, lightly beaten

Dissolve the yeast in the warm water in a small dish and let the mixture rest for 5 minutes.

In a large bowl combine the hot milk with the ½ cup butter and stir the butter until it is melted. Stir in the granulated sugar, salt, and cinnamon. Add 2 cups of the flour and beat the mixture until it is smooth. Stir in the yeast mixture, the beaten eggs, and enough of the remaining 2 cups flour to make a moderately stiff dough. Add the raisins and candied fruits, turn the dough out onto a lightly floured surface, and knead it for about 5 minutes, until it is satiny. Shape the dough into a large ball, put it in a buttered bowl, and turn it to coat it with butter. Loosely cover the dough with a cloth towel and let it rise in a warm place for 1 hour and 30 minutes.

Turn the dough out onto the floured surface, punch it down, and roll it out to a thickness of ½ inch. Cut the dough in rounds with a floured 2½-inch biscuit cutter and shape each round into a ball. Arrange the balls on a buttered baking sheet and brush them with the melted butter. With sharp scissors snip a deep cross in the top of each bun. Let the dough rise again for 1 hour, or until it is double in bulk.

Preheat the oven to 375° F. and bake the buns for 15 minutes.

In a small bowl combine the confectioners' sugar with enough of the beaten egg white to make a thick icing. Spoon the icing into a pastry tube and pipe crosses on top of the buns.

Serve the warm hot cross buns with butter. Makes 24 buns.

Soft Pretzels

1   *package active dry yeast*
1¼ *cups warm water*
1   *teaspoon sugar*
1   *teaspoon table salt*
5   *cups sifted all-purpose flour*
4   *cups cold water*
4   *teaspoons baking soda*
2   *tablespoons coarse salt*

In a large bowl dissolve the yeast in ¼ cup of the warm water; let the mixture rest for 5 minutes. Stir in the remaining 1 cup warm water, the sugar, and the table salt. Add 3 cups of the flour, a little at a time, and beat the mixture, adding more of the flour, until it becomes a stiff dough.

Turn the dough out onto a lightly floured surface and knead it, adding more flour as necessary, for 10 minutes, or until the dough is smooth and elastic. Shape the dough into a ball, put it in a buttered bowl, and turn it to coat it with butter. Cover the dough loosely with a cloth towel and let it rise in a warm place for 45 minutes, or until it is double in bulk.

Return the dough to the floured surface, punch it down, and shape it into long cylinders about half the desired thickness of the finished pretzels. Knot the dough into pretzel shapes, twisting the loose ends firmly together.

Preheat the oven to 475° F.

In a large kettle bring the 4 cups cold water to a boil and add the baking soda. Drop the pretzels into the water, two or three at a time, and boil them for 1 minute, or until they float to the surface. With a slotted spoon transfer the pretzels to cloth towels to drain.

Transfer the pretzels to buttered baking sheets, sprinkle them with the coarse salt, and bake them for 12 minutes, or until they are golden brown. Makes about 32 pretzels.

Hard Pretzels

1   *package active dry yeast*
1¼ *cups warm water*
    pinch sugar
2   *teaspoons table salt*
5   *cups all-purpose flour*
4   *cups cold water*
4   *teaspoons baking soda*
2   *tablespoons coarse salt*

Dissolve the yeast in ¼ cup of the warm water; let the mixture rest for 5 minutes.

In a large bowl combine the remaining 1 cup warm water, the sugar, and the salt. Stir in the yeast mixture. Add 4 cups of the flour, a little at a time, stirring, until the dough is stiff. Turn the dough out onto a lightly floured surface and knead it for 10 minutes, adding more of the flour, if necessary, until it is smooth and elastic. Roll the dough into a ball, loosely cover it with a cloth towel, and let it rise in a warm place for 1 hour to 1 hour and 30 minutes, until it is double in bulk.

Punch the dough down and roll it out into narrow panel about 18 inches long. Cut it into long strips and knot each strip loosely into a pretzel shape, twisting the loose ends firmly together.

Preheat the oven to 475° F.

In a large saucepan bring the cold water to a boil and add the baking soda. Drop the pretzels, three at a time, into the boiling water and cook them for 1 minute, or until they float to the surface. With a slotted spoon transfer the pretzels to a buttered pan. Repeat the procedure until all of the pretzels are cooked.

Sprinkle the pretzels with coarse salt and bake them for about 12 minutes, or until they are browned. Makes about 32 pretzels.

Cheese Pretzels

1   *package active dry yeast*
1½ *cups warm water*
1   *tablespoon sugar*
1   *teaspoon table salt*
2   *cups grated extra sharp Cheddar cheese*
4   *cups sifted all-purpose flour*
1   *egg, beaten*
2   *tablespoons coarse salt*

In a large bowl dissolve the yeast in ¼ cup of the warm water and let the mixture rest for 5 minutes. Stir in the sugar and table salt. Add the cheese and 3 cups of the flour, stirring and adding more of the flour until the mixture becomes a stiff dough. Turn the dough out onto a lightly floured surface and knead it, adding more of the flour as necessary, until it is smooth and elastic.

Preheat the oven to 425° F.

Pat the dough out into a rectangle about ¼ inch thick and cut it into 32 pieces. Roll each piece into a thin 7-inch rope and knot each rope into a pretzel shape. Transfer the pretzels to an unbuttered baking sheet, brush them with the beaten egg, and sprinkle them with the coarse salt. Bake the pretzels for 15 to 18 minutes, or until they are browned. Makes 32 pretzels.

Note: For thicker, chewier cheese pretzels, roll the dough into a ball after kneading, put it in a buttered bowl, and turn it to coat it with butter. Loosely cover the dough with a cloth towel and let it rise in a warm place until it is double in bulk. Punch the dough down, shape it into thick ropes, and knot the ropes into pretzel shapes. Allow the soft pretzels to rise, covered, for 20 minutes before baking as above.

Christmas Stollen

> 1 *cup milk*
> ½ *cup plus 2 tablespoons granulated sugar*
> ½ *teaspoon salt*
> 1 *package active dry yeast*
> ¼ *cup warm water*
> 5 *cups sifted all-purpose flour*
> ½ *cup finely chopped candied citron*
> ½ *cup finely chopped candied cherries*
> 1 *cup slivered almonds*
>   *grated rind of 1 lemon*
> 1 *cup seedless raisins*
> 2 *eggs, beaten*
> 1 *cup (2 sticks) butter, softened*
> ¼ *teaspoon nutmeg*
> ½ *teaspoon cinnamon*
> ⅔ *cup sifted confectioners' sugar*
> 2 *tablespoons hot water*

Pour the milk into a saucepan and heat it to scalding. Turn off the heat and stir in ½ cup of the granulated sugar and the salt. Let the mixture cool to lukewarm.

In a large bowl dissolve the yeast in the ¼ cup warm water and let the mixture rest for 5 minutes.

Pour the lukewarm milk mixture into the yeast solution and stir in 1 cup of the flour. Beat the dough with an electric mixture or an egg beater until it is smooth. Cover the bowl with a cloth towel and let the dough rise in a warm place for 1 hour and 30 minutes, or until it is double in bulk. Punch the dough down in the bowl and fold in the citron, cherries, almonds, lemon rind, and raisins. Add the eggs, ¾ cup (1½ sticks) of the softened butter, and the nutmeg. Stir in 3 more cups of the flour and mix the dough until it is smooth.

Turn the dough out onto a lightly floured surface and knead it, working in enough of the remaining flour to make the dough smooth and elastic. Divide the dough into halves and roll each portion out into an oval about ½ inch thick. In a small saucepan melt the remaining ¼ cup (½ stick) butter and brush it over the ovals. In a small bowl combine the cinnamon with the remaining 2 tablespoons granulated sugar; sprinkle the mixture over the ovals.

Fold the dough ovals in half lengthwise and place them on a buttered baking sheet. Twist the ends of each oval toward each other to form a crescent and loosely cover the ovals with wax paper and a cloth towel. Let the *Stollen* rise in a warm place for about 1 hour, or until they are double in bulk.

Preheat the oven to 350° F. Bake the *Stollen* for 45 minutes, or until they are golden.

In a small bowl combine the confectioners' sugar with enough of the hot water to make a thick icing. Dribble the icing over the hot *Stollen* and let the *Stollen* cool before slicing. Makes 1 *Stollen*.

Braided Christmas Wreath

2 packages active dry yeast
¼ cup warm water
1 cup milk
½ cup (1 stick) butter
4½ cups sifted all-purpose flour
⅓ cup plus 2 tablespoons sugar
1 teaspoon salt
1 teaspoon ground cardamom
3 eggs
2 tablespoons chopped almonds

Dissolve the yeast in the warm water and let the mixture rest for 5 minutes.

In a saucepan scald the milk. Turn off the heat, add the butter, and stir it until it is melted.

In a large bowl combine 1 cup of the flour with ⅓ cup of the sugar; stir in the salt and the cardamom. Add the yeast mixture and the melted butter and milk. With an electric mixer on high speed beat the mixture for 2 minutes. Add 2 of the eggs and 1 cup flour and beat the mixture for 2 minutes more. Stir in enough of the remaining flour to make a soft dough.

Turn the dough out onto a lightly floured surface and knead it for 8 to 10 minutes, adding more of the flour if necessary, until it is smooth and elastic. Shape the dough into a large ball, put it in a buttered bowl, and turn it to coat it with butter. Loosely cover the dough with a cloth towel and let it rise in a warm place for 1 hour, or until it is double in bulk.

Return the dough to the floured surface, punch it down, and knead it until it is smooth and elastic, adding more of the flour if

necessary. Divide the dough into three parts. Shape each portion into a rope 30 inches long. Braid the ropes loosely, transfer the braid to a buttered baking sheet, and shape it into a circle, pinching the ends together. Butter the outside of a 6-ounce custard cup and place the cup upside down in the center of the wreath. Loosely cover the wreath with a cloth towel and let it rise in a warm place for about 45 minutes, or until it is double in bulk.

Preheat the oven to 375° F.

In a small bowl beat the remaining egg until it is smooth. In a measuring cup combine the remaining 2 tablespoons sugar and the almonds. Brush the wreath with the beaten egg and sprinkle the nut mixture over it. Bake the wreath for 25 to 30 minutes, until it is golden. Transfer it to a rack and let it cool completely. Makes 1 large wreath.

Plum Kuchen

½ cup (1 stick) plus 2 tablespoons butter, softened
1¼ cups plus 2 tablespoons sugar
¼ teaspoon mace
¼ teaspoon salt
1 cup milk, scalded
1 package active dry yeast
¼ cup warm water
2 whole eggs, beaten
4 cups sifted all-purpose flour
6 tablespoons graham cracker crumbs
20 unpeeled purple plums, stoned and quartered
1 teaspoon cinnamon

2 *egg yolks*
2 *tablespoons heavy cream*
¼ *cup melted butter*

In a large bowl cream ½ cup (1 stick) of the butter with ¼ cup of the sugar and stir in the mace and salt. Add the hot milk, combine the mixture well, and let it cool to lukewarm.

Dissolve the yeast in the warm water, add 2 tablespoons of the remaining sugar, and let the mixture rest until it is frothy.

Stir the beaten whole eggs and the yeast mixture into the cooled milk mixture. Add enough of the flour to make a dough and stir the dough with a spoon until it is soft, adding more of the flour as necessary.

Turn the dough out onto a lightly floured surface and knead it until it is smooth and elastic, adding more flour if necessary. Shape the dough into a large ball, put it in a buttered bowl, and turn it to coat it with butter. Loosely cover the bowl with a cloth towel and let the dough rise in a warm place for about 1 hour, or until it is double in bulk.

Generously butter two 10-inch round baking pans. Divide the dough into two parts, shape each portion into a ball, and fit each ball into a baking pan. Pinch up the edges of the dough to form a 1-inch rim.

Spread each *Kuchen* with half of the remaining 2 tablespoons butter and spread each one with 3 tablespoons of the graham cracker crumbs. Let the *Kuchens* rest for 15 minutes.

Arrange the plum quarters, skin side up, in concentric circles on top of the crumbs. In a bowl combine the remaining 1 cup sugar with the cinnamon. In a separate bowl combine the egg yolks with the cream and the ¼ cup melted butter. Sprinkle the cinnamon mixture over the plums, brush the plums with the egg mixture, and let the *Kuchens* rest for 20 minutes more.

Preheat the oven to 350° F. and bake the *Kuchens* for 50 minutes. Makes 2 yeast cakes.

Pecan Griddle Cakes

1 *cup all-purpose flour*
1 *cup cake flour*
¼ *cup sugar*
4 *teaspoons baking powder*
1 *teaspoon salt*
2 *eggs*
2 *cups milk*
¼ *cup (½ stick) butter*
1⅓ *cups pecans, coarsely chopped*
   maple syrup, warmed

Into a large bowl sift together the all-purpose flour, the cake flour, the sugar, baking powder, and salt. In another bowl beat the eggs until they are smooth and stir in the milk. Turn the egg mixture into the dry ingredients and stir the batter until the flour is evenly moistened. Fold in the melted butter and the pecans.

Heat a lightly buttered griddle until it is very hot and drop the batter onto the griddle ¼ cup at a time. Cook the cakes until bubbles appear and break on top. Turn the cakes and brown the other side. Serve the griddle cakes at once with the maple syrup. Makes 16 pancakes.

German Apple Pancake

      3 large eggs
    ¾ cup milk
    ¾ cup all-purpose flour
    ½ teaspoon salt
  5½ tablespoons butter
      1 pound tart apples, peeled, cored, and
           thinly sliced
    ¼ cup granulated sugar
      1 teaspoon cinnamon
      3 tablespoons sifted confectioners' sugar

Preheat the oven to 450° F.

In a large bowl beat together the eggs and the milk. Add the flour and salt and stir the mixture until the dry ingredients are moistened.

In a heavy ovenproof 12-inch skillet melt 1½ tablespoons of the butter over medium-high heat. Pour in the batter and bake the pancake for 15 minutes, pricking any large bubbles with a fork. Lower the oven temperature to 350° F. and bake it for 10 minutes more, until it is lightly browned and crisp.

In a sauté pan melt the remaining 4 tablespoons butter over medium heat. Add the apples, the granulated sugar, and the cinnamon and cook the mixture for 10 to 15 minutes, until the apples are tender.

Slide the pancake out onto a platter and spoon the apple mixture over the top. Sprinkle the pancake with the confectioners' sugar, cut it into wedges, and serve it at once. Makes 4–6 servings.

Pennsylvania Dutch Rhubarb Coffee Cake

    ½ cup all-purpose flour
    ½ cup sugar
    ½ teaspoon baking powder
    ¼ teaspoon salt
      9 tablespoons (1 stick plus 1 tablespoon)
           butter, cut into small pieces
      1 egg
    ½ cup milk
      1 teaspoon vanilla
      3 cups thinly sliced rhubarb or 3 cups
           frozen sliced rhubarb, thawed and well
           drained
    ¾ cup brown sugar
    ½ teaspoon cinnamon

Preheat the oven to 400° F. and butter a 9-inch square baking pan.

In a bowl sift together the flour, sugar, baking powder, and salt. Cut in 6 tablespoons of the butter until mixture resembles cornmeal.

In a separate bowl beat the egg with the milk and vanilla. Turn the mixture into the dry ingredients and stir the batter just until it is well blended. Pour the batter into the baking pan, spreading it out with a spatula. Scatter the rhubarb over the top and press it into the batter gently.

In a small saucepan melt the remaining 3 tablespoons butter over medium-low heat and stir in the brown sugar and cinnamon. Sprinkle the streusel over the coffee cake and bake the cake for 25 to 30 minutes, or until a cake tester inserted in the center comes out clean. Let the cake cool in the pan on a rack for 10 minutes. Makes 8–12 servings.

Country Peach Coffee Cake

1   cup peeled sliced peaches
1   teaspoon lemon juice
1¼   cups plus 1 teaspoon sugar
½   cup (1 stick) plus 3 tablespoons butter,
        softened
1   egg
1   teaspoon vanilla
2⅓   cups all-purpose flour
1½   teaspoons baking powder
½   teaspoon salt
½   cup milk
¼   cup chopped pecans

Preheat the oven to 350° F. and butter a 9-inch square baking pan. In a bowl combine the peaches, the lemon juice, and 1 teaspoon of the sugar; set the mixture aside.

In another bowl cream ½ cup (1 stick) of the butter with 1 cup of the remaining sugar until mixture is smooth. Stir in the egg and vanilla.

Into a large bowl sift together 2 cups of the flour, the baking powder, and the salt. Add the dry ingredients and the milk alternately to the egg mixture, a little at a time, stirring just until the flour is moistened. Pour the batter into the baking pan and spread it out evenly with a spatula. Drain the peaches and arrange them on top of the batter.

In a small bowl combine the remaining ⅓ cup flour and ¼ cup sugar with the 3 tablespoons butter, cutting the ingredients together until the mixture is crumbly. Stir in the pecans and spread the streusel over the peaches. Bake the cake for 1 hour. Let the coffee cake cool in the pan for 10 minutes before serving. Makes 10–12 servings.

Poppy Seed Bread

1   cup milk
2   tablespoons butter
1   cup warm water
1   package active dry yeast
1   teaspoon salt
1   teaspoon sugar
6   cups all-purpose flour
1   egg, lightly beaten
¼   cup poppy seeds

In a small saucepan heat the milk and butter until the butter melts. Cool to lukewarm. In a large bowl mix together the warm water and the yeast. Let the yeast proof 5 minutes and add the salt, sugar, and 3 cups of the flour. Beat the dough with a wooden spoon until it is smooth. Gradually add the remaining flour until you have a soft, sticky dough.

On a lightly floured board knead the dough until it is smooth and elastic. Form the dough into a ball, place it in a large greased bowl, and turn it to coat it evenly. Cover the dough and let it rise until it is double in bulk, about 1 hour.

Punch the dough down, turn it out onto a lightly floured board, and let it rest 5 minutes. Knead the dough lightly for 2 minutes.

Lightly grease a jelly-roll pan. Roll out the dough and place it in the pan. Cut squares in the dough with a sharp knife and let it rise until it is double in bulk.

Preheat the oven to 400° F. Brush the bread with the beaten egg and sprinkle with the poppyseeds. Bake the bread about 15 minutes, or until it is lightly browned. Makes about 16 squares.

Amish Coffee Cake

2   cups brown sugar
¼   cup (½ stick) butter
1   egg, lightly beaten
2   cups all-purpose flour
2   teaspoons vanilla
1   teaspoon baking soda
1   cup hot coffee
¼   cup sifted confectioners' sugar

Preheat the oven to 350° F. Butter a
9-×-13-inch baking pan and dust it with flour.
   In a bowl cream the brown sugar and the
butter. Stir in the egg. Add the flour and
vanilla, and mix the batter until it is moistened.
In a measuring cup dissolve the baking soda in
the coffee and add the mixture to the batter,
stirring just until it is incorporated. Spread the
batter in the baking pan and bake the coffee
cake for 30 minutes, or until a tester inserted
in the center comes out clean. Let the cake cool
in the pan on a rack for 10 minutes. Dust it
with the confectioners' sugar and serve it
warm. Makes 12–16 servings.

German Almond Pancake

3   eggs
½   cup all-purpose flour
½   teaspoon salt
½   cup milk
4   tablespoons (½ stick) butter,
      melted
¼   cup sliced almonds
¼   cup sugar

Preheat the oven to 450° F. and generously
butter the bottom and sides of a 9- or 10-inch
ovenproof skillet.
   In a large bowl beat the eggs until they are
smooth. Into another bowl sift together twice
the flour and the salt. Add the dry ingredients
to the eggs, a little at a time, beating after each
addition just until the batter is smooth. Add
the milk, ¼ cup at a time, beating after each
addition. Lightly beat in half of the melted
butter.
   Pour the batter into the buttered skillet and
bake the pancake for 15 minutes. Scatter the
almonds over the surface of the pancake,
drizzle the remaining 2 tablespoons melted
butter over the almonds, and sprinkle the
pancake with the sugar. Bake the pancake for 5
minutes more. Cut the pancake into 4 wedges
and serve it at once. Makes 4 servings.

Sour Cream Coffee Cake

½   cup (1 stick) butter, softened
1¼   cups sugar
2   eggs, lightly beaten
½   cup sour cream
1   teaspoon vanilla
2   cups sifted all-purpose flour
1   teaspoon baking soda
1   teaspoon baking powder
⅛   teaspoon salt
1   tablespoon cinnamon
½   cup chopped pecans (optional)

Preheat the oven to 350° F. and butter a
10-inch tube pan.

In a large bowl cream together the butter and 1 cup of the sugar. Beat in the eggs one at a time. Stir in the sour cream and vanilla.

In a separate bowl sift together the flour, baking soda, baking powder, and salt. Stir the dry ingredients into the egg mixture, a little at a time, beating just until the flour is evenly moistened. In a small bowl combine the cinnamon, the remaining ¼ cup sugar, and the pecans, if desired. Turn half of the batter into the tube pan. Sprinkle half of the cinnamon mixture over it and pour in the remaining batter. Scatter the remaining cinnamon mixture atop the batter and bake the coffee cake for 45 minutes, or until a tester comes out clean. Makes 8–10 servings.

Mennonite Potato Muffins

½   *cup all-purpose flour*
¾   *teaspoon baking powder*
1   *teaspoon salt*
2   *egg yolks, well beaten*
2½   *cups grated potatoes*
3   *tablespoons grated onion*
4   *tablespoons (½ stick) butter, melted*
3   *egg whites*

Preheat the oven to 400° F. and grease 12 muffin tins.

Into a bowl sift together the flour, baking powder, and salt. Fold in the egg yolks, potatoes, onion, and melted butter. In a large bowl beat the egg whites until they hold stiff peaks. Gently fold them into the batter and spoon the batter into the muffin tins, filling the tins two-thirds full. Bake the muffins for 20 to 25 minutes, or until they are golden brown. Makes 12 muffins.

Date Bran Muffins

3   *cups bran*
½   *cup wheat germ*
1   *cup boiling water*
2   *eggs, well beaten*
2   *cups buttermilk*
½   *cup vegetable oil*
½   *cup honey*
1   *cup chopped pitted dates or 1 cup raisins*
¼   *cup sunflower seeds*
2½   *cups whole wheat flour*
5   *teaspoons baking powder*

Preheat the oven to 400° F. and butter 12 muffin tins.

In a bowl combine the bran and wheat germ with the boiling water; let the mixture cool for 10 minutes. Stir in the eggs, buttermilk, oil, and honey and fold in the dates or raisins and the sunflowers seeds. Into a separate bowl sift together the flour and the baking powder. Add the dry ingredients to the egg mixture all at once, stirring just until the flour is evenly moistened. Spoon the batter into the muffin tins, filling the tins two-thirds full. Bake the muffins for 15 to 20 minutes, or until a tester inserted in the center comes out clean. Turn the muffins out onto a rack and let them cool for 5 minutes before serving. Makes 12 muffins.

DESSERTS

*G*ERMAN DESSERTS cannot be character-ized as light. They tend to be rich, delicious and entirely unsuitable for any serious calo-rie counter, and they are usually irresistible. The tradition of the hefty dessert has also not been lost in this country. Delectable pies and puddings are an all important part of German-American cuisine, with strudel (which in fact originally came from Hunga-ry) as its crowning glory.

Cakes and cookies are the pride of good cooks everywhere, and German American cooks are no exception. The variety of cakes and cookies is endless, for every celebration or special occasion demands its own cake or torte. Many of these recipes have been hand-ed down from one generation to the next—carefully preserved and much beloved.

Strudel Dough

1   tablespoon vinegar
      Warm water
4   cups sifted flour
1   tablespoon butter, melted
      Melted butter
1   egg, lightly beaten

Place vinegar in a measuring cup and add enough water to make 1 cup. In a large bowl, make a well in center of flour. Add 1 tablespoon melted butter and the egg. Add liquid mixture gradually, mixing until the flour is moistened.

Turn the dough out onto a lightly floured pastry board and knead. Hold the dough high above the board and hit it hard against the board 100 or 125 times, or until the dough is smooth and elastic and small bubbles appear in the surface. Knead the dough occasionally during the hitting process. Shape the dough into a smooth ball and place it on a lightly floured board. Brush the top with melted butter and cover with an inverted bowl. Allow the dough to rest 30 minutes.

Cover a large table with a clean white cloth and sprinkle entire surface lightly with flour. Place the dough on center of cloth and sprinkle it very lightly with flour. Working with half the dough at a time, roll dough into a rectangle ⅛ to ¼ inch thick. Butter fingers and stretch dough until paper thin. Allow dough to dry 5 minutes, or until no longer sticky before filling and baking. Makes enough for 2 strudels.

Apple Strudel

4-5   *medium cooking apples, peeled and cored*
 ½   *cup melted butter*
 ¼   *cup dry bread crumbs*
     Strudel Dough
 ½   *cup raisins*
 ½   *cup sugar*
 1   *teaspoon cinnamon*
 1   *egg white, lightly beaten*

Cut apples into thin slices and set aside. Combine the melted butter and bread crumbs and sprinkle the crumbs evenly over the strudel dough. Cover the crumbs with the apple slices and raisins. Combine the sugar and cinnamon and sprinkle it over the fruit. Fold about three inches of one end of the dough over and continue to roll, brushing off any excess flour. Place the packet seam side down on a baking sheet and brush the top lightly with the egg white. Bake at 350° F. for 35 to 45 minutes, or until brown. Makes 1 strudel.

Cheese Strudel

 2   *egg yolks*
 ¼   *cup sugar*
 1   *teaspoon salt*
 2   *cups firmly packed dry cottage cheese*
 ¼   *cup raisins*
 ½   *teaspoon vanilla*
 ½   *teaspoon lemon peel*
 ½   *cup melted butter*
 ¼   *cup dry bread crumbs*
 1   *egg white, lightly beaten*

In a large bowl beat the egg yolks, sugar, and salt until thick and lemon colored. Gradually add the cottage cheese, blending after each addition. Mix in raisins, vanilla, and lemon peel.

Combine the melted butter and bread crumbs and sprinkle the crumbs evenly over the strudel dough. Cover the crumbs with the cheese filling. Fold about three inches of one end of the dough over and continue to roll, brushing off any excess flour. Brush the top lightly with egg white and bake at 350° F. 35 to 45 minutes, or until brown. Makes 1 strudel.

Prune Cake

 2   *cups all-purpose flour*
1½   *cups sugar*
 1   *teaspoon baking soda*
 1   *teaspoon cinnamon*
 1   *teaspoon allspice*
 1   *teaspoon ground cloves*
 1   *teaspoon nutmeg*
 3   *eggs*
 1   *cup vegetable oil*
 1   *cup buttermilk*
 ¼   *cup orange juice*
 1   *teaspoon vanilla*
 1   *cup chopped pecans*
 1   *cup chopped steamed prunes*

Preheat the oven to 325° F. and generously butter a bundt pan.

Into a large bowl sift together the flour, sugar, baking soda, cinnamon, allspice, cloves, and nutmeg. Add the eggs, oil, buttermilk, orange juice, and vanilla all at once, and beat until smooth. Stir in pecans and prunes and turn into bundt pan. Bake 45 minutes, or until a tester comes out clean. Makes 6–8 servings.

German Chocolate Cake

 1   *cup quick-cooking rolled oats*
1¼   *cups boiling water*
 ½   *cup (1 stick) plus 6 tablespoons (¾ stick)
       butter, softened*
 4   *ounces German sweet chocolate, broken
       into bits*
1½   *cups sifted all-purpose flour*
 1   *cup granulated sugar*
 1   *teaspoon baking soda*
 ½   *teaspoon salt*
1¾   *cups brown sugar*
 3   *eggs*
 ¼   *cup light cream*
 ½   *cup chopped pecans*

Preheat the oven to 350° F. Butter a
13- x 9- x 2-inch baking pan and dust the pan
with flour.

Put the oats in a large bowl and pour the
boiling water over them. Add ½ cup of the
butter and the chocolate. Let the mixture stand
for 20 minutes and then stir it until the
ingredients are well combined. Into a large
bowl sift together the flour, granulated sugar,
baking soda, and salt; stir in 1 cup of the
brown sugar. Alternately add the eggs and the
oatmeal mixture, beating well after each
addition. Beat the batter with an electric mixer
at low speed until the ingredients are
thoroughly combined. Turn it into the baking
pan and bake the cake for 35 to 40 minutes, or
until a tester comes out clean. Let the cake cool
in the pan for 20 minutes.

In a saucepan combine the remaining 6
tablespoons butter, the remaining ¾ cup
brown sugar, and the cream. Cook the mixture,
stirring constantly, until it boils. Reduce the
heat and simmer the topping for 2 to 3
minutes, until it is slightly thickened. Stir in the
pecans and spread the topping over the cake.
Makes 10–12 servings.

Fresh Apple Cake

 1   *cup sugar*
 ½   *cup vegetable oil*
 2   *eggs*
1½   *cups all-purpose flour*
 ½   *teaspoon salt*
 1   *teaspoon baking soda*
 2   *tablespoons hot water*
1½   *cups chopped nuts*
 1   *teaspoon vanilla*
 2   *cups peeled, cored, and chopped winesap
       or other similar apples*
 ½   *cup brown sugar*

Preheat the oven to 325° F. Butter a
10- x 14-inch baking dish or two loaf pans.
Dust the pan with flour and knock out excess.

In a large bowl combine the sugar with the
oil. Add the eggs and beat the mixture well.
Into another bowl sift together the flour, salt,
and baking soda. Add the dry ingredients and
the hot water alternately to the sugar mixture,
a little at a time, stirring well to combine the
ingredients. Stir in 1 cup of the nuts, the
vanilla, and the apples. Pour the batter into the
prepared baking dish or pans.

In a small bowl combine the brown sugar
with the remaining ½ cup chopped nuts.

Spread the mixture evenly over the cake. Bake the cake for 35 to 40 minutes, or until a tester inserted in the center comes out clean. Makes 12–16 servings.

German Apple Cake

3   large eggs, beaten
1   cup salad oil
2   cups sugar
1   teaspoon baking soda
2   cups all-purpose flour
2   teaspoons vanilla
1   cup chopped walnuts
4   cups thinly sliced apples (about 5 apples)
2   3-ounce packages cream cheese, softened
       and cut into pieces
3   teaspoons melted butter
2   cups confectioners' sugar

Preheat the oven to 350° F. and butter a 9- x 13-inch baking pan.

In a large bowl combine the eggs and oil and beat the mixture well. Add the sugar, baking soda, flour, and 1 teaspoon of the vanilla. Stir the mixture until the ingredients are blended. Beat the batter with an electric mixer until it is thick and smooth. Stir in the walnuts and apples, turn the batter into the pan, and bake the cake for 50 to 60 minutes. Let the cake cool for 20 minutes in the pan.

To make the icing, in the bowl of an electric mixer combine the cream cheese, butter, confectioners' sugar, and the remaining 1 teaspoon vanilla. Beat the icing until it is smooth and thick. Frost the cake while it is warm. Makes 8–10 servings.

German Gingerbread

¾   cup light or blackstrap molasses
¼   cup honey
⅔   cup hot water
     juice of 1 large lemon
     grated rind of 1 lemon
2½ cups sifted all-purpose flour
½   teaspoon salt
1½ teaspoons baking soda
1½ teaspoons cinnamon
1   teaspoon ground cloves
1½ teaspoons ginger
¼   teaspoon nutmeg
½   teaspoon cardamom
¼   teaspoon allspice
½   cup unsalted butter, softened
½   cup sugar
1   egg, beaten
     whipped cream

Preheat the oven to 350° F. and butter a bundt pan or a 9-inch square cake pan.

In a saucepan combine the molasses, honey, hot water, and lemon juice. Bring the mixture to a simmer and immediately remove it from the heat. Stir in the lemon rind and let the mixture cool.

Sift together the flour, salt, baking soda, cinnamon, cloves, ginger, nutmeg, cardamom, and allspice. In a large bowl cream the butter and sugar until the mixture is light and fluffy. Beat in the egg. Alternately add the dry ingredients and the molasses mixture, beating well after each addition. Pour the batter into the bundt pan and bake the cake for 45 to 50 minutes, or until a tester comes out clean. Makes 6–8 servings.

Zucchini Nut Cake

4   eggs
½   cup vegetable oil
¾   cup melted butter
3   cups sugar
1½   teaspoons cinnamon
1½   teaspoons baking powder
1   teaspoon baking soda
1   teaspoon salt
3   cups all-purpose flour
1   cup coarsely chopped walnuts
      or pecans
1   cup currants
3   cups stemmed, grated zucchini, loosely
      packed (3 small zucchini)
      vanilla ice cream or sweetened sour
      cream (optional)

Preheat the oven to 350° F. Butter a
9- x 13-inch tube pan and dust it with flour.

In a large bowl beat the eggs well. In a 2-cup measure combine the oil and the melted butter. Add the mixture to the eggs in a thin stream, beating constantly until the mixture is well combined. Add the sugar, beating constantly. Into another bowl sift together the cinnamon, baking powder, baking soda, salt, and 2½ cups of the flour. Stir the dry ingredients into the egg mixture and beat the batter until it is smooth.

In another bowl combine the remaining ½ cup flour, the nuts, and the currants. Fold the mixture into the batter. Stir in the zucchini and pour the batter into the tube pan. Bake the cake for 1 hour and 30 minutes, or until a tester comes out clean. Let the cake cool in the pan on a rack for 10 minutes. Turn the cake out onto the rack and let it cool completely, or serve it warm with ice cream or sweetened sour cream. Makes 8–10 servings.

Note: Choose small zucchini with barely visible seeds.

Grandmother's Buttermilk Cake

1   cup shortening
3   cups sugar
4   eggs
3   cups all-purpose flour
½   teaspoon baking soda
¼   teaspoon salt
1   cup buttermilk
1   teaspoon vanilla
2   teaspoons lemon extract
¼   teaspoon mace

Preheat the oven to 350° F. Butter a 9¼-inch tube pan and dust it with sugar.

In a large bowl cream the shortening and sugar. Add the eggs one at a time, beating well after each addition. Into another bowl sift together the flour, baking soda, and salt. Alternately add the dry ingredients and the buttermilk to the creamed mixture, stirring until the batter is well blended. Add the vanilla, lemon extract, and mace and stir the batter to blend. Pour the batter into the tube pan and bake for 1 hour, or until a tester comes out clean. Let the cake cool in the pan for 20 minutes. Invert it on a rack and let it cool completely before serving. Makes 6–8 servings.

Mocha Cake

½   *cup sugar*
3   *eggs*
¾   *cup sifted cake flour*
1   *tablespoon melted butter*
1   *recipe Mocha Butter Cream Frosting*
     (see below)
½   *cup chopped pecans or walnuts*
½   *cup whole pecan or walnut halves*

Preheat the oven to 425°. Generously butter and flour a 9-inch cake pan.

Beat the sugar and the eggs in a metal mixing bowl until just combined. Set the bowl over hot but not boiling water and beat with an electric mixer until the mixture is light yellow and has increased at least three times in volume (about 6–8 minutes). When the batter is ready, it will fall in sheets or ribbons from the beaters.

Remove the bowl from the hot water and gently fold in the flour (do not stir or beat). Mix the flour in thoroughly, then fold in the melted butter. Pour into the prepared cake pan.

Bake for about 20 minutes or until the center springs back when touched and the cake has begun to pull away from the sides of the pan. Let the cake cool for 5 minutes; turn it out onto a rack covered with waxed paper and cool completely.

Using a serrated knife, split the cake horizontally into two layers. (The cake will not be tall, but it is very rich.) Place the bottom layer on a round of cardboard the same diameter as the cake. Cover the first layer with a thin layer of the frosting and top with the second cake layer. Spread a thin layer of the frosting over the top and sides of the cake. Sprinkle the top with the chopped nuts and press the nut halves into the frosting around the base of the cake. Makes 6–8 servings.

Mocha Butter Cream Frosting

2   *cups sugar*
½   *cup water*
4   *egg yolks, beaten*
3   *tablespoons strong coffee*
1   *cup butter, softened*

Melt the sugar in the water in a heavy saucepan. Cover and cook for 10 minutes. Uncover and continue to boil until the syrup reaches 235° (the "soft ball" stage) on a candy thermometer (15 to 30 minutes or longer depending on the temperature and humidity). Cool slightly.

Slowly beat the cooled syrup into the egg yolks, whisking constantly. Whisk or beat with an electric mixer until the mixture is light and creamy, about 5 minutes. Add the coffee and butter and blend to the consistency you want.

Bundt Kuchen

½ pound (2 sticks) butter
1¾ cups sugar
5 eggs at room temperature
½ teaspoon mace
½ teaspoon vanilla
2 cups all-purpose flour
½ teaspoon baking powder
    pinch salt
1 cup chopped pecans
1 cup chopped dried apricots, apples, or
    currants
¼ cup sifted confectioners' sugar

Preheat the oven to 325° F.

In a large bowl cream butter and sugar. Add the eggs one at a time, beating thoroughly after each addition. Stir in the mace and vanilla. Into another bowl sift together the flour, baking powder, and salt and gradually add the dry ingredients to the egg mixture. Fold in the pecans and fruit and turn the batter into a bundt pan. Bake the cake for 1 hour and 30 minutes. Let the cake cool in the pan for 30 minutes. Turn it out onto a rack, let it cool completely, and dust it with confectioners' sugar. Makes 6–8 servings.

German Chocolate Pound Cake

1 4-ounce package German sweet baking
    chocolate
1 cup (2 sticks) butter
2 cups sugar
4 eggs
2 teaspoons vanilla
1 cup buttermilk
3 cups all-purpose flour
½ teaspoon baking soda
1 teaspoon salt
    whipped cream

Preheat the oven to 300° F. and butter a 9-inch tube pan.

In the top of a double boiler melt the chocolate over hot water, stirring occasionally.

In a large bowl cream the butter, shortening, and sugar, beating with an electric mixer until smooth. Add the eggs one at a time, stirring to blend the batter. Stir in the vanilla and the buttermilk. Into another bowl sift together the flour, baking soda, and salt. Gradually add the dry ingredients to the creamed mixture, beating well after each addition. Add the melted chocolate and stir the batter until it is smooth. Pour the batter into the tube pan and bake the cake for 1 hour and 30 minutes. Turn the cake out onto a rack while it is hot. Serve the pound cake with whipped cream. Makes 6–8 servings.

Peach Kuchen

1½   *cups all-purpose flour*
½   *teaspoon salt*
½   *cup (1 stick) cold butter, cut into small pieces*
2   *tablespoons plus ⅓ cup sour cream*
3   *large egg yolks*
1   *cup sugar*
6   *medium-size peaches, peeled, pitted, and thickly sliced*

Preheat the oven to 375° F.

Put 1¼ cups of the flour, ¼ teaspoon of the salt, and the butter in a food processor fitted with the steel blade. Process the mixture until it is crumbly. Add the 2 tablespoons sour cream and run the motor until the dough forms a ball, about 4 to 6 seconds.

Press the dough out into a 9-inch pie pan, covering the bottom and sides of the pan evenly. Bake the shell for 20 minutes, or until it is lightly browned. Let the shell cool.

Lower the oven temperature to 350° F.

In the food processor, using the steel blade, combine the egg yolks, the remaining ⅓ cup sour cream, the remaining ¼ cup flour, the sugar, and the remaining ¼ teaspoon salt. Process the ingredients for 5 seconds. Scrape down the sides of the container and process the mixture for 10 seconds more.

Pour half of the filling into the baked pie shell. Arrange the peach slices in concentric circles on top of the pie filling and carefully pour the remaining filling over the peaches.

Bake the *Kuchen* for 40 to 50 minutes, or until the custard is set and the top is lightly browned. Let the *Kuchen* cool for 10 minutes before serving. Makes 6–8 servings.

Plum Cake

1   *cup flour*
½   *teaspoon baking powder*
1   *cup plus 3 tablespoons and 2 teaspoons sugar*
⅓   *cup butter*
2   *egg yolks*
⅓   *cup cold water*
½   *cup bread crumbs*
2   *pounds plums, halved and pitted*
2   *egg yolks, well beaten*
2   *tablespoons cream*

Into a bowl sift together the flour, baking powder, and 2 teaspoons of the sugar. Cut in ⅓ cup butter until the mixture is crumbly. Make a well in the center and add the egg yolks and water. Blend the mixture well, knead it thoroughly, and refrigerate it, wrapped in plastic, for 1 hour.

Preheat the oven to 350° F.

On a lightly floured surface roll the dough out into a thin sheet. Transfer dough to a jelly-roll pan. Sprinkle it with bread crumbs and dot it generously with butter.

Arrange the plum halves, skin side up, in rows on the dough. Sprinkle them with 1 cup of the remaining sugar. In a bowl combine the egg yolks with the remaining 3 tablespoons sugar and the cream. Pour the mixture over the plums and bake the cake for 45 minutes. Makes 6–8 servings.

Honey Cakes

1   quart honey
3   cups sugar
½   pound citron, chopped
2   pounds pecans, chopped
2   tablespoons brandy
1   scant teaspoon baking soda
½   teaspoon cinnamon
½   teaspoon ground cloves
½   teaspoon nutmeg
    pinch salt
6   cups all-purpose flour

Preheat oven to 350° F. and butter 2 baking sheets.

In a saucepan bring the honey to a boil and cook it slowly until it is deep golden. In a large bowl combine the sugar, citron, pecans, brandy, baking soda, spices, and salt. Add the hot honey and mix well. Mix in 5 cups of the flour and work the mixture until it becomes a stiff dough, adding as much of the remaining flour as necessary. Roll the dough out on a lightly floured surface. Cut into rounds with a cookie cutter and bake for 15 to 20 minutes or until golden brown. Makes 4 dozen cookies.

Spicy Lebkuchen

3   large eggs
2¼   cups dark brown sugar
¼   pound citron, chopped
1   teaspoon cinnamon
½   teaspoon ground cloves
2½   cups flour

½   teaspoon baking soda
    confectioners' sugar

Preheat the oven to 350° F. Butter an 8- x 10-inch baking pan and dust it lightly with flour.

In a large bowl add the eggs one at a time to the brown sugar, beating well after each addition. Stir in the citron, cinnamon, and cloves. Into another bowl sift together the flour and baking soda. Add the dry ingredients, a little at a time, to the egg mixture, beating well to combine. Turn the cookie batter into the baking pan and bake it for 15 minutes.

To the confectioners' sugar add enough water to make a thick icing. Spread the icing over the warm cookie loaf and cut the loaf into squares. Makes 2 dozen cookies.

German Ginger Bars

2   cups flour
½   teaspoon baking soda
½   teaspoon cinnamon
    salt
½   cup shortening
¼   cup plus 3 tablespoons butter
¾   cup firmly packed light brown sugar
½   cup light molasses
1   egg
2   tablespoons grated fresh ginger
½   cup raisins
1   tablespoon heavy cream
2   tablespoons brandy or cognac
2   cups confectioners' sugar
½   teaspoon vanilla

Preheat the oven to 375° F. and butter a 13-×-9-inch baking pan.

Into a large bowl sift together the flour, baking soda, cinnamon, and a pinch of salt. In a large bowl with an electric mixer cream the shortening, ¼ cup of the butter, the brown sugar, and the molasses until the mixture is light and fluffy. Beat in the egg. Gradually add the dry ingredients, beating well after each addition. Stir in the ginger and the raisins. Spread the mixture in the baking pan and bake it for 25 minutes. Let the cake cool for 10 minutes and cut it into 2-×-1-inch bars.

In bowl combine the cream, brandy, confectioners' sugar, and vanilla and stir the mixture until it is smooth. Pour the glaze over the warm ginger bars. Makes about 54 cookies.

Kringles

2   teaspoons baking powder
    dash salt
2   cups sifted flour
1   cup granulated sugar
½   cup unsalted butter, softened
1   egg, beaten
½   tablespoon caraway seeds
3½ tablespoons brandy
½   cup confectioner's sugar

Preheat the oven to 375° F.

Into a large bowl sift together the baking powder, salt, and 1½ cups of the flour. In a separate bowl, cream the sugar and butter. Beat in the egg, caraway seeds, and brandy.

Add the dry ingredients to the butter mixture. Stir in enough of the remaining ½ cup flour to make a stiff, manageable dough.

On a lightly floured surface roll the dough out ⅛ inch thick and cut it into crescent shapes with a floured cutter. Sprinkle the cutouts with the confectioner's sugar and bake them for 12 minutes. Makes 4 dozen cookies.

Pfefferkuchen (Ginger Cookies)

1¼ cups sugar
3   eggs
3   cups flour
1½ tablespoons ginger
1½ tablespoons grated lemon rind

In a large bowl beat together the sugar and the eggs until they are thoroughly blended. Into another bowl sift the flour and ginger. Gradually add the flour mixture to the sugar and eggs until the dough is well blended. Stir in the lemon rind and divide the dough into two portions. On a lightly floured surface roll one portion of dough out about ⅛ inch thick. Cut it into 2-inch circles with a floured cutter or drinking glass and arrange the cookies about 1 inch apart on a foil-covered baking sheet. Repeat the procedure with the remaining dough. Let the unbaked cookies stand at room temperature for 45 minutes.

Preheat the oven to 325° F. and bake the cookies for 12 minutes, or until they are golden. With a wide spatula transfer the cookies to a flat surface and let them cool. Makes 5 dozen cookies.

Pfeffernusse

1 cup molasses
1 cup light corn syrup
1 cup plus 2 tablespoons firmly packed
      brown sugar
½ cup (1 stick) butter
½ cup lard
¼ teaspoon pepper
½ teaspoon ground cloves
½ teaspoon allspice
1 teaspoon cinnamon
1 teaspoon ground anise
2 eggs, well beaten
8 cups sifted flour
3 teaspoons baking powder
½ teaspoon baking soda
¼ teaspoon salt
      confectioners' sugar to garnish

In a large saucepan combine the molasses, corn syrup, and brown sugar. Heat the mixture until it begins to bubble. Turn down the heat, add the butter and lard, and stir the mixture until it is well blended. Remove the mixture from the heat and let it cool slightly. Stir in the pepper, cloves, allspice, cinnamon, and anise. Add the beaten eggs and stir the mixture well.

Into a large bowl sift together the flour, baking powder, baking soda, and salt. Gradually add the dry ingredients to the molasses mixture, stirring after each addition, until the dough is smooth. Let the dough stand, covered, overnight.

Preheat the oven to 350° F. and butter two baking sheets.

Turn the dough out onto a lightly floured surface and shape it into balls about the size of marbles. Transfer the balls to the cookie sheets and bake them, in batches, for about 12 minutes. Let the cookies cool, sprinkle them with confectioner's sugar, and place them in cloth bags. Let them ripen in a cool, dry place for several weeks. Makes 4 pounds, or about 270 cookies.

Steve's Family Speculaci

4½ cups flour
2 teaspoons baking powder
½ teaspoon salt
1 cup sugar
2 teaspoons cinnamon
¼ teaspoon cardamom
½ teaspoon ground cloves
3 eggs
½ pound (2 sticks) butter,
      softened and cut
      into pieces

In a large bowl combine the flour, baking powder, salt, sugar, cinnamon, cardamom, and cloves. Add the eggs one at a time, beating after each addition. Beat in the butter until the mixture is smooth. Refrigerate the dough, covered, for 1 hour.

Preheat the oven to 325° F. and butter two baking sheets.

On a lightly floured surface roll the dough out very thin and cut it into various shapes with cutters or press it into German *Speculatius* molds, which may be purchased at specialty shops, and trim off the excess dough. Transfer the cutouts or the molds to the baking sheets and bake the cookies for 15 to 20 minutes, or until they are lightly browned.

German Chocolate Cookies

2 4-ounce bars German sweet chocolate
1 tablespoon butter
2 eggs
3/4 cup sugar
1/4 cup flour
1/4 teaspoon baking powder
1/8 teaspoon salt
1/2 teaspoon cinnamon
1 teaspoon vanilla
3/4 cup chopped pecans

Preheat the oven to 350° F. and butter two baking sheets.

Melt the chocolate and butter in the top of a double boiler over hot water, stirring occasionally. Let the mixture cool.

In a bowl beat the eggs until they are foamy. Add the sugar, 2 tablespoons at a time, and beat the mixture until it is thickened. Stir the melted chocolate and butter into the egg mixture. Into another bowl sift together the flour, baking powder, salt, and cinnamon. Gradually add the dry ingredients to the chocolate mixture, stirring well after each addition. Stir in the vanilla and pecans. If the batter is too dry, beat in a few drops of water. Drop the batter by teaspoonfuls onto the baking sheets and bake the cookies for 8 to 10 minutes, or until they are set. Makes 3 dozen cookies.

Linzer Bars

1 cup whole almonds
1 1/4 cups rolled oats
1 1/2 cups flour
1 cup brown sugar
3/4 teaspoon nutmeg
1/2 teaspoon cinnamon
3/4 cup (1 1/2 sticks) butter, softened and cut into pieces
1 1/2 tablespoons lemon juice
3/4 cup raspberry jam or preserves, or 1/2 cup raspberry and 1/4 cup apricot jam or preserves
1 egg white

Preheat the oven to 350° F.

Grind the almonds in a blender or in a food processor fitted with the steel blade. Add the oats, flour, brown sugar, nutmeg, and cinnamon and process the mixture until it is well blended. Turn the dry ingredients into a bowl and cut in the butter until the mixture is crumbly. Press two thirds of the dough into a 13-×-9-inch baking pan and bake it for 20 minutes.

In a small bowl combine the lemon juice and the jam; spread the mixture over the baked dough. In a large bowl combine the remaining one-third of the dough with the egg white and spoon the mixture into a pastry bag fitted with a number 1 plain tube. Pipe the dough in a lattice pattern over the jam. Bake the loaf for 30 minutes more. Let it cool for 15 minutes and cut the loaf into 2- by-1-inch bars. Makes about 54 cookies.

Moravian Christmas Cookies

1   cup unsulfured molasses
¼   cup shortening
1   cup brown sugar
1   tablespoon cinnamon
1   tablespoon ground cloves
1   tablespoon nutmeg
½   tablespoon baking soda
½   tablespoon hot water
4   cups flour

In a large heavy pan combine the molasses, shortening, brown sugar, cinnamon, cloves, and nutmeg. Heat the mixture slowly until the sugar is dissolved and the shortening is melted. Remove the pan from the heat and let the mixture cool slightly. In a measuring cup or a small bowl dissolve the baking soda in the hot water. Pour the molasses mixture into a large mixing bowl and add the soda solution. Stir in enough of the flour, 2 cups at a time, to make a stiff dough. Refrigerate the dough, covered, overnight.

Preheat the oven to 300° F.

Turn the dough out onto a lightly floured pastry cloth and roll it out wafer thin, in batches. Cut the dough into the desired shapes with a floured cutter, transfer the cookies to buttered baking sheets, and bake for 5 to 10 minutes, just until they are done. Let the cookies cool for a few minutes on the baking sheets.

Ginger Snaps

1   cup sugar
1   cup dark molasses
1   cup (2 sticks) butter
1   tablespoon lemon juice
1   egg
1   teaspoon ginger
½   teaspoon cinnamon
1   teaspoon baking soda
5   cups flour

In a saucepan combine the sugar, molasses, butter and lemon juice. Heat the mixture to a simmer and cook it, stirring, until the sugar is dissolved. Turn off the heat and let the mixture cool, stirring frequently. Transfer the cooled mixture to a large bowl and add the egg, stirring until it is well combined.

Preheat the oven to 400° F.

In a large bowl combine the ginger, cinnamon, baking soda, and 4 cups of the flour. Gradually add the dry ingredients to the molasses mixture. Stir in enough of the remaining 1 cup flour to make a stiff dough. Turn the dough out onto a lightly floured surface and roll it out very thin. Cut it into 1- to 1½-inch rounds with a floured cutter and transfer the rounds to a baking sheet. Bake the ginger snaps until they are done, about 5 minutes.

Springerle (Anise Cookies)

2 eggs
1 cup sugar
2½ cups sifted flour
4 teaspoons anise seeds

Beat the eggs with an electric mixer until they are pale and light. Gradually add the sugar, beating well after each addition. Continue to beat the mixture for 10 to 15 minutes with an electric mixer or 30 minutes by hand. Add 2 cups of the flour and stir the mixture until it becomes a stiff dough, adding more of the flour if necessary.

Turn the dough out onto a lightly floured surface and roll it out to a thickness of ⅛ inch. Dust two *Springerle* molds or a patterned rolling pin with flour. Press the dough into the mold, trim away the excess dough, and turn the cookies out onto a lightly floured surface, or run the rolling pin firmly over the dough and cut the cookies apart. Sprinkle the cookies with the anise seeds and arrange them on buttered baking sheets. Let the cookies stand, uncovered, in a cool place for 12 to 24 hours.

Preheat the oven to 300° F.

Place the cookies in the oven, set the oven door slightly ajar, and bake the cookies for 8 to 10 minutes, or until they are pale yellow. Let the cookies cool completely on the baking sheets. The number of cookies the recipe makes depends on the size and shape of the molds.

Fastnachts

1 envelope dry yeast
1 cup warm water
6 cups flour, approximately
2 cups milk
½ cup sugar
   salt
3 eggs, beaten
4 tablespoons butter
   Pinch of nutmeg
   Fat for deep frying
   Granulated sugar

In a bowl dissolve the yeast in the warm water. Add ½ cup of flour to the yeast and stir until smooth. Add the milk. Stir in 1 tablespoon sugar and half of the remaining flour. Put the dough in a warm place and let it rise. When the sponge is at least double in bulk, stir in the salt, eggs, butter, the remaining sugar, nutmeg, and enough flour to make a firm dough. Let the dough rise until it is double in bulk. Punch down the dough and roll it out on a floured board. Cut the dough into squares or normal doughnut shapes. Set the squares on a floured board and let them rise. Fry the squares in hot deep fat until light and golden. Drain them on absorbent paper and roll them in granulated sugar while still warm. Makes 12–18 doughnuts.

Black Forest Cherry Torte

TORTE

2	*cups cake flour*
2	*teaspoons baking powder*
6	*eggs*
2	*cups granulated sugar*
4	*teaspoons lemon juice*
¾	*cup hot milk*

CHERRY FILLING

1	*1-pound can of pitted tart red cherries in syrup, or 1 pound pitted and stemmed fresh cherries tossed with 1½ cups sugar*
2	*tablespoons cornstarch*
8–10	*drops red food coloring (optional)*

CHOCOLATE FILLING

1	*4-ounce package German chocolate*
1	*cup heavy cream*

KIRSCH FLAVORED FILLING

2	*cups heavy cream*
	pinch salt
3	*tablespoons kirsch*

GARNISH

whole cherries
chocolate shavings

Preheat the oven to 350° F. and lightly butter three 9-inch round cake pans.

To make the torte, sift the flour and baking powder together three times. In a large bowl beat the eggs with an electric mixer until they are light and thick, about 10 minutes. Gradually add the sugar and then the lemon juice, beating constantly. Alternately fold in the dry ingredients and the milk, a little at a time, beating constantly until the batter is smooth. Pour the batter into the pans and bake the layers for 25 minutes, or until a tester comes out clean. Invert the pans on a rack and let the cakes cool upside down in the pans.

To make the cherry filling, in a saucepan combine the cherries and cornstarch and heat the mixture, stirring constantly, until it is smooth, thick, and clear. Add enough food coloring, if desired, to tint the mixture a bright red. Let the filling cool.

To make the chocolate filling, in the top of a double boiler melt the chocolate over boiling water, stirring occasionally. In a bowl beat 1 cup of the heavy cream until it holds stiff peaks. Fold the melted chocolate into the whipped cream and chill the mixture for 15 minutes.

To make the kirsch-flavored filling, with the electric mixer beat the 2 cups heavy cream with the pinch salt until the mixture holds stiff peaks. Fold in the kirsch.

Remove the cakes from the pans and slice each layer in half horizontally. Place one half-layer smooth side down on a serving plate and spread it with about half of the chocolate filling. Add another half-layer, smooth side up, and spread it with half of the cherry filling. Arrange a third half-layer on top of the cream and spread it with half of the kirsch-flavored filling. Repeat the procedure, topping the torte with kirsch-flavored whipped cream and spreading the remaining cream over the sides of the cake. Garnish the torte with whole cherries and chocolate shavings. Refrigerate it for at least 1 hour. Makes 6–8 servings.

Nut Torte with Fabulous Frosting

TORTE

4 egg yolks
1 cup sugar
2 tablespoons all-purpose flour
½ teaspoon salt
½ teaspoon baking soda
1 tablespoon rum
2 cups ground pecans
4 egg whites

TOPPING

6 ounces semisweet chocolate
½ cup sour cream
pinch salt
½ cup whipped cream
whole pecans for garnish

Preheat the oven to 350° F. Butter two 8-inch cake pans and line them with wax paper.

To make the torte, beat the egg yolks until they are thick and light. Add the sugar and beat the mixture until it is light and fluffy. Stir in the flour, salt, baking powder, rum, and ground pecans. In another bowl with clean beaters, beat the egg whites until they are stiff. Fold the whites into the yolk mixture and pour the batter into the cake pans. Bake the cakes for 25 minutes, or until they spring back when lightly touched. Let the layers cool in the pans on a rack.

To make the topping, melt the chocolate in the top of a double boiler over boiling water. Stir in the sour cream and the salt.

Turn the cakes out of the pans. Arrange one layer, smooth side up, on a serving plate and spread half of the whipped cream over it. Set the other layer on top of the cream and spread the chocolate cream over it. Garnish the torte with whole nuts and serve it within 3 hours. Makes 6–8 servings.

Bitter Chocolate Torte

½ cup plus 1 tablespoon unsalted butter, softened
¾ cup sugar
7 egg yolks
8 ounces bittersweet or semisweet chocolate, melted and cooled slightly
7 egg whites
¼ cup raspberry preserves
sweetened whipped cream (optional)

Preheat the oven to 350° F. Butter a 9-inch springform pan and dust it lightly with flour.

In a large bowl with an electric mixer, cream the butter with the sugar until the mixture is light and fluffy. Add the egg yolks and beat the mixture until they are incorporated. Add the melted chocolate and beat the mixture until it is smooth.

In another bowl beat the egg whites until they hold stiff peaks. Fold them into the chocolate mixture. Turn the batter into the springform pan and bake the torte for 40 minutes, or until the center springs back when lightly touched. Place the cake pan on a rack and remove the sides. Let the torte cool to room temperature. Spread the preserves over the top and serve it with the sweetened whipped cream. Makes 6–8 servings.

Old-Fashioned Berried Hazelnut Torte

 5   *extra-large egg yolks*
 1   *cup sugar*
1½ *cups ground Zweibach*
 1   *cup ground hazelnuts*
 3   *teaspoons baking powder*
 5   *extra-large egg whites*
1½ *teaspoons vanilla*
 2   *cups heavy cream, whipped*
 1   *pint fresh strawberries, hulled*

Preheat the oven to 350° F. Lightly butter two 8- or 9-inch round cake pans and line the bottoms of the pans with wax-paper rounds.

In a large bowl with an electric mixer, beat the egg yolks with the sugar until the mixture is light and thick. In another bowl combine the ground Zweibach with the hazelnuts and baking powder. Add the dry ingredients to the creamed mixture and beat the batter until it is well blended and stiff. In a large bowl with clean beaters, whip the egg whites until they form stiff peaks; beat in the vanilla. Fold half of the egg whites into the batter; then add the remaining whites.

Half-fill the cake pans with batter and bake the layers for 25 minutes, or until the center of the cake springs back when touched lightly. Let the layers cool in the pans on a rack for 10 minutes. Invert the cakes onto the rack, peel off the wax paper, and let them cool to room temperature.

Transfer one layer, smooth side down, to a serving plate, spread it with a layer of whipped cream, and scatter about half of the strawberries over the cream. Arrange the second layer on top of the first. Spread top and sides of torte with remaining whipped cream and arrange the remaining strawberries on and around the torte. Makes 6–8 servings.

Variations: Use blueberries, blackberries, or red cherries in place of the strawberries, or use a mixture of ground walnuts and pecans instead of the hazelnuts.

Lemon Meringue Torte

 4   *egg whites, room temperature*
1¾ *cup sugar*
 ½   *teaspoon vanilla extract*
 4   *egg yolks*
 3   *tablespoons fresh lemon juice*
 2   *teaspoons fresh lemon rind*
 ½   *pint whipping cream*
 2   *teaspoons vanilla extract*
     whipped cream and fresh strawberries to garnish

Cover cookie sheets with brown paper and using a plate as a guide, draw three 8-inch circles. Beat the egg whites, adding 1 cup sugar slowly, until stiff and sugar is incorporated. Fold in vanilla. Fill a pastry bag with the meringue. Beginning in the center, pipe the mixture onto the circles until the entire area has been filled. Bake at 250° F. for approximately 60 minutes, or until the meringues are dry and stiff but not brown.

In the top of a double boiler, beat the egg yolks and ½ cup sugar until smooth. Beat in the lemon juice and rind. Cook over gently boiling water, stirring constantly, until the mixture is smooth and thick as mayonnaise. Cool the mixture. In a large bowl whip the cream until it holds stiff peaks. Gradually add the remaining ¼ cup sugar and the vanilla. Fold the cream into the lemon mixture. Spread this filling between meringue layers and refrigerate the torte for several hours. Just before serving, garnish with whipped cream and strawberries. Makes 8–12 servings.

Taimi's Dobosch Torte

5	*egg yolks*
1¾	*cups sugar*
¾	*cup all-purpose flour*
5	*egg whites*
½	*pound (2 sticks) butter*
½	*pound German sweet chocolate*
4	*whole eggs*

Preheat the oven to 500° F. and generously butter and flour the *outside* of the bottom of one or more 9-inch cake pans.

Beat together the egg yolks, 1 cup of the sugar, and the flour. In another bowl beat the egg whites until they hold stiff peaks. Fold the whites into the yolk mixture. Pour 1 tablespoon of the batter, as for pancakes, onto the back of a cake pan and smooth it out with a spatula. Bake the torte layer for 3 minutes. Repeat the procedure until 10 layers are baked, using several pans, if desired. Remove the thin layers from the pans right away and let cool on racks.

In the top of a double boiler melt the butter with the chocolate. Add the whole eggs and the remaining ¾ cup sugar and beat the icing with a rotary beater until it is thickened. Let the icing cool for 10 minutes.

Arrange one torte layer on a serving plate and spread about one tenth of the icing over it. Add the remaining layers, frosting each one, until the torte is assembled. Refrigerate for 12 hours before serving. Makes 6–8 servings.

Marzipan

1	*pound blanched almonds*
1	*pound plus ½ cup confectioners' sugar*
1	*egg white*
4	*tablespoons rosewater or orangewater*
	chocolate bits
	colored sugar

In a blender or a food processor grind the almonds into a fine powder. Transfer the ground nuts to a large bowl and stir in the 1 pound sugar and the egg white. Work in enough of the rosewater or orangewater, 1 tablespoon at a time, to make a stiff but pliable dough. Dust a pastry board with some of the remaining ½ cup confectioners' sugar, turn the dough out onto the board, and knead it a few times until it is smooth. Divide the dough into 3-inch balls and color some of the balls with food coloring.

Mold the dough into miniature apples, peaches, strawberries, or other shapes, adding a few drops of the remaining rosewater if it becomes too stiff to handle. Dust the figures with bits of chocolate or colored sugar.

Let the candies dry in a cool, airy place for 24 hours. Wrap each candy separately or place all of the candies in a serving dish or basket and cover the whole dish with plastic wrap. Makes 2 pounds candy.

Sacher Torte

CHOCOLATE TORTE

> ³/₄   cup (1¹/₂ sticks) butter, softened
> ³/₄   cup sugar
>   7   ounces semisweet chocolate, melted and cooled
> ¹/₄   teaspoon salt
> ¹/₂   teaspoon vanilla
>   2   egg yolks
>   1   cup sifted all-purpose flour
> 10   egg whites
>   1   cup apricot jam

CHOCOLATE GLAZE

>   2   tablespoons butter
>   2   ounces unsweetened chocolate
>   2   tablespoons confectioners' sugar
> ¹/₈   teaspoon salt
>   1   cup heavy cream, whipped

Preheat the oven to 325° F. Generously butter an 8-inch springform pan and dust it with flour.

To make the cake, cream the butter and sugar until the mixture is light and fluffy. Stir in the chocolate, salt, and vanilla. Add the egg yolks one at a time, beating well after each addition. Gradually beat in the flour and continue beating until the batter is smooth. In another bowl beat the egg whites until they are stiff but not dry. Fold them into the batter and spread the batter evenly in the pan. Bake the cake for 50 to 55 minutes, or until a tester comes out clean. Let the cake cool in the pan on a rack for 15 minutes. Remove the sides of the pan, invert the cake on a rack, lift off the bottom of the pan, and let the cake cool completely.

In a saucepan heat the apricot jam, stirring frequently, until it boils. Remove the melted jam from the heat and press it through fine sieve or purée it in a blender. With the cake bottom side up on the rack, brush top and sides with the apricot jam.

To make the glaze, melt the butter and unsweetened chocolate in the top of a double boiler over hot water. Stir in the confectioners' sugar and the salt and cook the glaze over simmering water, stirring constantly, until it is smooth. Spread the warm glaze over the top and sides of the cake and refrigerate the torte until the frosting is hardened. Transfer the torte to a serving plate and serve it with the whipped cream. Makes 8–12 servings.

Pie Crust

> 3-3¹/₂ tablespoons butter plus enough shortening to equal 1 scant cup
>   2   cups sifted flour
> ¹/₂   teaspoon salt
> ¹/₄   teaspoon sugar
> 3-4 tablespoons ice water

Blend together the butter and shortening. Refrigerate the mixture 1 hour or more. Mix the flour, salt, and sugar. Cut in the shortening mixture until it is the size of small peas. Add the water and mix lightly with a fork until the dough holds together. Roll out the dough on a floured pastry board. Makes 1 double crust.

Buttermilk Pie

4   tablespoons all-purpose flour
4   tablespoons water
1   cup buttermilk
¾   cup dark brown sugar
2   eggs, separated
2   tablespoons butter, softened
    pastry for 1-crust pie, baked 15 minutes
        or until golden
2   tablespoons sugar

Preheat the oven to 350° F.

In a small bowl beat the flour and water together until smooth. Pour the mixture into the top of a double boiler, add the buttermilk, and cook the mixture over boiling water until thick, stirring frequently. Beat in the sugar, egg yolks, and butter and continue to cook until the mixture is thick and clear. Remove from heat.

Pour the mixture into the cooled pie shell.

In a large bowl beat the egg whites with 2 tablespoons sugar until stiff peaks form. Pour the meringue over the custard in the pie shell and bake 8 to 10 minutes, or until meringue is golden. Chill before serving.   Makes 1 pie.

Pecan Maple Pie

2   cups pecan halves
3   eggs
⅛   teaspoon salt
¾   cup sugar
⅔   cup maple syrup
⅓   cup dark corn syrup
½   cup (1 stick) butter, melted
½   teaspoon vanilla
1   unbaked 9-inch pie shell

Preheat oven to 350° F.

Chop about ¼ cup pecans and set them aside. In a medium bowl beat the eggs and the salt with a wooden spoon until the mixture thickens. Gradually beat in the sugar. Add the maple syrup, corn syrup, melted butter and vanilla; stir well to combine. Stir in the chopped pecans. Pour the mixture into the pie shell, spread the remaining pecans over the top, and bake the pie for 1 hour. Makes 1 pie.

Fancy Cherry Pie

    Pastry for 2-crust pie
2   cups sour red cherries, stoned (fresh or
        canned), or 2 cups fresh Bing
        cherries, stoned
1   large apple, peeled, cored, and thinly
        sliced
2   tablespoons raisins, plumped in 3
        tablespoons rum
2   tablespoons flour
⅔   cup sugar
½   teaspoon almond extract
2-3 tablespoons butter
3   tablespoons rum

Preheat the oven to 425° F. Roll out half the pastry and line a 9-inch pie pan.

In a bowl toss the cherries, apple, and raisins with the flour, sugar, and almond extract. Pile the mixture into the pie shell, dot with butter, and pour in the rum. Roll out the remaining pastry and cut it into 1-inch strips. Weave the strips into a lattice crust. Crimp the edges and bake the pie for 35 minutes. Makes 1 pie.

Rhubarb Custard Pie

2   eggs
3   tablespoons milk
2   cups sugar
6   tablespoons flour
½   teaspoon ginger
¼   teaspoon nutmeg
5   cups cut-up rhubarb
1   unbaked pastry shell plus pastry for a
    lattice crust

Preheat the oven to 375° F.

In a bowl beat the eggs until they are smooth. Add the milk, sugar, flour, ginger, and nutmeg and beat the mixture until it is light and fluffy. Stir in the rhubarb and pour the mixture into the unbaked pie shell. Add a lattice top crust and bake the pie for 50 to 60 minutes, until it is nicely browned. Makes 6 servings.

Strawberry Rhubarb Pie

    Sweet pastry for 2-crust pie
1   pound rhubarb, leaves trimmed, stalks
    cut into ½ inch pieces
1   pint fresh strawberries, hulled and sliced
¾   cup sugar
2   tablespoons all-purpose flour
1   teaspoon cinnamon
1   teaspoon lemon juice
    Sugar

Preheat the oven to 450°F. Roll out half of the pastry and line a 9-inch pie plate.

In a large bowl toss together the rhubarb, strawberries, sugar, flour, cinnamon, and lemon juice. Pile the mixture into the lined pie shell. Roll out the remaining pastry and cut it into 1-inch strips. Arrange the strips in a lattice pattern on top of the filling and crimp the edges. Bake the pie for 10 minutes, reduce the heat to 350° F. and bake 30 to 45 minutes longer. Sprinkle the top of the pie with sugar as soon as it comes from the oven. Makes 1 pie.

Amish Creamy Raisin Pie

3   eggs
1   cup sugar
1   cup dairy sour cream
¼   teaspoon salt
1½   teaspoons ground cinnamon
½   teaspoon ground nutmeg
1   cup seedless raisins
1   unbaked 9-inch pie shell
    sweetened whipped cream (optional)

Preheat the oven to 450° F.

Beat the eggs until they are thick and pale. Add the sugar, a little at a time, beating well after each addition. Continue to beat the mixture until it is thick and light. Add the sour cream, salt, cinnamon, and nutmeg, stirring until the filling is well blended. Fold in the raisins and spoon the filling into the pie shell. Bake the pie for 10 minutes. Reduce the oven temperature to 350° F. and bake it for 30 minutes more, or until a knife inserted halfway between the center and the edge comes out clean. Let the pie cool on a rack for at least 15 minutes before slicing. Serve the pie, warm or cool, topped with whipped cream, if desired. Makes 8 servings.

Schnitz Pie

1 **pound dried apples**
4 **cups water**
1/3 **cup orange juice**
   Rind of one orange, cut in a fine julienne
1 **tablespoon cinnamon**
1 1/2 **cups sugar**
   Pinch of salt
   Pastry for 2-crust pie
   Sugar

In a saucepan combine the dried apples with the water and simmer until the apples are very soft. Add the orange juice and orange rind. Stir in the cinnamon, sugar, and salt and cool.

Preheat the oven to 375° F.

Roll out half the pastry. Line a 9-inch pie plate with the pastry. Pour in the cooled filling and sprinkle the top crust with sugar. Bake the pie for 35 minutes. Makes 1 pie.

Gooey Shoofly Pie

   Pastry for 1-crust pie
1 1/2 **cups flour**
1 **cup brown sugar**
1/4 **cup butter**
1/2 **teaspoon baking soda**
1/2 **cup hot water**
1 **egg**
1/2 **cup molasses**

Preheat the oven to 350° F. Line a pie plate with the pastry.

In a bowl combine the flour, brown sugar, and butter until the mixture resembles coarse meal. Dissolve the baking soda in the hot water.

In a separate bowl beat the egg and stir in the molasses and the baking soda and water mixture.

Alternate layers of liquid and crumb mixture in the lined pie tin, finishing with a layer of crumbs. Bake until firm, about 35 to 45 minutes. Makes 1 pie.

Sour Cream Apple Pie

9 **tart cooking apples**
2 **tablespoons lemon juice**
1 1/4 **cups sugar**
1/2 **cup all-purpose flour**
2 **teaspoons cinnamon**
1 **10-inch unbaked pie crust**
1/2 **cup sour cream**
2 **tablespoons butter, cut up**

Preheat the oven to 350° F.

Peel and slice the apples and place the slices in a large bowl. Toss them with the lemon juice to prevent discoloration. In a small bowl combine the sugar, flour, and 1/2 teaspoon of the cinnamon and add this to the apple slices. Toss until the apples are well coated.

Line the bottom of the pie crust with one third of the apples. Spoon 1/4 cup of the sour cream over them and top with another layer of apple slices. Spoon on the remaining sour cream and top with a final layer of apple slices. Dot the top with butter. In a small bowl combine the remaining sugar and cinnamon and sprinkle this over the top of the pie.

Bake for 15 minutes, lower the heat to 325° F., and continue baking for about 1 hour or until the apples are tender and the top of the pie is lightly browned. Makes 1 pie.

Deep Dish Apple Cider Pie

2 cups apple cider
1 cup sugar
1 cinnamon stick, crushed
3 pounds Granny Smith or Cortland apples
2 tablespoons lemon juice
2 tablespoons butter
1 tablespoon nutmeg
  pastry for a 2-crust pie or one 11-ounce package pie crust mix
1 egg yolk
1 tablespoon water
1 6-ounce jar apple jelly
  vanilla ice cream or sweetened whipped cream

In a large skillet combine the cider, sugar, and crushed cinnamon stick. Bring the mixture to a boil and cook it, stirring, until the sugar is dissolved. Continue boiling the filling, uncovered, for 15 minutes more.

Preheat the oven to 400° F.

Peel and core the apples, cut them into ¼-inch slices, and drop them into a large bowl (apples should measure about 10 cups). Sprinkle the apples with the lemon juice and add them to the cider mixture. Return the filling to a boil over medium heat, stirring frequently. Reduce the heat and simmer the filling, uncovered, for 5 minutes. With a slotted spoon lift the apples out of the syrup and mound them in the center of a shallow 12- by 7½-inch glass or Teflon 2-quart baking pan. Return the syrup to a boil and cook it for 10 minutes, or until it is thickened. Pour the syrup over the apple slices, dot the filling with the butter, and sprinkle the nutmeg over it.

On a lightly floured surface roll half of the pastry into a 12-inch circle. With a knife or a pastry wheel cut a 2-inch-wide strip of pastry and fit it around the circumference of the baking pan so that it rests on the edges of the filling. Roll out the remaining pastry and cut it into long strips ½ inch wide. Place the strips over the pie in a lattice pattern, pressing them into the surrounding collar of pastry. With the remaining pastry add decorative touches to the pie crust. In a small bowl beat the egg yolk with the water and brush the mixture over the lattice of pastry. Bake the pie for 35 to 40 minutes, or until it is lightly browned and bubbling. Let the pie cool in the pan on a rack for 20 minutes.

Over low heat melt the apple jelly. Brush the glaze over the lattice and let the pie cool until serving time. Serve the pie with whipped cream or ice cream. Makes 6 servings.

Streusel Apple Pie

¾ cup firmly packed brown sugar
3 tablespoons cornstarch
2 tablespoons lemon juice
½ teaspoon nutmeg
⅛ teaspoon ground cloves
⅛ teaspoon plus a dash of salt
1½ teaspoons cinnamon
2 pounds tart cooking apples, peeled, cored, and sliced (6–7 cups)
1 9-inch unbaked pie shell
3 tablespoons butter, melted
½ cup flour

3 tablespoons granulated sugar
½ teaspoon baking powder

Preheat the oven to 400° F.

In a large bowl combine the brown sugar, cornstarch, lemon juice, nutmeg, cloves, the dash of salt, and 1 teaspoon of the cinnamon. Add the apples and toss them until they are well coated. Spread the apple mixture evenly in the pie shell.

In a glass bowl combine the melted butter with the flour, sugar, baking powder, the remaining ½ teaspoon cinnamon, and the remaining ⅛ teaspoon salt. Spread the streusel evenly over the pie filling.

Bake the pie for 40 to 45 minutes, or until the apples are tender and the streusel topping is lightly browned. Cool the pie on a rack before serving. Serves 8.

Lemon Chess Pie

¼ cup (½ stick) butter
1½ cups sugar
4 eggs
 juice of 2–3 lemons
1 scant tablespoon cornmeal
1 unbaked pastry shell

Preheat oven to 350°F.

In a mixing bowl cream together the butter and sugar until light. Add the eggs and stir until blended. Add the lemon juice and cornmeal. Pour the mixture into the pie shell and bake the pie for about 25 minutes. Serve warm or cold. Makes 1 pie.

Plum Tart

2 cups flour
½ teaspoon salt
½ teaspoon baking powder
2 teaspoons sugar
1 cup (2 sticks) butter, softened and cut
 into pieces
5 egg yolks
⅓ cup cold water
¼ cup bread crumbs
2 pounds fresh plums, halved and pitted
1 cup plus 2 tablespoons sugar
2 egg yolks
2 tablespoons cream

Preheat the oven to 325° F.

Sift together the flour, salt, baking powder, and sugar. Cut in two thirds of the butter and blend the mixture well. Make a well in the center and add 3 of the egg yolks and the water. Stir the mixture until it becomes a dough. Knead the dough thoroughly, cover it with plastic wrap, and refrigerate it for 1 hour.

Turn the dough out onto a lightly floured surface and roll it into a thin circle. Crimp the edges to form a 1-inch collar. Transfer the shell to a baking sheet, sprinkle it with bread crumbs, and dot it with the remaining butter.

Arrange the plum halves in rows, cut side down, in the shell. Sprinkle them with 1 cup of the sugar. In a bowl beat the 2 egg yolks until they are smooth. Stir in the remaining 2 tablespoons sugar and the cream and pour the mixture over the plums. Bake the tart for 45 minutes. Makes 6 servings.

Cherry Tart

2   1-pound cans pitted sour red cherries
      packed in water
2   tablespoons kirsch
1   cup sugar
2   cups flour
⅛   teaspoon salt
⅔   cup butter
1   egg, lightly beaten
1   tablespoon water
2   teaspoons grated lemon rind
4   teaspoons cornstarch
¼   teaspoon almond extract
½   cup heavy cream, whipped

Drain the cherries, reserving the liquid, and sprinkle them with the kirsch and ⅔ cup of the sugar. Let them stand at room temperature for 1 hour, stirring occasionally.

Into a large bowl sift together the flour, the salt, and the remaining ⅓ cup sugar. Cut in the butter until the mixture resembles fine meal. Make a well in the center of the dry ingredients and add the egg, water, and lemon rind. Combine the mixture until the dough sticks together and forms a ball. Turn the dough out onto a lightly floured board and knead it three or four times. Reshape the dough into a ball, wrap it in wax paper or plastic, and chill it for 30 minutes.

Pat the dough into a 9-inch tart or pie pan, pressing it out evenly over the bottom and up the sides of the pan. Crimp the edges of the pastry, prick the bottom with a fork, and refrigerate the shell for 10 minutes.

Preheat the oven to 350° F.

Drain the cherries well, pour the kirsch marinade into a measuring cup, and add enough of the reserved liquid from the cherries to make one cup. In a saucepan combine the kirsch mixture with the cornstarch. Bring the liquid to a boil, stirring, and simmer it for 2 to 3 minutes, or until it is clear and thickened. Pour it over the drained cherries, add the almond extract, and stir the mixture gently. Pour the cherry mixture into the chilled tart shell and bake the tart for 50 minutes, or until crust is golden and the filling is bubbly. Serve the tart, warm or cold, with the whipped cream. Makes 8 servings.

Sour Cream Apple Tart

    pastry for a 1-crust 9-inch tart
1   pound tart cooking apples
2   tablespoons lemon juice
1   cup sour cream
½   cup granulated sugar
2   eggs
2   tablespoons flour
½   teaspoon cinnamon
½   teaspoon grated lemon rind
¼   cup firmly packed dark brown sugar

Preheat the oven to 375° F.

Line the bottom of a 9-inch shallow tart pan with pastry dough, crimp the edges of the pastry, and prick the bottom of the shell with a fork. Bake the shell for 15 minutes, or until it is slightly browned. Let the tart shell cool on a rack.

Peel and core the apples, thinly slice them into a bowl, and toss with the lemon juice. Arrange the apple slices in the tart shell in concentric circles. In a bowl combine the sour cream, granulated sugar, eggs, flour, cinnamon, and lemon rind, stirring to blend the mixture well. Pour the filling over the apples and sprinkle it with the brown sugar. Bake the tart for 40 to 45 minutes, until the filling is set, rotating it once during the baking time. Let the tart cool on a rack and chill it thoroughly before serving. Makes 8 servings.

Vanilla Bavarian Cream with Raspberry Sauce

BAVARIAN CREAM

- 1 *tablespoon (1 envelope) unflavored gelatin*
- ½ *cup sugar*
- ⅛ *teaspoon salt*
- 2 *egg yolks*
- 1¼ *cups milk*
- 1 *teaspoon vanilla*
- 2 *egg whites*
- 1 *cup heavy cream, whipped*

RASPBERRY SAUCE

- 1 *10-ounce package frozen raspberries, thawed and their liquid reserved*
- ¼ *cup sugar*
- ¼ *cup Port wine*
- 1 *tablespoon cornstarch*
- 1 *tablespoon lemon juice*
- ⅛ *teaspoon salt*
- 2 *tablespoons butter*

To make the Bavarian cream, in the top of a double boiler combine the gelatin, ¼ cup of the sugar, and the salt. In a small bowl beat the egg yolks with the milk; stir the mixture into the dry ingredients in the double boiler. Cook the custard over hot water, stirring constantly, until the gelatin is dissolved, about 6 minutes. Remove the custard from the heat and stir in the vanilla. Refrigerate the mixture until it mounds slightly when dropped from a spoon.

In a large bowl beat the egg whites until they are stiff but not dry. Gradually beat in the remaining ¼ cup sugar and continue to beat the meringue until it is very stiff. Fold the gelatin mixture into the beaten egg whites. Gently fold in the whipped cream and turn the mixture into an oiled 5-cup mold. Refrigerate the Bavarian cream for at least 2 hours, or until it is set.

To make the raspberry sauce, in a saucepan combine the raspberries and their liquid with the ¼ cup sugar and the Port. In a measuring cup combine the cornstarch with the lemon juice. Pour the paste into the raspberries and cook the sauce over low heat, stirring often, until the sauce is thickened and clear. Remove the sauce from the heat, add the ⅛ teaspoon salt and the butter, and stir the sauce until the butter is melted. Strain the sauce and chill it until serving time, or serve it warm, without straining.

Rap the gelatin mold sharply against a hard surface, submerge the bottom of the mold in warm water for a few seconds, and invert the mold on a serving plate. Serve the raspberry sauce as an accompaniment. Makes 8 servings.

Rum Puff Pudding

3   eggs
3/4 cup sugar
1/4 teaspoon salt
3/4 cup half-and-half
2/3 cup flour
1/2 cup butter
1/4 cup dark rum

Preheat the oven to 350° F.

In a large bowl with an electric mixer on high speed, beat together the eggs, sugar, and salt for about 6 minutes. Reduce the mixer speed to low and beat in the half-and-half and the flour just until they are blended. With a wooden spoon fold in the butter and rum. Pour the pudding into a 1½-quart soufflé dish or casserole.

Bake the pudding for 45 to 50 minutes, until it is lightly browned and set. Serve it warm. Makes 6 servings.

Strawberry Bavarian Cream

2   eggs
2   tablespoons sugar
1½   cups milk, scalded
3   envelopes unflavored gelatin
1/2 cup water
4   cups strained strawberry purée (about 3 pints berries)
3/4 cup sugar
1   cup heavy cream, whipped

In a large bowl beat the eggs with the sugar until the mixture is smooth. Gradually stir in the hot milk. Pour the mixture into a saucepan and heat it over low heat, stirring constantly until the custard coats the spoon. Strain the custard through a sieve and refrigerate it until it is cool.

In a small saucepan dissolve the gelatin in the water. Heat the mixture over low heat, stirring constantly, until the gelatin is melted. In a large bowl combine the strawberry purée and the sugar and stir the mixture until the sugar is dissolved. Stir in the gelatin mixture and chill the pudding until it begins to set. Fold in the chilled custard and the whipped cream. Turn the Bavarian cream into a serving bowl and chill it until it is set. Makes 12 servings.

Frozen Raspberry Mousse

1   envelope gelatin
1/4 cup cold water
2   egg yolks
1¼   cups milk
1/2 cup sugar
     pinch of salt
     vanilla
1½   cups raspberry purée
2   egg whites
1   cup heavy cream
     whipped cream to garnish

Sprinkle the gelatin over the water and let it soften for 5 minutes. Beat the egg yolks slightly. In a heavy bottomed saucepan heat the milk until hot but not boiling. Stir about ½ cup of the hot milk into the egg yolks, then return this mixture to the saucepan. Add the sugar, salt, and gelatin, stirring constantly over medium heat until it is slighlty thickened. Take care not to boil the mixture or the yolks will curdle. Remove the pan from the heat and chill the mixture until cool, about 20 minutes. When cool, add vanilla and raspberry purée.

Beat the egg whites until stiff and fold them into the custard. Beat the cream until it holds stiff peaks and fold it into the custard. Spoon the mixture into a 2-quart mold, cover it, and freeze it until firm. Unmold before serving and garnish with whipped cream.

German Rice Pudding

2 cups water
½ teaspoon salt
½ cup raw long-grain rice
3 cups milk
1 tablespoon butter
½ cup sugar
½ cup raisins (optional)
1 teaspoon vanilla
  cinnamon (optional)

In a large saucepan, bring the water and salt to a boil. Add the rice and return the water to a boil. Reduce the heat and continue cooking the mixture until the water is absorbed and the rice is tender.

In another saucepan, cook the milk and the butter over low heat until the butter is melted and the milk is scalded. Pour the hot milk into the cooked rice. Bring the mixture just to a boil, lower the heat, and simmer it for 15 to 20 minutes, stirring occasionally. Sprinkle the mixture with the sugar and add the raisins, if desired. Cook the pudding over medium heat for 15 to 20 minutes more, or until it is creamy. Stir in the vanilla.

Serve the pudding warm, sprinkled with cinnamon, if desired. Makes 6 servings.

Red Fruit Pudding

1 1-pound can pitted tart red cherries in heavy syrup
1 10-ounce package frozen raspberries, thawed, juice reserved
1½ tablespoons cornstarch
1 tablespoon lemon juice
1 tablespoon currant jelly
1 cup sweetened whipped cream

Drain the cherries and raspberries, reserving and combining the liquids. Purée the fruits in a blender or in a food processor fitted with the steel blade. Force the puréed fruits through a fine sieve to remove the raspberry seeds. In a saucepan, stir together the cornstarch and about ½ cup of the reserved raspberry-cherry juice. Add the remaining juice and bring the mixture to a boil, stirring, until it is thickened and bubbly. Stir in the lemon juice and currant jelly. Fold in the fruit, let the pudding cool, and refrigerate it until it is cold. Serve the pudding in a glass bowl or in individual sherbet dishes and top each serving with whipped cream. Makes 5–6 servings.

Lemon Sherbet

2 cups sugar
3 cups water
1 lemon, very thinly sliced
   juice of 6 lemons
4 egg whites

In a saucepan combine the sugar, 2 cups of the water, and the lemon slices. Bring the mixture to a boil and cook it, stirring, for 5 minutes. Strain the syrup into a bowl. Combine the lemon juice with the remaining 1 cup water and stir the mixture into the syrup. Freeze the mixture in an electric ice cream freezer according to the manufacturer's instructions until it is half frozen.

With an electric mixer beat the egg whites until they hold stiff peaks. Fold the meringue into the half-frozen sherbet. Spoon the sherbet into freezer trays and freeze it completely. Makes 10 servings.

Fresh Peach Sherbet

1½ cups sugar
½   cup water
3   cups sliced fresh peaches
    juice of 2 oranges
1   teaspoon fresh lemon juice
2   egg whites, stiffly beaten
1   cup heavy cream, whipped

In a saucepan combine the sugar and water and cook the mixture until it forms a thread when dropped from a wooden spoon. Remove

the pan from the heat and let the mixture cool. In a bowl mash the peaches coarsely with a fork or the back of a wooden spoon, but do not purée them. Stir the cooked syrup into the mashed peaches. Add the orange juice and the lemon juice and blend the mixture well. Turn the mixture into freezer trays and freeze it until it is almost firm. Transfer the sherbet to a large bowl, beat it well, and fold in the beaten egg whites and then the whipped cream. Return the sherbet to the freezer and let it harden, stirring several times during the freezing process. Makes 8 servings.

Strawberry Ice Cream

2   pints strawberries, hulled
1   cup granulated sugar
½   cup framboise (raspberry liqueur)
1   large egg
1   cup half-and-half
3   cups heavy cream

In a saucepan combine half of the strawberries with ½ cup of the sugar and heat the mixture over low heat for 10 minutes. Purée the mixture in a blender and let it cool. Put the remaining strawberries in a bowl, pour the framboise over them, and let them marinate for 10 minutes. In another bowl with an electric mixer, combine the egg, the half-and-half, and the remaining ½ cup sugar and beat the mixture until it is smooth and the sugar is dissolved. Gradually add the heavy cream and beat the mixture for 1 minute more. Transfer the mixture to an ice cream maker and freeze it according to the manufacturer's directions. When the mixture is half frozen, add the strawberry purée. Fold marinated strawberries into the frozen ice cream end. Makes 6 servings.

Fresh Apricot Ice Cream

2   pounds apricots, peeled, pitted, and
        halved
1¼ cups sugar
⅛   teaspoon salt
1   tablespoon vanilla
2   cups heavy cream
2   cups light cream
1   cup milk

Purée the apricots in a blender or in a food processor fitted with the steel blade. In a large bowl combine the purée with the sugar, salt, vanilla, the heavy and light cream, and the milk, stirring to blend the mixture well. Freeze the mixture in a 4-quart ice cream maker. Makes 8–12 servings.

Apple Dumplings

1   cup granulated sugar
1   teaspoon cinnamon
⅛   teaspoon ground cloves
¼   teaspoon salt
¾   cup plus 1 tablespoon water
      Pastry for 2-crust 9-inch pie
6   medium-size tart apples
1   egg white
6   tablespoons brown sugar
6   tablespoons raisins
3   tablespoons butter
1   cup heavy cream, whipped
      (optional)

In a 9- x 13-inch flameproof baking pan combine the granulated sugar, cinnamon, cloves, salt, and the ¾ cup water. Cover the pan and cook the mixture on top of the stove, stirring, until it is syrupy. Remove the pan from the heat and set it aside.

Preheat the oven to 425° F.

Cut the pastry into 6 equal pieces. On a lightly floured surface roll each piece into a round large enough to enclose one apple. Peel and core the apples. In a small bowl beat the egg white with the remaining 1 tablespoon water and brush the mixture around the edge of each round of dough. Place one apple on each pastry circle. Spoon 1 tablespoon brown sugar and 1 tablespoon raisins into each apple. Gather the pastry up around each apple, leaving it open at the top, like a sack. Brush the remaining egg white around the inside of the pastry-sack opening and press the dough together, closing the package. Set the dough-wrapped apples in the syrup in the baking dish. Top each apple dumpling with ½ tablespoon butter.

Bake the dough-wrapped apples for 10 minutes. Reduce the oven temperature to 350° F. and bake them for 40 minutes more, or until they are tender and the pastry is browned. Let the apples cool until they are just warm and serve them topped with the syrup and the whipped cream, if desired. Makes 6 servings.

Apples Baked in Apricot Sauce

BAKED APPLES

6 *tart baking apples*
½ *cup honey, heated*
⅓ *cup sliced blanched almonds*
2 *1-pound cans pitted apricots in syrup*

VANILLA APRICOT SAUCE

1 *cup heavy cream*
1 *pint vanilla ice cream, softened*
2 *tablespoons apricot brandy*

To make the baked apples, core the apples and peel them, leaving a 1-inch strip of skin around the bottom. Arrange them in a well-buttered shallow casserole or gratin dish just large enough to hold them. Fill the cavity of each apple with 1 tablespoon honey and brush the remaining honey over the apples. Sprinkle the apples with the slivered almonds.

Preheat the oven to 400° F.

Drain the apricots, reserving ½ cup of the syrup. Purée the apricots with the reserved syrup in a food processor or blender. Pour the apricot purée around the apples and bake the apples for 45 minutes, basting them every 10 minutes. Let the apples cool in the casserole 30 minutes and transfer them to a serving dish.

To make the Vanilla Apricot Sauce, in a chilled bowl beat the heavy cream until it stands up in soft peaks. In another bowl beat together the ice cream and the apricot brandy until the mixture is smooth. Fold the whipped cream into the ice cream and chill the sauce for at least 1 hour.

Serve the baked apples, warm, with the sauce. Makes 6 servings.

Apple Crisp with Eggnog Sauce

EGGNOG SAUCE

12 *egg yolks*
¾ *cup granulated sugar*
4 *cups half-and-half, scalded*
3 *tablespoons rum*
1 *teaspoon vanilla*
¼ *teaspoon nutmeg*

APPLE CRISP

9 *large Granny Smith apples*
9 *large Golden Delicious apples*
1½ *cups (3 sticks) unsalted butter, cut into pieces*
½ *cup granulated sugar*
¼ *teaspoon cinnamon*
1 *teaspooon vanilla*
2 *cups flour*
2 *cups dark brown sugar*

To make the eggnog sauce, in a bowl whisk together the egg yolks and granulated sugar until they are well blended. Gradually whisk in the half-and-half. Pour the mixture into the top of a double boiler and cook it over simmering water, stirring constantly, for 10 to 15 minutes, until it is thick enough to coat the back of a metal spoon or until a thermometer registers 180° F. Strain the sauce through a fine sieve into a medium bowl. Place the bowl in a larger bowl half filled with ice water. Stir in the rum, vanilla, and nutmeg and let the sauce cool to room temperature, stirring occasionally. Refrigerate the sauce, covered, for 3 to 4 hours.

To make the apple crisp, peel and core the apples and cut them into ¾-inch chunks. In a large heavy saucepan melt ½ cup (1 stick) of the butter over high heat. Add the apples and sauté them, stirring constantly, for 5 minutes. Reduce the heat to medium and stir in the sugar. Cook the apples, stirring frequently and mashing them slightly with a wooden spoon, for 30 to 35 minutes, until all of the liquid is evaporated and the apples form a chunky sauce. Remove the apples from the heat, stir in the cinnamon and vanilla, and add more sugar, if desired. Set the apples aside to cool slightly.

Heat the oven to 375° F. and butter a 15- x 9½- x 2-inch baking pan.

In a bowl combine the flour and brown sugar. Cut in the remaining 1 cup (2 sticks) butter until the mixture is crumbly. Spread the applesauce evenly in the pan and top it with a layer of the flour mixture. Bake the crisp for 45 to 60 minutes, until the topping is set and golden and the applesauce is bubbling. Let the crisp cool to lukewarm on a rack and serve it with the sauce. Makes 12–16 servings.

Pink Applesauce

3/4 *cup water*
1/2 *cup sugar*
1/4 *cup red currant jelly*
2 *tablespoons lemon juice*
6 *tart apples*

In a heavy saucepan combine the water, sugar, jelly, and lemon juice. Cook the mixture over high heat, stirring constantly, until the sugar is dissolved. Bring the syrup to a boil, reduce the heat, and simmer it for 5 minutes.

Peel, core, and thinly slice the apples. Stir them into the syrup and simmer them for 10 to 15 minutes, until they are soft. With a slotted spoon transfer the apple slices to a blender or food processor and purée them. Cook the syrup over high heat until it is reduced and thickened. In a bowl combine the puréed apples with the syrup. Refrigerate the sauce and serve it with gingerbread. Makes 6 servings.

Glazed Baked Apples

1 *cup sugar*
1/2 *teaspoon cinnamon*
1½ *cups water*
1 *tablespoon fresh lemon juice*
2 *tablespoons fresh orange juice*
6 *baking apples*

Preheat the oven to 350° F.

In a saucepan combine 1 cup of the sugar with the cinnamon, water, lemon juice, and orange juice. Bring the mixture to a boil and cook it at a fast simmer for 5 minutes, stirring occasionally until the sugar is dissolved and the mixture becomes a syrup. Remove the syrup from the heat.

Remove three-fourths of the core from each apple and peel a 1½-inch strip from around the stem end. Arrange the apples in a baking pan or dish, pour the syrup into and over them, and bake the apples for 1 hour, or until they are tender, basting occasionally with the syrup. Makes 6 servings.

Peach Cobbler

FILLING

5	tablespoons cornstarch
2–2½	cups sugar
8	cups sliced fresh peaches
½	teaspoon almond extract
¼	cup (½ stick) butter, melted

PASTRY

½	cup shortening
2	cups flour
4	tablespoons sugar
	Pinch salt
4–5	tablespoons ice water
3	tablespoons butter, melted

To make the filling, blend the cornstarch and 2 cups of the sugar and toss in the peaches, almond extract, and melted butter. Taste the mixture and add the remaining sugar, if desired.

Preheat the oven to 400° F. and butter a 9-×-13-inch baking pan.

To make the pastry, cut the shortening into the flour until the mixture is mealy. Add 2 tablespoons of the sugar and the pinch of salt. Gradually add enough of the ice water to make a dough that will hold its shape. Roll the dough out on a floured surface and cut it into five 1-×-13-inch strips and seven 1-×-9-inch strips.

Pour the peach mixture into the baking pan. Crisscross the dough strips over the filling, brush the dough with the melted butter, and sprinkle it with the remaining 2 tablespoons sugar. Bake the cobbler for 30 minutes, or until the crust is browned. Makes 10–12 servings.

Zesty Fruit Compote

1	pound dried apricots
⅔	cup sugar
½	teaspoon salt
	juice of 1 lemon
	rind of 1 lemon in large pieces
	juice of 1 orange
	rind of 1 orange in large pieces
2	cups dry white wine
1½	cups pitted and halved prunes
1	cup diced pineapple with its juice
1	can drained white peaches
½	cup slivered almonds
2	tablespoons grated candied ginger
½	cup rum or Grand Marnier
1–2	cups seedless white grapes
1–2	cups sliced strawberries, if desired

In a saucepan combine the apricots, sugar, salt, lemon juice and rind, orange juice and rind, and white wine. Bring the mixture to a boil, reduce the heat, and simmer it until the apricots are tender, about 20 minutes. Stir in the prunes and cook the mixture for 5 minutes more, or until the prunes are tender. Remove the lemon and orange rind and stir in the pineapple with its juice, the peaches, and the almonds. Add the ginger, rum, grapes, and, if desired, the strawberries. Heat the mixture through and serve it warm with whipped cream as a dessert or chilled with roast meat or poultry. Makes 8–10 servings.

Apricot Poached Pears

6 medium-size pears (about 2 pounds)
1 tablespoon lemon juice
1 cup water
1 cup white wine
½ cup sugar
⅓ cup chopped dried apricots
1 teaspoon grated orange rind
1 cinnamon stick
2 tablespoons toasted sliced almonds

Preheat the oven to 300° F.

Peel the pears, leaving the stems intact. Use a grapefruit knife and small spoon to hollow out the cores, working from the bottom of the fruit. In a bowl combine the lemon juice with ½ cup of the water. Dip the pears in the lemon juice mixture and set them aside to drain. In a 2- to 2½-quart casserole with a cover, combine the wine, sugar, apricots, orange rind, cinnamon stick, and the remaining ½ cup water. Arrange the pears stem end up in the sauce and bake them, covered, for 1 hour, or until they are tender, adding more water if necessary. Let the pears cool in the cooking liquid.

With a slotted spoon transfer the cool pears to a serving dish. Remove the cinnamon stick from the sauce and purée the sauce in a blender or food processor until it is smooth and thick. Spoon the sauce over the pears and sprinkle the dessert with the almonds. Makes 6 servings.

Almond-Apple Crunch

1¼ cups flour
¾ cup (1½ sticks) butter, softened
½ cup almond paste
1½ cups sugar
¼ cup soft fine bread crumbs
6 tart apples
juice of 1 lemon
pinch salt
½ teaspoon ground cinnamon
pinch ground cloves
pinch nutmeg

Combine the flour, butter, almond paste, and 1 cup of the sugar in a bowl and refrigerate the mixture for 2 hours.

Preheat the oven to 350° F. Butter a 9- x 13-inch baking dish and coat it with the bread crumbs.

Peel and core the apples and slice them thinly into a large bowl. Toss the apples with the lemon juice, salt, cinnamon, cloves, nutmeg, and the remaining ½ cup sugar. Turn the apple mixture into the baking dish and crumble the almond paste mixture over it. Bake the crisp for 45 minutes, or until the top is golden brown. Makes 6–8 servings.

RESOURCE GUIDE

Many department and specialty stores throughout the country often carry, especially at holiday times; special molds, forms and utensils for traditional baked goods and other German-American specialties. Mail-order culinary catalogues, such are those listed below, are also often good resources for such items.

Lekvar by the Barrel, 1577 First Avenue, New York, New York 10028.

Williams-Sonoma, P.O. Box 3792, San Francisco, California 94119.

The Silo, Upland Road, New Milford, Connecticut 06776.

Many state and local organizations have issued attractive and interesting regional cookbooks. The following are among the many excellent ones available.

Big Valley Amish Cookbook: A Cookbook from Kishacoquillas Valley. Available by mail from Mr. and Mrs. Joe A. Zook, R1, Box 207, Belleville, Pa., 17004

Colorado Cache Cookbook, available by mail at a cost of $12.95 per copy plus $1.30 per copy for postage and handling from The Junior League of Denver, Inc., 3372 South Broadway, Englewood, Colorado 80110.

Guten Appetit!, available by mail at a cost of $11.43 plus $1.25 for postage and handling (Texas residents please add $.57 per copy for local sales tax) from The Sophienburg Memorial Association, Inc., New Braunfels, Texas 78130.

The Mennonite Maid Cookbook, available by mail from Legacy Book Publishers, Route 2, Dayton, Virginia 22821.

San Francisco a la Carte, available by mail at a cost of $19.95 plus $2.50 for postage and handling (plus tax in California) from The Junior League of San Francisco, Inc., 2226 Fillmore Street, San Francisco, California 94115.

Soupçon II, available by mail at a cost of $11.95 plus $1.55 for postage and handling (Illinois residents please add $.72 per copy for local sales tax) from The Junior League of Chicago, Inc., 1447 Astor Street, Chicago, Illinois, 60610.

INDEX

(page numbers in italics indicate illustrations)

ACKNOWLEDGMENTS

We wish to thank the following individuals for their help and cooperation:

Benjamin House of Rolf's German-American Restaurant, New York City; Mrs. William S. Covington, Ms. Donna Ryan, Ms. Donna Coates, Mr. Jeff Grunewald, Mr. Dan Barba.

Our thanks to the Tourist Information Bureau of the Chamber of Commerce of Fredericksburg, Texas, for the festival photographs that accompany the Introduction.

The staff of Media Projects Incorporated would like to acknowledge the help, support and cooperation of Robert Frese, Dominique Gioia and Kathy Ferguson of Taylor Publishing Company.

Kuby's Restaurant, Dallas, for their expert preparation of the food shown in the dust jacket photograph.

For information on how you can have *Better Homes and Gardens* delivered to your door, write to: Mr. Robert Austin, P.O. Box 4536, Des Moines, IA 50336.